AT THE FIRST TABLE

Early Modern
Cultural Studies

SERIES EDITORS

Carole Levin
Marguerite A. Tassi

At the
First Table

*Food and Social Identity
in Early Modern Spain*

JODI CAMPBELL

UNIVERSITY OF NEBRASKA PRESS

LINCOLN AND LONDON

Publication of this volume was assisted by
the Virginia Faulkner Fund, established
in memory of Virginia Faulkner, editor in
chief of the University of Nebraska Press.

Library of Congress
Cataloging-in-Publication Data
Names: Campbell, Jodi, 1968– author.
Title: At the first table: food and social identity
in early modern Spain / Jodi Campbell.
Description: Lincoln: University of Nebraska
Press, 2017. | Series: Early modern cultural studies
| Includes bibliographical references and index.
Identifiers: L C C N 2016010863 (print)
L C C N 2016033152 (ebook)
I S B N 9780803290815 (paperback: alk. paper)
I S B N 9780803296596 (epub)
I S B N 9780803296602 (mobi)
I S B N 9780803296619 (pdf)
Subjects: L C S H : Food habits—Social aspects—
Spain—History—16th century. | Food habits—Social
aspects—Spain—History—17th century. |
Gastronomy—Spain—History—16th century. |
Gastronomy—Spain—History—17th century. |
Food—Symbolic aspects—Spain. | Spain—Social
life and customs—16th century. | Spain—Social life
and customs—17th century. | B I S A C : H I S T O R Y /
Europe / Spain & Portugal. | S O C I A L   S C I E N C E
/ Sociology / General. | C O O K I N G / History.
Classification: L C C G T 2853.S 7 C 36 2017 (print) | L C C
G T 2853.S 7 (ebook) | D D C 394.1/2094609031—dc23
L C record available at https://lccn.loc.gov/2016010863

Set in Garamond Premier by John Klopping.
Designed by N. Putens.

CONTENTS

ACKNOWLEDGMENTS

THEY SAY THAT TOO MANY COOKS SPOIL THE BROTH, BUT in this case quite the opposite is true. This project was greatly improved by the many hands that have helped season and stir it over the years. Texas Christian University granted me a semester sabbatical in 2010, which allowed me to dedicate substantial research time to the Spanish archives. I would like to thank my colleagues in TCU's Department of History and Geography for awarding me the Pate Professorship in 2013–14, which provided time, financial support, and encouragement. Additional and much-appreciated funding was provided by TCU's Research and Creative Activities Fund and the Program for Cultural Cooperation between Spain's Ministry of Culture and United States Universities. Graduate assistants Amanda Milian, Scarlet Jernigan, and Chad McCutchen helped with the early stages of research and sifting through sources. Ken Albala, Ray Ball, Amanda Milian, and Kathleen Kennedy contributed thoughtful and constructive feedback on several chapters. Rachel Shaw gave invaluable advice on how to help the whole thing come together, as did the readers for UNP. Input from Patty Scarborough and Michael Campbell was heartening and helpful. This book is much the better for the contributions of all the people named here; any remaining errors, gaps, or misunderstandings are entirely my own. I am grateful to Kathy McDorman and Becca Sharpless for their friendship, encouragement, and the occasional kick in the pants; to Pablo Gómez for the rivalry; to Alisa Plant for her patience and unflagging support of this project from the very first time we discussed it over lunch several years ago; and to Juan Carlos for everything.

AT THE FIRST TABLE

Introduction

ANTONIO MORENO DE LA TORRE WAS A SEVENTEENTH-
century merchant in Zamora, a city in northwestern Spain. Like many
businessmen of his time and place, Moreno kept a diary for several years
in which he recorded his business ventures, travels, social activities, and
key events in the lives of his family and friends. The entries are brief and
direct, without much detail or personal reflection. Nevertheless, as he
wrote about these events, his descriptions indicate the extent to which
an awareness of food and its symbolic importance was woven into the
social, festive, and business activities of early modern Spaniards.

Moreno's observations on his social and business contacts nearly always
included meals as an important element, celebrating religious or other
festive events and demonstrating valuable social connections. On the
feast day of San Atilano in May 1675, his entry read, "Sermon from the
famous Franciscan, and then a fulsome meal, especially at the first table,
with the dean, the priests, the aldermen and myself." In the spring of
1676, after the Palm Sunday procession, he noted that "Valmaseda gave
a dinner in the house of Don Francisco Valderas, which I attended, very
successful."[1] Moreno's entries most often referred to the context of the
meals he attended (a festival day, family celebration, or meeting of business

partners) and the other people who attended, but occasionally the quality or quantity of the food itself was impressive enough to earn commentary. He described the Corpus Christi festival of 1675 as "audacious in everything. . . . There were fountains of wine, *aloja* and flavored waters for all, and the chapter went to great expense in providing food and drink, which must have cost eight thousand *reales*."[2] He noted approvingly that the baptism of his nephew's son "was carried out with great ostentation, as there was a fine spread of good food" and registered a festival celebrating the founding of the local church for which "the government prepared a grand dinner."[3]

Moreno's commentaries illustrate the ways in which food registered in the quotidian imagination and experience of ordinary Spaniards as part of a series of displays of status, power, wealth, identity, religion, and social connection. For upwardly mobile merchants like Moreno, the dinners he attended were markers of social ascent. His inclusion at the "first table" for the San Atilano feast was a public sign of his acceptance among the town's most important personages.[4] Just as often, however, food was used to define and maintain social boundaries between different groups and social levels: rich and poor, urban and rural, Christians and non-Christians. In either case, food was an integral part of people's social, cultural, and religious lives and an important element of the performance of individual and group identity.

Early modern Europe was a society of orders, in which everyone had a clearly cast social role that was determined by factors such as age, gender, religion, social position, occupation, and region. These factors in turn generated a set of expectations about one's appearance, behavior, and interactions with others. Such expectations may be unfamiliar to modern readers, especially in a context where we emphasize at least the rhetoric and appearance of equality. In the twentieth-century United States, civil rights protests argued that individuals had the legal and social right to be treated equally and to pursue their individual preferences in the marketplace regardless of their race or status. It is telling that one of the most powerful and symbolic forms of these protests happened at lunch counters, an important intersection of social space and the provision of food, where students demanded an end to racial segregation. In premodern Europe, though, such a goal would have been unthinkable. This was a society for which inequality was the norm, and this inequality needed to be visible and maintained in daily practice. These requirements generated a kind of choreography of everyday life that is rather more complicated than what we are accustomed to today. It was also important for this choreography to be publicly displayed—for Antonio Moreno to be seated "at the first table" with the priests and aldermen, for example, or for the city government's support of the church to be displayed in the form of a "grand dinner."

Therefore in this book I interpret the intersection of food and social relationships as a form of performance, through which early modern Spaniards established and communicated their individual and collective identities. The acquisition, preparation, and consumption of foodstuffs are rich with symbolism related to the places and people involved. Many food-related words draw on the Latin root *edere*, from which we get *eat* and *edible*. Adding the prefix *com-* gives us *comestible* in English, French, and Spanish, emphasizing the companionable and community aspect of eating; the literal meaning of the word *companion* means "one with whom you eat bread." We tend to think of food first in terms of nutrition, but in the words of anthropologist Jesús Contreras, food functioned "as sustenance, pleasure, medicine, poison, a means to honor or offend God, as much as a form of maintaining health."[5] At the most intimate level, home is symbolized by the preparation of food. In medieval France the kitchen was known as the "house within a house," while *hogar*, the Spanish word for home, is the same as the word for hearth, the center of both cooking and sociability.[6] The ways in which people choose food, share it with others, and the forms, places, and occasions in which they consume it, are all part of displaying who they are, what their connections are, and where they fit in.

Mary Douglas has argued for understanding the cultural function of food as a kind of grammar, in which its meaning is constructed via the elements of chronological location (time of day, season, place in the festival cycle, relationship to important life events, or some combination thereof), ingredients (meat, fish, or vegetables; sweet or savory flavors), and the location where it is consumed (in a home, restaurant, outdoors, or on the street).[7] If we add to these elements the dimension of the categorized nature of early modern European society, food becomes an ideal way to perceive and understand social relationships. This is not an ahistorical perception imposed by scholars; Spaniards themselves understood their relationships with food in terms of social categorization and connection. Sources from medical treatises to conduct books all agreed that different kinds of foods were appropriate to different kinds of people and occasions. Some foods were best suited to monks, others to sailors, students, prisoners, or royalty; some were considered appropriate according to a person's gender or age. There were foods suitable for events such as weddings, funerals, or the cycles of the liturgical calendar—fish days, meat days, fasting for Lent, feasting for Carnival and other religious holidays. Meals were an important component of the establishment of groups and relationships: each year the peasants who worked on land owned by someone else would display their loyalty and service by sharing a communal meal with their landlord. City councils celebrated the signing of important contracts with a meal; social and religious organizations such as guilds and confraternities celebrated their founder's day or patron saint day with a banquet for their members. The thirteenth-century jurist Albert of Ghent argued that it was impossible for one person to accuse another of a crime or try to bring him to trial if the first person had shared food or drink with the second after the alleged crime had occurred, because the sharing of food implied a bond of mutual support and reconciliation.[8]

Studying the role of food as a mechanism in these relationships provides us with not only a more nuanced picture of early modern Spanish society but also a better lens through which to view changes in social structure over time. The early modern period in Europe was fundamentally a period of transition—indeed, it was invented (in the sense of being identified by scholars as a historical period) as a way to acknowledge its characteristics of instability and change. Traditional periodization of European history considered the period following the fifth-century fall of Rome to be "medieval" and the Renaissance to be the beginning of "modern." However, since historians increasingly came to appreciate the long transition and connection between the two—as well as the difficulty of lumping together such disparate worlds as those of Chaucer and Churchill in the "modern" era—it became more useful to label the period between the Black Death in the fourteenth century and the French and Industrial Revolutions at the turn of the nineteenth as a separate one, "early modern." This allows us to acknowledge its significance as a period of complexity and transition, including changes in labor relationships and the increasing economic and political role of the third estate following the Black Death; the growth of urban populations; the rise of the printing press and corresponding developments in education, religion, and communication; the development of the modern state and the personality cult of monarchs; dramatic growth in trade, exploration, and the growth of European colonial empires; and the Reformation and the changing position of the church vis-à-vis the state across Europe. By the eighteenth century, western Europeans were more connected to each other by trade, print culture, and infrastructure than they had ever been, while at the same time they began to develop distinct national identities and cultures.

Such changes were expressed through and reflected in Europeans' production and consumption of food. By around the year 1000, a broadly common European food culture had developed, based on the fusion of classical Roman and medieval Germanic foodways. These common foodways were not perfectly uniform or unchanging, but they rested on the central assumption that meals were centered on bread accompanied by meat and other items, what the Romans knew as *companatico*, "the idea that bread is the basis of the meal that everything else *goes with*."[9] There were also geographical variations, as one would expect, based on the availability and ease of cultivation of different foodstuffs. Medieval food historians suggest that social and class variations were relatively insignificant. Elites and masses ate mainly the same foods, and the principal difference in their consumption of food was in the quantity of what they ate, rather than kind. In the High Middle Ages (the eleventh through thirteenth centuries), however, a series of factors led to greater social differentiation within that common culture, one that was reflected in changing foodways. Demographic growth, the expansion of cultivated lands, and increased consumption of grain led to the increased importance of land ownership, and therefore to greater control over land and grain, as well as uncultivated areas, by wealthy elites. With the expansion of grain cultivation and the corresponding loss of pasture and hunting land, access to meat became more limited, and its consumption became a symbol of social prestige. Agrarian expansion also meant that a greater variety of food was exchanged via trade, so that those with money had access to much more culinary variety, especially in urban areas, rather than depending entirely on what was produced locally. By the sixteenth century, these changes led to an important turning point in European food culture in terms of the growing differentiation between the lifestyles and foodways of people at different economic and social levels. This differentiation was expressed through tactics such as the acquisition of unusual or expensive foods, a new emphasis on table manners, and changing approaches toward charity and hospitality.

The symbolic value of food in early modern society is underscored by the wide range of sources in which Spaniards recorded information about food and its role in social relationships. The most direct, of course, are those recording the purchase of food and its uses. Such purchases are noted in the household accounts of elite families, which contain lists of food typically purchased and served for ordinary days when the family dined at home, as well as more elaborate menus for when the family entertained guests. The account books of universities include lists of rations provided for their residential students, including the purchase of food of higher quality for rectors and other officials, and the stipulation that poorer scholarship students were to receive the leftovers from the tables of the wealthier students. The constitutions of *cofradías* (lay religious brotherhoods) and monasteries often dedicated several chapters to the organization of meals, ranging from special banquets for festival days to the daily meals they provided to the poor. Municipal regulations governed the storage, sale, and prices of various kinds of essential foodstuffs, as well as the kinds of foods that could be provided by different kinds of urban establishments. Dietary and medical treatises described the qualities of different foods and made recommendations about those that were appropriate to different categories of people according to their age, status, gender, and physical condition.

Other, less literal sources suggest the social and cultural symbolism of food. Food had a prominent place in Golden Age literature, used sometimes to evoke a particular context and more often to illustrate a character's status or relationships. Lope de Vega's play *La dama boba* begins with a scene that associates sweet foods with the refinement, femininity, and elegance of the court lady, and different kinds of foods in the same author's *Fuenteovejuna* highlight the difference between city and country culture.[10] Religious conformity was judged by the things people ate: no one was allowed to share his table with a person who had been excommunicated, and Inquisition records suggest that people were most likely to denounce their neighbors for heresy or crypto-Judaism because of their food practices (not cooking with pork fat, not following Lenten dietary restrictions, etc.)[11] The pursuit of social advancement was aided by the publication of conduct books that associated cultivation and social superiority with cleanliness and self-control at the table. These books also described the necessary sensitivity to social rank in seating arrangements, table settings, and the proper distribution of food. Sumptuary laws provide evidence about social display and competition, as governments sought to place limits on the number of guests that could be invited to weddings and other feasts as well as the number of dishes that could be served at each.

In spite of these rich veins of historical evidence, food history has only fairly recently been a topic of interest to scholars. Food studies developed in the 1960s and 1970s, led by Annales historians who studied large-scale patterns and quantitative elements of the production and consumption of food, statistical studies of nutritional value, and the structures of agricultural systems.[12] In the 1980s, anthropologists and sociologists led the way toward evaluating the cultural elements of food and its connections to material culture, social identity, and symbolism and ritual.[13] More recently, historians have picked up on these approaches, studying food as a window onto cultural habits and expressions in particular regional and chronological contexts. For early modern Europe, these contributions are beginning to come together in a broad synthesis of themes relating food to the rise of urban elites, changes in health and medical ideas, manners and conduct books, developments in taste and culinary style, banquets and status, and the interaction between public and private life.[14] While unquestionably valuable, these studies draw largely on research and sources from France, Germany, Italy, and England, with very few references to Spain. Spanish historians have not neglected food history, but so far their work has principally delved into narrow areas, groups, or time periods, such as food supplies and preparation in the royal palace of Madrid, food as represented in late medieval Castilian chronicles, and the rural culinary traditions of Almería.[15] There is a rich scholarly tradition in Spain of archive-based local history, often supported by local political and cultural foundations whose support guarantees publication but not necessarily a wide audience, especially for works published in Catalan or Gallego.[16] The few general works of synthesis of early modern Spanish cuisine have not been translated to English.[17] Therefore, what I hope to accomplish with this study is to provide an overview of food and social identity in early modern Spain for readers interested in food history, Spain, and early modern Europe. It draws on archival research in the sources described in the previous paragraphs, as well as incorporating valuable material from local studies that would not otherwise be accessible to an English-speaking audience.[18] This is not a history of food per se; instead I intend to demonstrate the performative elements of food in early modern Spain (particularly the sixteenth and seventeenth centuries) and how these were intertwined with social and cultural change.

This analysis suggests that Spain generally fits into the overall patterns for western Europe, though it will highlight the elements that are unique to the peninsula. Spanish society at the beginning of the early modern period, like that of the rest of Europe, was firmly hierarchical and patriarchal. Its economy was mostly rural and agrarian; most peasants, while freer than they had been before the great plague of the fourteenth century, still owed dues and services to the lords whose land they worked. What made Spain distinct was its rich heritage of Jewish and Muslim culture and the legacy of the Reconquest. While the medieval period saw a fair degree of *convivencia*, or cultural tolerance and cooperation, between the

Muslims who conquered much of the peninsula in the eighth century and the Christians who slowly brought that territory back under their control over the following centuries, tensions between the two populations grew in the early modern period as Spain increasingly tried to define itself as Christian. The process of the Reconquest made its greatest headway from the eleventh through thirteenth centuries, creating a powerful land-based elite as well as close ties between political power and Christian religious identity. Politically it resulted in a sort of patchwork of kingdoms: the Crown of Castile (Galicia, Asturias, the Basque provinces, Leon, Old Castile, New Castile), the Crown of Aragon (Catalonia, Aragón, Valencia, Majorca), Navarre, and Granada. By the early 1700s, all of these had come together via conquest or marriage to form what we now refer to as Spain, though their regional identities remained strong and distinct. For the sake of simplicity, unless there is reason to do otherwise, my references to "Spain" are meant to include the various historical kingdoms that compose today's Spain.[19]

With the end of the Reconquest, the authority of the traditional landed nobility gradually lost ground in favor of that of a single centralized state, and these elites needed to adapt or find ways to defend their status and privilege. The clearly defined social structures of the medieval period became more fluid due to growth in trade and education, which provided opportunities for people of talent and ability to make a place for themselves rather than being limited to the position associated with the status of their family. New urban elites leveraged their wealth and connections to create a place for themselves, competing in prestige with the traditional nobles. Early modern Spaniards at all social levels emphasized their "old Christian" identity in opposition to Spanish Jews and Muslims as well as those who were relatively recent converts to Christianity. In all of these tensions and competitions, Spaniards used food to perform their identity and to negotiate their place within society. As Ken Albala has argued, "the social meaning of food grows in intensity when the class structure is in danger of disruption by social mobility."[20] Food could be both an agent of change and a method of defense, as members of any given social group sought to penetrate the barriers above them even as they reinforced the barriers below. In contexts from funerals to festivals to their treatment of the poor, Spaniards used food as a mechanism to display and leverage their sophistication, social connections, religious affiliation, regional heritage, and membership in various groups and institutions.

We will begin with an overview of the basic characteristics of early modern Spanish food customs: what foods were eaten, how they were prepared, the perceived cultural hierarchy of food, and who controlled food in the urban environment. The chapters that follow will demonstrate the connections between food and various kinds of social identity and how these changed over the course of the fifteenth to seventeenth centuries. Early modern Spaniards had particular expectations of each other based on categories such as gender, political authority, and religion, and these categories had explicit connections to food customs. In the case of more mutable forms of identity for elective groups such as universities, monasteries, and confraternities, their members used food to distinguish themselves from the rest of society and to perform the particular purpose of the group, as well as to maintain hierarchy and order within the group. Such expressions of identity through food did not remain static. Individuals could use table manners, privileged access to food, and the treatment of guests to improve their own social status, limit that of others, or both. As the boundaries between traditional nobility and rising urban elites became increasingly blurred during this time, both groups used dining practices to jockey for social position.

The final section of this book addresses the symbolic value of food as it related to vice, virtue, and self-control. Early modern Spaniards were concerned about the broader trajectory of their empire, and food was closely interwoven into their discussions of morality, politics, and the economy. Gluttony was not just an individual sin but one that threatened the moral and economic health of the nation. Virtue (both individual and collective) could be pursued through the self-restraint of fasting as well as through charitable provisions to the poor. In both cases, attitudes toward food reflect Spaniards' concerns about their collective future and the proper relationship between the individual and society.

I

Basic Food Practices and Beliefs

FOR PREINDUSTRIAL EUROPEANS, IN THE AGE BEFORE THE convenience of supermarkets, refrigeration, and preservatives, a substantial part of every day was taken up by the acquisition and preparation of food. This also represented a substantial part of the household budget; in one typical Barcelona merchant household, nearly 80 percent of the family's yearly essential spending was for food.[1] The vast majority of this food came from local gardens and pastures. García Gómez estimates that in the early sixteenth century up to 90 percent of the food consumed by an average rural family came from a radius of ten miles around their home, and cities drew most of their food from their immediate surroundings as well.[2] Most households kept stores of staples such as grain, flour, and legumes that could be maintained in a cool, dry pantry. Given the lack of good storage options for perishable items, townspeople generally made daily purchases of meat, fish, fruits, and vegetables in the markets. Hunting was also a common pastime; part of elite privilege was the right to hunt large game animals, but ordinary people especially in rural areas hunted rabbits and birds.[3] Basic food preparation was also more complicated than we are accustomed to. The responsibilities of feeding an early modern household were labor-intensive, and they included fetching water, carrying grain back and forth from a local mill, carrying prepared dough to and from a neighborhood oven, maintaining a vegetable garden, caring for domestic animals such as chickens and perhaps a pig, fetching fuel (firewood or coal) and tending the kitchen fire, and purchasing other needed items at the local marketplace. Those who maintained a household's food supplies needed to be familiar with techniques for cleaning and dressing animals, smoking or curing meat, and making fruit and vegetable preserves. Such processes were often described in basic recipe collections and books on household maintenance.

Most houses had only a very simple kitchen with a cooking fire and an iron tripod or chain to support a copper cooking pot, or a three-legged bronze pot set directly over the fire. A typical household would also have earthenware pots for cooking soups, stews, and legumes over a low fire and a simple turnspit or gridiron for roasting. Humble families would have a small selection of wooden or clay pots and bowls; wealthier ones used metal serving dishes (silver or gold in the finest cases, for special occasions) and glass drinking vessels. Tables were likely to be mounted on trestles, easy to set up and remove, rather than permanent pieces of furniture. (Medieval French folk tales describe the ownership of a permanent table as a mark of prosperity.[4]) The "dining room" is a modern phenomenon. Medieval and early modern houses did not have a separate space dedicated exclusively to eating, so members of the household would eat around the kitchen fire or in whatever area of the house (or outdoors) was most convenient depending on the number and rank of those sharing the meal. Diners carried and used their own personal knives, used for cutting food as well as other quotidian tasks. At the table, they would eat with their fingers or a spoon, usually sharing food out of a common bowl. Large forks were used for supporting meat that was to be carved, but individual forks did not come into use until the sixteenth century and were not common in ordinary houses until much later.

Given the simplicity of kitchens and cooking utensils, the most common Spanish dishes in humble households were stews and pottages. Cooking in one pot preserved both fuel and nutrients and allowed a vegetable and legume-based diet to be easily flavored with the addition of small amounts of meat or fat. These dishes were also readily available outside the home. Madame d'Aulnoy, the French baroness who visited Spain in the late seventeenth century, noted that "there are Cooks Shops almost at every Corner of a Street: these have great Kettles set upon Trivets; there folks may have such ordinary Things as Beans, Garlick, Leeks, or a little Broth, in which they steep their Bread."[5] The most famous of these dishes was the *olla podrida*, or "rotten pot," a stew of any combination of meats, vegetables, and legumes. Its curious name, according to the sixteenth-century lexicographer Sebastián de Covarrubias, came from the fact that it was cooked slowly until "its contents start to fall apart and for this reason it is called rotten, like fruit that is too ripe, although in this case this 'rottenness' is what gives the dish its flavor and attribute."[6] Olla podrida was remarkably adaptable, incorporating individual preferences, seasonal ingredients, and regional differences.[7] Covarrubias sang its praises in a full column in his dictionary, noting that while it provided a common supper, it was also substantial enough to provide the main meal of the day: "It satisfies with meat, and everything else that is added.... In some houses they prepare olla only at midday, and then for supper they get by with a salad and some fruit."[8] Prepared by those with few resources, its dominant ingredients were likely to be garbanzos or turnips. It could also hold its own as part of a fine banquet: when the Countess of Olivares hosted a dinner for the visiting Cardinal Barberini in 1626, she provided olla podrida alongside chicken, squab, capon, and other roasted meats, and the royal cook Francisco Martínez Montiño included it as part of a suggested menu for a Christmas banquet.[9] Vegetables (most frequently cabbage, leeks, eggplant, and spinach) were generally criticized by Renaissance medical treatises as being too cold and moist to be entirely healthy, but they played a significant role in the diets of ordinary people and were frequently incorporated into soups and stews. A complete meal was rounded out with fruit, nuts, olives, and sheep or goat cheese.

Early modern Spaniards enjoyed strong flavors and combinations of tart and sweet, achieved by combining acidic liquids (most frequently wine, citrus, vinegar, or *agraz*, the juice of unripe grapes) with sugar or honey. The Benedictine monks of San Martín of Madrid regularly purchased "vinegar and honey for the spinach," and early modern recipe books featured meats and vegetables seasoned with various combinations of sugar, cloves, pepper, saffron, ginger, nutmeg, and cinnamon.[10] Such spices were used for flavor as well as for color, an important factor in the visual presentation of meals. Sauces were common, often made with a wine base thickened with blood, almonds, or bread crumbs and sweetened with honey or sugar. Martínez Montiño, head cook to King Philip IV and author of one of the seventeenth century's principal cookbooks, recommended a sauce of quince, onion, black pepper, cinnamon, wine, vinegar, and sugar for all kinds of game birds and rabbits.[11] In a list of popular dishes from 1617, the most common seasoning combination for roast meats was lemon, pepper, and cloves.[12] Sugar (usually mixed with wine or vinegar) appeared among the seasonings for several roast meats and as an ingredient in stuffings and soups. Spaniards quickly developed a taste for the combination of almonds, cinnamon, and sugar, as these ingredients became more widely available after the 1400s. The Benedictine monks of San Martín in the seventeenth century celebrated holidays and the presence of guests with substantial purchases of sugar, almonds, honey, raisins, marmalades, and marzipan, and the Portuguese traveler Pinheiro da Veiga marveled that in Valladolid in 1605 he found over a hundred shops specializing in sweets.[13] Travelers from the rest of Europe often found that Spanish food was rather heavily spiced for their taste. Madame d'Aulnoy in the late seventeenth century complained that Spaniards took excellent fish and made pastries that "would be good, were they not stuffed with Garlick, Saffron and Pepper."[14] The predominance of sugar and imported spices in recipe books and household accounts reflects the taste of those with greater financial means; the rest of the population was more likely to rely on honey and locally available herbs such as thyme, marjoram, basil, bay leaf, fennel, and sage.[15] There were of course other significant variations in what people ate by region, season, and status, a fact that shall be discussed at greater length later, but these were the basic patterns familiar to households across Spain.

THE MOST IMPORTANT ELEMENT ON MOST EARLY MODERN European tables was bread. Consider the symbolic weight that it carries in religious and community identity: one "breaks bread" in sharing a meal with family and friends; family and household units are often described in medieval texts as "those who share bread." In the Judeo-Christian tradition, bread as manna represents the generosity of God and, for Christians, becomes the body of Christ in the Eucharist. Bread and wine for the Romans were important symbols of civilization and cultural advancement, and their consumption throughout Europe followed Roman settlement patterns. Early Christian writers cultivated bread as a religious metaphor, as in the case of St. Augustine, who described new Christians as being ground into flour through exorcism, leavened into dough through baptism, and baked in the oven of the Holy Spirit.[16] Similarly, the omnipresent stories of saints' lives in late medieval and early modern Europe frequently drew upon the image of spreading Christian faith as planting and harvesting wheat. The religious symbolism of bread was strengthened with the rise of Islam, when bread-eating Christians could contrast themselves with Muslims who consumed grain in other forms. The treatise describing the management of the household of the fifteenth-century Dukes of Burgundy, admired across Europe for its elegance and its cuisine, explained that *panetiers* and cup-bearers ranked more highly than the cooks in the kitchen hierarchy, because the bread and wine they served were symbolic of the Eucharist.[17]

Bread thus functioned as a metaphor for spiritual as well as material sustenance—and reasonably so, since it was the predominant foodstuff in the early modern diet. Scholars estimate that while the medieval diet may have been relatively varied, there was an increasing shift toward the production of grain, especially in the Mediterranean regions. By the year 1000, bread was the most important dietary component for most of the European population, and by the sixteenth and seventeenth centuries grain provided up to 70 percent of the daily calories consumed by early modern Europeans. Grain-based soups (such as *gachas* in Castile and *farinetes* and *ordiates* along the Mediterranean coast) were also common, following the influence of the Arabic *harisa*.[18] Estimates of bread consumption agree that an average adult in Spain could expect to eat close to one kilogram (2.2 pounds) of bread each day. Even in difficult years in the seventeenth century, when grain supplies in Mallorca were rationed, authorities still promised a minimum of 810 grams (1.8 pounds) per person per day.[19] Regardless of the season, feast days or fast days, bread and wine provided the foundation of the diet of groups who resided and dined together, such as students and monks, and it was also the central element of offerings to the poor by charitable groups or at funerals. In the larger context, bread (as grain) was also the largest engine of the European economy, both as measured by the value of the domestic grain grade and the proportion of the labor force engaged in agricultural production.[20]

Bread was also a symbol of community, not just out of religious symbolism but in a more practical way, as mills and ovens were communal structures shared by a village or urban neighborhood. Individual households could possess mortars for the grinding of small amounts of softer grains, or hearths that maintained simple cooking fires, but the tasks of milling flour and baking bread required large amounts of energy and were most efficient when shared.[21] The number of mills grew dramatically throughout Europe in the late Middle Ages; they were usually water-driven and required a certain amount of specialized labor and maintenance of the millstones. Mill operators would transport, weigh, and grind the grain and then return the ground flour to its owner, keeping in payment the *maquila*, a predetermined percentage, as a fee. Communal ovens were similarly specialized: they were large, brick-lined structures, often up to twenty feet wide and fired by wood, to which family members or servants would bring prepared dough to be baked, in return for a set fee or a proportion of the finished product.[22] For those who had no access to grain or for other reasons preferred to buy baked bread, licensed bakers were contracted to provide certain quantities for sale daily in public plazas. In Valencia, there were separate terms for bakers according to whose bread they produced: *forners*, who baked the dough brought to them in return for a portion in kind, and *flequers*, who sold for coin the bread they prepared themselves.[23] Municipal regulations in Morón (Andalusia) established that the communal ovens had to be heated by dawn each morning to bake the dough brought by residents or anyone else. If anyone needed to bake after that time, they were to inform the baker, who was obliged to maintain the oven ready until nightfall.[24] Such communal ovens, used by a large percentage of the population, thus became important centers of gathering and communication.

The centrality of bread production also meant that control of these structures was important and potentially profitable. During the course of the Reconquest, mills and ovens in newly conquered areas were appropriated by the crown and redistributed as gifts to key supporters. When licenses were granted for the construction of new ones, these tended to go to members of the local governing council.[25] Whether old or new, privately or publicly owned, they were generally operated on yearly contracts and were subject to close municipal regulation of the price and weight of both the grain and final baked products. City officials recognized the importance to social order of maintaining the bread supply. In the book of aldermen's guidelines for Madrid, the chapter on bread shortages is one of the longest, emphasizing that city officials were responsible for supervising the importation of bread into the city and making sure one alderman stayed in each bakery to make sure the bread was properly and fairly distributed. The guidelines acknowledged that "aldermen face the most work during bread shortages, which are common when it rains or snows too much in the spring, and in the months of April, May and June."[26] Even in times of plenty, city officials were concerned about avoiding fraud in the production and sale of bread.

What was this bread like? *Pan* in Spanish is today a mass noun, as *bread* is in English—one eats *some* bread, not *a* bread. However, in the early modern period, it was a count noun, and while "a bread" could be as large as five to six kilos (thirteen pounds), pan generally referred to a round, hard loaf of slightly less than a kilogram in weight, while a *panecillo* or "little bread" was a quarter that size.[27] Even the best-quality bread would have been harder and darker than that to which we are accustomed. Part of its usefulness lay in the fact that it could keep for several days or even weeks, though in noble or court households it was more customary to bake every day, if only for the lord's table.[28] The durability of ordinary bread made it somewhat difficult to manage gracefully at the table. Conduct books and other guidelines for any group that shared communal meals, such as monks and students, all emphasized the importance of cutting off small, manageable pieces of bread and not tearing them off with the teeth.[29] However, its hardness also made it useful as a utensil. Food was often served in communal dishes rather than individual plates, and one's slab of bread could be used essentially as a plate.

Wheat was considered to be the best of the grains, and finely ground white flour was used to prepare bread for those of the most wealth and status. (Wheat flour becomes lighter in color as the germ and bran are sifted out, resulting in a finer and softer but less nutritious bread.) Elites had access to a much greater variety of foodstuffs, especially meat, so that bread probably formed a smaller percentage of their overall diet than it did that of the majority of the population. It was ubiquitous enough to not merit specific mention in most banquet descriptions or festival accounts, but the panter, responsible for the provision and serving of bread, was a key member of any elite kitchen staff. Curiously, this office was also responsible for the provisioning of lettuce, radishes, and peaches, though this may be simply because these were grown along rivers where mills and ovens were situated, and consequently those who regularly purchased flour or bread would have easy access to these products as well.[30] In Madrid, once the court was established there in the sixteenth century, bakers produced what was known as "court bread" made from *trigo candeal*, a variety of wheat known for its soft, white flour, as well as delicate *panecillos de leche*, or "milk breads." Both were exclusive enough that bakers were required to register the names of those for whom such breads were made.[31]

Bread could also be made from other grains, such as rye, millet, oats, spelt, barley, and, in times of greater need, acorn, chestnut, or garbanzo flour. Here too there was a hierarchy: in some cases the grains used for bread depended on what was most available in the region, but more commonly bread was determined by social class within any given community. The *ministros mayores*, or ecclesiastical officials, of the Royal Hospital of Santiago de Compostela received substantial daily rations of wheat bread, even though wheat was relatively rare in the region, while the nurses and servants received smaller rations of rye.[32] Even peasants who grew wheat usually used it in payment to landowners, while the bread they made for their own consumption was made from the "lesser" grains. This was especially true in regions with lower wheat production, such as Galicia, in the northwest corner of Spain: the accounts of landowners there show that wheat flour was reserved for only elite families and their guests, while servants and day laborers consumed bread made from rye or millet. These divisions reflected deeply embedded social habits at least as much as they did price differences, as they held true even in times when more wheat was available.[33] The coastal areas of the Basque country to the east were similarly lacking in wheat until they began to import the grain in the fifteenth century; this is one of the few regions that developed the production of corn.[34] Meanwhile, in Valencia, Jaén, and parts of Catalonia, wheat production was high enough that even the most humble urban residents could depend on wheat bread, though their rural counterparts were likely to rely on lesser grains.[35] In parts of rural Catalonia, not as in most of the rest of Spain, even peasants could regularly eat wheat: rye was consumed only in times of genuine dearth, and donations of bread to the poor specified that they should receive wheat bread.[36] On the whole, though, wheat bread, and especially that made from soft candeal wheat, was a crucial symbol of status and wealth.

BREAD'S MOST IMPORTANT COMPANION AT THE TABLE was wine; both had deep roots in Roman and Christian culture that were maintained throughout the medieval period. *Pan y vino*, bread and wine, was the shorthand used for basic sustenance across the social spectrum from wealthy monasteries to rough poorhouses, and both were present in the strictest religious fasts as well as at fine banquets. Until the rise of water treatment facilities in the nineteenth century, drinking water was more dangerous than healthful, so preindustrial Europeans satisfied their thirst with beer and wine. Their levels of alcoholic consumption sound startlingly high to us, though we must keep in mind that the average alcohol content of both beer and wine was much lower than it is today.

Average wine consumption could reach a liter and a half per person per day, or more for elites; its purchase represented nearly a fourth of an average family's total expenditure on food.[37] Even in convents and monasteries, daily rations were often as much as one liter per person.[38] Wine was believed to give strength, and thus it was thought to be particularly appropriate for soldiers, manual laborers, and those who suffered from poor health. When in November of 1429 Queen Blanca of Navarre received complaints that her army was having difficulty with provisions, she ordered her suppliers to redress the problem and to "make sure they do not lack wine."[39] Lobera de Ávila wrote approvingly in his sixteenth-century treatise on health that wine "facilitates the mind, gladdens the heart, gives good color, makes proficient the tongue, and provides good maintenance and substance."[40] The guidelines for the Hermandad del Real Hospicio de Pobres Mendigos del Ave María y San Fernando, a brotherhood established for the care of the poor in seventeenth-century Madrid, prescribed regular rations of wine for everyone except children and those considered to be demented.[41]

The only times when medical and dietary treatises recommended avoiding the consumption of wine was during times of plague, when "cold" foods (in the Galenic sense) were prescribed to avoid infection.[42] There were occasional criticisms of the dangers of excess consumption of wine, which we will consider in a later section.[43] For the most part, though, wine was considered to be an important and necessary element, as Granada's municipal authorities noted in 1559 regarding the Alhambra's five wine taverns, commenting that they provided "great utility and advantage to its residents and visitors, as is well known."[44] The consumption of wine was an integral part of Spanish social activities and celebrations: while under normal circumstances wine brought into a city had to be taxed, during important religious festivals in Toledo that drew large numbers of pilgrims and travelers, individuals were allowed to bring in up to half an *arroba*, or approximately eight liters of wine, as long as they drank it themselves rather than selling it.[45] Indeed, a common (and greatly feared) punishment for misbehavior in groups such as soldiers, monks, and university students was to lose their ration of wine for a period of time.

As with all other foodstuffs, wine served to indicate and emphasize social differences. Murcia, for example, produced its own wine, but finer wine from other regions was imported for special occasions. In the summer of 1465, the city celebrated the naming of a new set of public officials by buying six and a half *cántaras* of white Aragonese wine for the members of the city council (a cántara equaling roughly eleven liters) and three cántaras of local wine for "the people of the town."[46] In the Galician convent of San Payo in 1650, the daily ration of wine for the abbess was over two liters per day, while the nuns who had been longest in residence received one, and their servants got just over a quarter of a liter.[47] While plain wine was the predominant social drink, the Spanish taste for spices was reflected in a variety of wine-based drinks, which probably made good use of wine of lower quality. These included *carraspada*, a watered wine simmered with honey and spices, and hippocras, red wine warmed with brown sugar, cinnamon, cloves, and essences of amber and musk; the same mixture with white wine was a *clarea*. The ingredients in these "mixed" drinks, since they were a combination of sweet, spicy, and alcoholic, sparked some conflict over the rights to production and sales as they grew more popular through the seventeenth century. Taverns were licensed to sell wine but not food; therefore they did not have access to the additional ingredients for drinks such as hippocras. Its production therefore fell to confectioners and apothecaries, who monopolized sales of hippocras in the seventeenth century, in spite of the ongoing protests of tavernkeepers, who thought they should be the ones profiting from sales of the wine-based drink.[48]

The technique of distillation led to the growing popularity of brandy and *aguardiente* (distilled from fruit or grains, especially barley and rye) across Europe by the fourteenth century. These never reached the level of popularity of wine, but just as the Spanish taste for a variety of spices and sweets seemed to expand in the seventeenth century, so did the consumption of spirits. The emerging taste for aguardiente can be seen in Madrid city regulations, which tentatively allowed its production in 1599 with "a license to sell during four months, with reports on whether its use seems to be advantageous," while just a few years later the city's concerns were more about collecting the appropriate taxes on its sale and determining whether it could be sold at all hours.[49] A small cup of liquor, often accompanied by *letuario* (a sweet paste made from honey and orange peel), purchased from street stands, became a customary breakfast for early modern city-dwellers. In regions like Mallorca that did not produce their own wine, aguardiente was actually cheaper. Diluted with water, it formed the principal drink of the populace as wine did elsewhere. In its social associations, aguardiente was a masculine drink, considered most appropriate for soldiers and workers.[50]

Beer has one of the longest histories of any manmade beverage, having existed in Europe for millennia, though it was largely replaced by ale (brewed without hops) in the Middle Ages. It regained popularity in northern Europe first, and was reintroduced to Spain in the 1530s by the emperor Charles V, who had been raised in Flanders and was accustomed to drinking beer. It did not, however, achieve much popularity there. Until the eighteenth century it was only consumed by the northern European residents of the court and a handful of nobles who drank it in imitation of the emperor.[51] Lobera de Ávila included a chapter on beer in his *Vergel de sanidad*, but he kept it brief, noting that "as in Spain there is much good wine and water, there is little need of beer and it is not customary, so I will say no more on this matter."[52] Many Spanish Benedictine monastic communities recommended beer only when there was no possibility of obtaining wine, and indeed they found it sufficiently uninteresting that they decided it was an appropriate beverage for Lent.[53] One seventeenth-century recipe book at least found it useful in raising chickens, noting that after a week of giving them beer, they would end up "as fat as turtledoves."[54] While English recipe and household books of the sixteenth and seventeenth centuries regularly included information on domestic beer production (and in fact brewing became one of the more respected professions associated with women in England), similar recipe collections in Spain almost never mentioned beer. It occupied very little of the attention of the *alcaldes de casa y corte* in Madrid, the officials whose responsibilities included licensing and regulating the prices and sales of food and drink. In fact, it was difficult enough to find that in

1624 the ambassador of Denmark requested permission to grind barley in the mills of the court in order to produce his own beer.[55] Even in the late eighteenth century, the Enlightenment writer Benito Bails noted that it was simply foreign to Mediterranean culture.[56]

While most drinks had some alcoholic content, a variety of non-alcoholic drinks were common in Spain, especially those that favored the Spanish taste for spices. Even though drinking plain water was uncommon, Spaniards were fond of flavored waters made with cinnamon, rosemary, lemon, orange blossom, or fennel. One of the most popular urban drinks among all social ranks was aloja, a mildly fermented mixture of water, honey, yeast, cloves, cinnamon, nutmeg and pepper. This was most frequently sold at street stands; by 1671 there were forty-six different licensed sellers of aloja in Madrid alone. (As we will see later, as their popularity grew, aloja and flavored waters came to be associated with idleness and frivolity in the eyes of local authorities.) Fresh milk was too challenging to preserve to be a common drink, though it was often used in recipes; almond milk appeared more frequently. In the early seventeenth century, the popularity of aloja and flavored waters was boosted by the use of ice (*nieve*, literally snow), which could be brought down from nearby mountains, packed in straw and stored in special wells. Ice of course was not a new invention, but it was expensive and difficult to obtain in the sixteenth century.[57] Entrepreneurial landowners with estates near the mountains soon dedicated themselves to collecting and storing snow for urban markets, and a veritable ice craze began in the early seventeenth century. Especially in the court, ice became a prized commodity, given occasionally as a stipend to palace servants and granted by the royal family to convents and monasteries during the summer months as alms. Aloja vendors used it to make flavored sorbets and drinks with shaved ice in an early modern antecedent of the snow cone. Chroniclers noted its popularity among all social ranks: municipal authorities in Madrid noted that "everyone, from the rich to the poor, uses ice," and when the royal family prepared a lunch to take to an Inquisition ceremony in July of 1632, they did not neglect to pack their own ice.[58] Some Spanish physicians attempted to preserve the elite connotation of ice, suggesting that while cold drinks were appropriate for those who heated their brains through intellectual endeavors, they could be dangerous to manual laborers whose stomachs were not well prepared for the cold.[59] While medical opinion was initially opposed to the new fashion of drinking iced beverages, physicians eventually incorporated it favorably into their Galenic framework, arguing that it "protects against the plague, cures burning fevers, is good for irregular heartbeats, gladdens the sad, represses the vapors of wine, and therefore lengthens life."[60]

In the sixteenth and seventeenth centuries, Europeans experienced their first encounters with the stimulant beverages that would become essential to the modern world: coffee, tea, and chocolate. Spain was the conduit by which chocolate, cultivated by the Aztecs, first reached Europe in 1520.[61] Prepared with ground cocoa beans as a bitter drink, it was one of the few New World products to catch on quickly in Spain. The seventeenth century saw the increasing addition of sugar, though it was not customary to prepare chocolate in solid form until the nineteenth century. Curiously, its reception was rather the reverse of the pattern we have seen with beer: chocolate became popular in Spain and Italy at least a century before it was accepted in the rest of Europe. As we shall see in chapter 3, chocolate took on particular significance in Spain as a social drink, prepared at home to share with guests or sold at numerous street stands.

Coffee also made its first appearance in Europe in the late sixteenth century, and coffeehouses developed as spaces for social and political interaction. In spite of its quality and omnipresence in today's Spain, coffee caught on much more slowly there than in the rest of Europe. By the eighteenth century in England and France, coffeehouses had become inextricably intertwined with public debate and Enlightenment ideas, and coffee went so far as to replace wine as the essential drink of social gatherings. Nevertheless, in Spain the wine tavern remained the most important site for social engagement. Some coffeehouses appeared in cities in the mid-eighteenth century, but they never became the hotbeds for political discussion that they were elsewhere.[62] Very few Spanish treatises on food mention it, and then not until the eighteenth century; its first appearance in Madrid's food-licensing regulations is in 1760.[63] Benito Bails in the late eighteenth century described the differences in coffee drinking across Europe (Spaniards drink one cup with sugar after a meal; Swedes drink three with milk; the Dutch drink it in the morning with bread and butter) but he dismissed the concoction as useless and without nutritious value.[64] Coffee gained some ground with Spanish elites after the rise of the Bourbon royal family and their cultural ties to Italy, but it could not replace wine as a drink of the common people. Similarly, when the first shipment of tea reached English shores in 1657, it was quickly transformed from an exotic, unfamiliar brew into the cornerstone of British culture—but it hardly registered in the minds or kitchens of early modern Spaniards.

IF THE MAJORITY OF SPANIARDS SHARED THESE ELEMENTS of a common food culture, to what degree can we speak about a national cuisine in the early modern period? Although I have been using the terms "Spain" and "Spanish" to refer to the people and culture that are part of today's modern nation and have tried to paint a general picture of patterns across the peninsula, it is important to remember that such a nation did not exist in the early modern period. Even in the 1500s, after the heirs of Ferdinand and Isabella inherited the kingdoms of Castile and Aragon together, and following the annexation of the Crown of Navarre and the Kingdom of Granada, "Spain" combined (and continues to reflect) a group of historically distinct regional cultures.

On the largest scale there was a continental western European cuisine, especially in the medieval period. Montanari and others argue that the earliest cookbooks, from fourteenth-century Spain, France, Germany, England, and Italy, feature generally the same recipes, flavors, and ingredients.[65] An important subset of western Europe was the Mediterranean region, which maintained some elements of the classical Greco-Roman tradition as well as incorporating Arab contributions following the spread of Islam in the seventh and eighth centuries. Elements of culinary culture were shaped of course by climate and geography as well as regional culture. Trade networks, political influences, even intermarriage between members of ruling families also came into play, and sometimes particular cities such as Naples or Venice seemed to have strong enough individual personalities to have a distinctive cuisine. Early modern cooks themselves referred to particular cuisines, sometimes by nationality and sometimes by more specific influence. Ruperto de Nola's *Llibre del coch* has recipes identified as French-style mustard and Genovese torte, while the seventeenth-century collection of the royal chef Martínez Montiño mentions Aragonese soup, Savoyard pastries, Portuguese-style spinach, and English fish pie, though in both cases these are just a few recipes out of many, and their labels may be for snob value more than an indication of an actual regional style. Still, Teresa Vinyoles argues that as early as the fourteenth century there were clearly defined regional tastes, at least at elite levels, and that courts thus become important sites of culinary exchange.[66]

What were the characteristics of these regional cuisines? One would think that Andalusia, the region that had been longest under Muslim control in the medieval period, would retain a culinary culture distinct from that of the rest of Castile (into which it was incorporated over the period 1212–1492). Castilians who settled in this region during the Reconquest did adopt and maintain many Arab food products and ingredients, such as sugar, rice, citrus fruits, couscous, and eggplant, but they also worked to impose their own. As the Castilian conquerors were generally a minority (only forty thousand came from the north to settle in the kingdom of Granada over the period 1485–1499), they struggled with conflicting priorities.[67] They needed to rely on the existing Andalusian agricultural workforce and infrastructure, especially in rural areas, but at the same time to adapt it as quickly as possible to Castilian control and preferences, and to pressure the resident population to adopt Christian customs. This meant maintaining citrus and rice production while adding livestock and wheat and establishing separate Christian marketplaces and storehouses. The result was a mix of Muslim and Castilian culinary traditions, or perhaps it would be better to say that Castile incorporated Muslim elements and established them as part of its own cuisine.

The Basques of northeastern Spain arguably have the most distinct historical tradition, with roots in that region going back to the Stone Age and a language that bears no clear relation to any other. In the Middle Ages their territory was relatively geographically isolated from the rest of the peninsula and relied on a largely subsistence economy, and so they did not develop a distinctive cuisine. With the founding of new cities like San Sebastián and Bilbao in the late twelfth century, however, they developed increasing trade connections with Castile. After the incorporation of the Basque kingdom of Navarre into the kingdom of Castile in the early 1500s, they imported foodstuffs that were most valued by Castilian society, particularly oil, wine, and wheat.[68] The sole early modern cookbook produced in the Basque country, *El cocinero religioso*, written by an Augustinian friar under the pseudonym Antonio Salsete in the late seventeenth century, was representative of monastic cuisine more than of Basque cuisine. It incorporated elements from across Spain, copying several recipes from Nola and Martínez Montiño, incorporating a few typical Andalusian plates and including one of the first references to tomatoes and potatoes, all of which suggest that Basques were receptive to influences from all over the peninsula. The influence did not seem to go in the other direction, however. The only particularly Basque recipes mentioned in Salsete, for mushrooms and turtle meat, had almost no influence outside the Basque region in the early modern period, and Castilian and Catalan cookbooks did not identify any particular preparations as being in the Basque style. Lope de Isasti's 1625 chronicle of Navarre includes several descriptions of local food, but he refers to apples, cabbage, onions, and chestnuts, which were characteristic of the entire peninsula. In sharp contrast to the reputation the Basque country holds today as a center of high-quality and innovative cuisine, in the early modern period the region did not seem to have a unique culinary identity.

The biggest divide, both in potential culinary difference and in regional identity, was that between Catalonia and Castile. Catalonia, the region in eastern Spain surrounding Barcelona, was a relatively independent county in the Middle Ages until it became a principality of the Crown of Aragon in the early twelfth century. After the dynastic union of Castile and Aragon and the establishment of a permanent court in Madrid, in the center of Castile, many Catalans resented what they saw as an undue

outside influence on their affairs. Today's Catalan independence movement draws on this longstanding resentment as well as on the Catalan
perception of possessing a distinct culture and history from the rest of
Spain. Catalan food scholars point to the region's culinary history as
part of the evidence for this difference.[69] The earliest peninsular recipe
books, the early fourteenth century manuscript *Llibre de Sent Soví* and
Ruperto de Nola's *Llibre del coch*, published in 1520 but probably written
in the late 1400s, were both written in Catalan. Naples for a time in the
fifteenth century was part of the Kingdom of Aragon, and the style of
these cookbooks reflects Catalonia's strong cultural ties to Italy. Nola
identified himself as having been a cook in the court of King Ferdinand
of Naples, and the Roman culinary writer Maestro Martino da Como
borrowed a good deal of his fifteenth-century *Libro de arte coquinaria*
from the *Llibre del coch*. So Catalan cuisine, at least the elite version as it
was identified by written recipe collections, was firmly rooted in a broader
western Mediterranean regional cuisine. If we follow the cookbook trail
within Spain, most of the direction of influence does seem to have been
from the Catalan coast toward the Castilian interior. Nola's *Llibre del coch*
was published in the sixteenth century in at least five Catalan editions and
ten Castilian ones, becoming the first cookbook to be printed in Castile.
García Marsilla has argued that these early Catalan cookbooks did not
reflect any Castilian influences, although since there are no contemporary
existing Castilian recipe collections, the absence of influence is difficult
to prove.[70] Similarly, the Castilian Diego Granado Maldonado copied
many of the recipes in his 1599 *Libro del arte de cozina* from both the
Catalan Nola and the Italian Bartolomeo Scappi.

With the Catalan economic crisis of the fourteenth century and the
establishment of the court in Madrid in the sixteenth, Castile became the
dominant political and economic power of the growing Spanish empire.
Its culinary influence seems to have followed suit, though by this time it
had incorporated many elements of Catalan cuisine. To the extent that
there was such a thing as an early modern "Spanish" cuisine, it seems to
have been a compilation of Italian, Catalan, and Castilian influences, such
as those pulled together in Granado Maldonado's *Libro del arte de cozina*,

as well as contributions from Muslim Andalusia, Portugal, and the Low Countries, as reflected in Martínez Montiño's 1611 *Arte de cozina*.[71] This blended "Spanish" cuisine, while not yet what one would call a distinctly national cuisine, was recognized and influential throughout Europe in the early seventeenth century.

FOOD HIERARCHIES: THEORY AND PRACTICE

In addition to its basic nutritious benefits, food was associated with a wide range of medical, social, and religious characteristics. In early modern Europe, foods were identified in terms of their place in the traditional Galenic framework, perceived as being hot, cold, wet, or dry in accordance with their association with the bodily humors of choler, black bile, blood, and phlegm.[72] Galen perceived the principal causes of illness to be external, such as corrupted water or air, and so food was an important corrective. A well-balanced, healthy human, rather than being at the precise center of the Galenic axes of cold/hot and wet/dry, tended a little bit toward the warm and the moist. Foods that aligned with that tendency, or helped to draw the body back to it from an excess of cold or dryness, were therefore considered to be the most beneficial. Most of the written evidence about food reflects these ideas; treatises on food and health identified the qualities of various foods and provided guidelines for the proper quantity, proportion, and timing of their consumption as well as how they could best be combined.[73] Eggs, for example, being hot and moist, should not be consumed with wine, which shares the same characteristics. Red meats tend to generate choler, and so they should be eaten with sauces that temper that inclination. Greens and fruits, cool and more easily digested, should be eaten before heat-generating meats. This understanding also influenced the preparation of foods, particularly those that fell in the more dangerous cold and wet categories: fish could be improved by frying, and fruits such as grapes were better dried as raisins. (The latter idea coincided nicely with the Muslim culinary preference for dried fruit, adopted in southern Spain.) The Spanish preference for sauces also fit well with this system, as they could be used to balance any unhealthful qualities of the foods they dressed.

These humoral characteristics determined a body's personality as well as its physical health. According to the preponderance of humors in the body, those who were of a sanguine character were cheerful and had strong digestive systems that were not easily upset; their only concern was to avoid excessive consumption of alcohol. The choleric were outgoing and possibly quarrelsome and were advised to avoid fasting. Those with an imbalance favoring black bile were thought to be easily angered and unsociable; they had a more delicate digestion and should avoid overeating, especially of meat. Finally, phlegmatics had a tendency to be overweight because of their slow digestion, and it was recommended that they eat light foods and seek regular exercise.[74] When King Ferdinand VI became feverish and depressed in 1758 following the death of his wife, his physician noted that the monarch's natural temperament was melancholic, having an excess of black bile, and that he had exacerbated this imbalance by being inclined toward the consumption of meat and thick soups. The doctor supervised a limited diet, based on his careful study of the works of Hippocrates, hoping to rid the king's body of the excess bile that troubled it. When this was not successful, after consulting with other doctors, he settled on the remedy of a broth with the most potent cool and wet characteristics—including tortoise, frog, and serpent—but the king "was not willing to try this more than once."[75] While challenges to the Galenic model of the four humors arose as early as the 1530s with the work of Paracelsus, it remained influential in medical thinking through the mid-nineteenth century.

Early modern Spaniards drew on these concepts and blended (or even contradicted) them with their own regional preferences and ideas of social organization and power relationships. Indeed, the ubiquitous olla podrida went against all the Galenic recommendations; it was "a food fit to kill a man," in the words of the Dominican physician Scipione Mercurio.[76] Beginning in the fifteenth century, in a combination of Aristotelian and Christian ideas, western Europeans began to overlay the Galenic system with the perception that the natural world and the world of human beings were both created by God in a parallel vertical hierarchy of society and nature. Among fruits and vegetables, those that were lowest to the ground, such as bulbs and roots, were considered to be the most base. Those grown on bushes or vines were slightly better, and orchard fruits, being the highest, were superior. Therefore garlic and turnips, being low and earthy, were best suited to peasants, while tree fruits were only appropriate for lords. The same vertical hierarchy held true of creatures, so that birds were superior to land animals, which in turn were preferable to fish.[77] Chicken occupied the curious position of being considered a superior food, belonging to the category of winged creatures, while in a practical sense the birds themselves were earthbound and widely available even to poor and rural residents. Elites managed this contradiction by preferring game birds and doves to domestic poultry, while prosperous peasant families raised and ate hens as a key sign of social differentiation to separate them from their poorer counterparts.[78] An eighteenth-century refrain listed in the *Diccionario de Autoridades* held that "carne de pluma quita del rostro la arruga," meaning that the flesh of fowl, being the most delicate and pleasant, could erase the wrinkles from one's face.[79] The cultural value of poultry even led it to be suspected of being overly luxurious; fowl ranked high in the fears of those who were concerned about the moral dangers of gluttony.[80] A Florentine notary complained about a gift of partridges from a friend, suggesting that the gift would have been appropriate had he still been serving on the city council but that coarser and less luxurious foods should be his lot now that he was out of that prestigious position.[81]

Similar cultural associations as well as economic and agricultural patterns affected the consumption of meat animals.[82] The population growth of the High Middle Ages, combined with the necessary expansion of land cultivated for cereals, resulted in a sharp decline in pasture land and thus meat consumption in the twelfth and thirteenth centuries, especially for urban populations.[83] Europeans were more carnivorous in the fourteenth and fifteenth centuries, following the population collapse of the Black Death, which made more natural resources available per capita. As the population recovered over the next two centuries, however, pasture land and forest were again brought under cultivation to produce wheat, and relative meat consumption declined.[84] In the sixteenth and seventeenth centuries, then, consumption of meat came to differentiate between social groups, as a privilege of the wealthy, as well as between urban and rural populations. In the medieval period, game animals (both birds and beasts) were prized because of their association with noble privilege. Actual consumption of them dropped in the early modern period with the increase in pasture animals, but they still retained their symbolic value. Within the category of domestic meat animals, sheep and lamb ranked highest, then beef and pork.[85] Rural families tended to send calf, lamb, kid, and other such profitable meats to urban slaughterhouses while relying on pork, chicken, and older sheep and cows for their own consumption.[86] Goats were raised throughout Spain but were used more to produce milk and cheese than for meat. Kid goat was a valued delicacy for special occasions, but mature goats were rarely consumed. Beef was valued in other parts of Europe, but in Spain it was cheaper and generally of poorer quality than other meats since oxen and dairy cows were used principally for labor and milk production and would not be consumed until they had outlived their usefulness.[87] Pork did not appear as often as other meats in documentary evidence, but this does not mean it was not frequently consumed. Since it was possible for many families to keep their own pigs, pork consumption could have been fairly high without leaving much of a paper trail.[88] The Valencian town of Gandía limited its residents to two pigs on each property and repeated decrees in Madrid requiring people to keep their pigs off the streets as late as the mid-seventeenth century suggest that this was common practice even in a fairly large urban center.[89] Its lower position in the meat hierarchy may have been due simply to this wider availability, especially to the poor, who had less access to fresh meat but could slaughter perhaps one pig a year and preserve much of it in the form of sausage and cured ham throughout the year.

There were certainly regional and particular variations on these themes, but in general they reflect early modern social attitudes, and this food hierarchy was clearly incorporated into people's choices and behaviors. The fourteenth-century Catalan scholar Francesc Eiximenis used the example of a medieval Italian king, of peasant origins, who became seriously ill when he tried to eat the refined foods of the court. He was able to recover only when he returned to the simple, plain food of his youth. The moral for Eiximenis was that each man should eat foods appropriate to his nature—although according to his example, one's origins trumped one's eventual acquired position, since the king in his story was physically not able to eat foods considered appropriate to royalty.[90] In general, though, it was considered appropriate for those in power to eat more of everything, especially meats of quality; for a ruler, eating too little could be perceived as a failing.[91] Such divisions applied to both gender and status. The anthropologist Claude Lévi-Strauss suggested that roasted foods were perceived to be best for men, while boiled foods were more appropriate to women. Similarly, sweet flavors were associated with women and salty ones with men.[92] Eiximenis's conduct book for women, *Llibre de les dones*, suggested that they be allowed only dry wine rather than sweet, assuming that their natural attraction to sweet wine would lead them to drink it in excess.[93] In rural Catalonia, where it was customary for lords to provide their laborers with food, the lords of the Catalan castle of Montesquiu purchased lamb for themselves, while they provided meals of pork to the men who served in their ironworks.[94] Provisions for the Navarrese army in the early fifteenth century included both mutton and chicken, but the records indicate that the chickens (and the highest-quality wine) were reserved for the officers and noblemen.[95] Juan de Soto's 1619 treatise *Obligaciones de todos los estados*, with its chapters on the proper behaviors associated with different categories of people, emphasized repeatedly that one's food consumption should not overreach one's status. Soto admonished scribes and notaries "not to eat more feathers for the sake of the one they carry," in other words, not to consume so much poultry in an attempt to display their status as legal authorities. "An ordinary and moderate diet is enough. . . . There is fish for them on Fridays, without needing to bring trout and eel and oysters and salmon and all such things that are suited to kings, princes and lords."[96] Similarly, the physician Giacomo Albini warned that elites (such as the princes of Savoy, whom he served) should avoid legumes and tripe, which were not refined enough for them to digest, while the stomachs of the poor were better suited to such rough fare.[97]

The proportion of meat in any meal rose sharply according to one's position in the social hierarchy. Roasted meats and combinations of meat and bread or pastry (empanadas or tortes) were prevalent among those with greater resources. Elites prided themselves on their high levels of meat and poultry consumption, reflecting both their superior purchasing power and their elevated social status. Charlemagne, revered as an icon of kingly and warrior virtues, was said to prefer roast game to any other food, and he required four hunters and a falconer to provide meat for his table. Whether or not these accounts are strictly accurate, they reflect the popular associations made between masculinity, power, strength, and meat.[98] We know that by the beginning of the early modern period, the regular consumption of meat had risen through urban and rural communities across all of western Europe, but were the poor able to purchase meat? We often assume that peasant life was plagued with poverty and malnutrition, particularly a lack of protein. Literary portrayals of early modern society convey images of peasants desperate for crusts of bread and elites stuffing themselves at sumptuous banquets, but both are likely to be exaggerated and not representative of ordinary quotidian dining habits. Spanish picaresque literature is full of people scrounging for crumbs (some of the most memorable scenes in the anonymous novella *Lazarillo de Tormes* are of the main character and his blind master matching wits to filch scraps of food from each other). Certainly peasants would not have feasted regularly on lamb chops or steaks, but given the predominance of stew-like dishes and one-pot meals, it would not have been too challenging for poorer families to regularly include at least small amounts of bacon, lard, or what were considered lesser meats (beef, pork, organ meats) in their meals.[99] The Portuguese chronicler Fernão Lopes noted in his description of the siege of Lisbon in 1384 that the poor went without meat, which suggests that normally they did have access to it.[100] Even in the seventeenth century, when average meat consumption was lower, descriptions of Madrid suggest that the poor were able to purchase meat on a regular basis. In Cristóbal Pérez de Herrera's recommendations to Philip III about improving the city of Madrid, he argued for having at least two meat-market stands (one for mutton and one for beef) in the main marketplace and two more near the slaughterhouse. The addition of the latter was important since the slaughterhouse "has become so large that it is difficult for the poor who live nearby to have access to only one butcher's shop."[101] If authorities did not assume meat to be a regular part of their diet, surely lack of access to a butcher would not have registered as a problem. Similarly, the records of that city's municipal authorities show the proprietors of *bodegoncillos* (small taverns or cantinas) arguing that their services were important for supporting the poor, since they provided cheap meals "for the sustenance of poor people and workers who have no one to cook for them," such as a serving of chopped liver for only two *maravedís*.[102] Meat was important enough to require the introduction of millions of sheep and cattle to the Americas, and by 1600 Spanish colonists there consumed more meat than any other sedentary population in the world. When Gaspar Castaño de Sosa embarked on an unauthorized expedition to New Mexico in 1590 with over one hundred and seventy men, women, and children, even as their rations ran low, he managed to provide each of his followers with at least a pound and a half of meat daily.[103] The viceroy Francisco de Toledo in 1575 proclaimed that indigenous laborers should receive each day half a pound of mutton, beef, or pork.[104] In Spain, it is possible that the urban poor may have had more access to meat than their rural counterparts, due to the concerns of city authorities who wanted to avoid unrest due to food shortages and the presence of slaughterhouses that processed enough animals to guarantee a supply of cheap cuts of meat and offal. However, the rural poor may have had more flexibility in raising their own chickens and pigs (though they were likely to sell the most valued parts of these) and having some access to hunting rabbits, small birds, and such.

FOR THE MOST PART, THE CONCEPTIONS OF FOOD ACCORD-ing to the Galenic tradition coincided harmoniously with popular ideas, particularly in relation to basic elements such as meats and vegetables. Occasionally, however, the two systems came into conflict with each other, or with people's individual or collective preferences. The position of tripe and offal is an interesting example of conflict within the cultural hierarchy of meat. *Despojos*—the organs and offal of meat animals and poultry including necks, lungs, intestines, gizzards, feet, and muscle meats such as heart and tongue—were the least expensive meats, theoretically ranked lowest in the meat hierarchy. They were considered appropriate only for the poor, for whom they were often the most accessible form of animal protein. Offal was considered to be a food category unto itself; there was a separate stand in the Plaza Mayor of Madrid, distinct from the fish, poultry, and meat stands, where despojos were sold.[105] (The animal hierarchy was reflected here as well, as the innards of sheep and poultry were more valued than those of pigs or cows.) Early modern food treatises as well as practical urban customs indicated that such meats were best suited to the lowest ranks of society. Of the names of the various categories of offal, several carried negative connotations: "menudo" (tripe) also meant "despicable, or of little consequence; plebeian," and "despojos," offal, was a term also used for any sort of unwanted surplus.[106] This attitude was reflected in the social use of such foods. In Antequera, in southern Spain, butchers were not allowed to sell organ meats and blood until the poor had had a chance to purchase them first; city ordinances there emphasized that "the poorest . . . are those who sustain themselves on said entrails and offal because of their low price."[107] Similarly, Madrid's municipal regulations reserved offal from the slaughterhouse to feed the poor who were held in the city jail or who lodged in the city's hospitals.[108] The constitutions of the city's Hermandad del Real Hospicio de Pobres Mendigos (Brotherhood of the Royal Hospice of Poor Beggars), dedicated to providing regular meals for the poor, stipulated that mutton heads and sweetbreads should be provided for their dinners.[109] As late as the 1780s, the results of a questionnaire about food consumption in Cataluña stated that the wealthy ate lots of meat, especially lamb, while the poor consumed organ meats.[110]

Nevertheless, several clues indicate that elites had a particular taste for offal and sought to procure it in spite of its association with poverty. While in theory despojos were principally reserved for the poor and the provision of hospitals, they appear in the kitchen accounts of the queens of Aragon and the barons of Pinos i Mataplana in the fourteenth century.[111] The alcaldes of Madrid, whose job included the appropriate distribution of slaughterhouse products in the markets, received frequent petitions from high-ranking officials for a share of organ meats, and twenty beef tongues were set aside for the commissary-general of the Santa Cruzada for the annual meal that he offered to the members of the Council of Castile.[112] Part of the appeal of offal in the early modern period may have been that it occupied an uncertain zone between foods that were clearly prohibited on fast days and those that were allowed. Fridays required total abstinence from meat, but Saturdays were days of semi-fasting, where "Saturday foods," including despojos, were allowed. These became popular enough, perhaps simply for being a form of meat that could be consumed during Lent and fast days, that the price of offal in the public markets was regularly higher on Saturdays than during the rest of the week.[113]

Fruit was another food category whose position in early modern society was different in theory than it was in social and cultural practice. Fruit is one of the most difficult foodstuffs for the historian to trace, since it does not leave much of a paper trail: unlike wine, oil, meat, and grain, it was not considered essential enough to include in records of city contracts, and most fruit production and trade were local and informal. In general, commentaries on fruit placed it low on the food hierarchy in terms of its practical and moral characteristics. Galenic theory viewed fruit more as a condiment than a true source of nourishment, and not a favorable one at that: too cold and wet, bad for digestion, potentially a cause for fever, and even encouraging of "wanton appetite" and moral weakness.[114] Eiximenis in a chapter on remedies for gluttony wrote that one should abstain from fruit because of its moral dangers.[115] The seventeenth-century jurist León Pinela attributed the death of the crown prince Carlos in 1568 to, among other things, having eaten an excess of fruit.[116] Vilanova directed that fresh fruit could be eaten for medicinal purposes (usually as either a laxative or a costive, depending on the fruit) but that it should not be eaten simply for pleasure.[117] In 1612 Pedro Aznar Cardona wrote a treatise supporting the expulsion of the *moriscos* (those of Muslim background who had converted to Christianity), justifying his arguments in part by saying that the morisco community possessed valuable land but used it to cultivate fruit rather than anything of real value.[118]

In spite of these negative connotations, elites seem to have favored the consumption of fruit, at least in southern Europe. Bartolomeo Scappi, the sixteenth-century Italian who wrote one of the most influential cookbooks of the early modern period, included descriptions of typical meals and menus—"typical" for the Vatican, at least, where he served as personal chef to Pius V. These menus, probably designed for groups of fifty or sixty people, included substantial amounts of fruit, such as a first cold course consisting of twenty pounds of sugared strawberries, thirty pounds of cherries, three hundred plums, and one hundred and fifty apricots.[119] These tastes were reflected in the principal Spanish cookbooks. Diego Granado Maldonado's 1599 *Libro del arte de cozina* was greatly influenced by Scappi, and Domingo Hernández de Maceras's early seventeenth-century recipe collection includes a variety of preparations of cherries, melons, peaches, and pears.[120] Aragonese court guidelines recommended that each diner should be served fruit at the beginning of a meal and that those seated at the royal table should be given an additional serving after dinner.[121] Individual tastes seem to reflect these values. Ferdinand I of Aragon wrote to the *batle general* (a royal official) of Valencia with requests for fruit for his personal consumption and received regular shipments of cherries, peaches, lemons, figs, oranges, and pomegranates.[122] Teresa Vinyoles relates a case of an Aragonese lady in the late fourteenth century who asked a visiting friend to bring her pears; when the friend forgot the request, the lady wept for her loss.[123] The Dukes of Gandía in the seventeenth century regularly consumed fruit, and even more so when honored guests shared the table, suggesting that it was considered to be a particular delicacy.[124]

It seems then that early modern Spaniards not only enjoyed fruit but also associated it with elite status. The charitable institution Pia Almoina of Barcelona provided regular meals for hundreds of poor residents, and though meat was included in these meals during most days of the year, fruit was not served, as they considered it not appropriate for the needy.[125] Sumptuary laws in Castile in 1563 placed limits on the number of servings of fruit that could be included in banquets, as part of an ongoing effort to control the growing expenses of weddings and other formal occasions.[126] This distinction may have arisen because orchard fruits had to be cultivated, and they were generally produced on seigneurial lands; they required careful tending and produced relatively little in relation to the land they occupied.[127] They were therefore inaccessible to peasants and relatively expensive for town dwellers. In elite households, expenditures on fruit were nearly always higher than those on vegetables, suggesting both greater expense and higher consumption. Moving down the social scale, such expenditures even out between fruits and vegetables at the level of urban merchants, while the poor almost certainly consumed far more vegetables than they did fruits.[128] All of this suggests that despite the disdain of medical and dietary treatises, fruit was informally a luxury item.

Nevertheless, not all fruits were created equal. Fruit, like other categories of food, contained its own social hierarchy: sour cherries (*guindas*) and peaches were on the more expensive end of the spectrum and favored by elites, while melons and black grapes were considered more appropriate for the humbler classes.[129] Similarly, Felicity Heal has noted in English gift-giving patterns that fruit was valued enough to be a common gift but that easily acquired fruits such as apples and pears were perceived as "gifts of the poor," while greater pride was taken in offering rarer fruits such as apricots and peaches.[130] As we will see with other elite foods, the acceptability of fruit seems to have become more widespread through the early modern period. In the sixteenth century, the university students of Alcalá de Henares had access to seasonal plums, pears, and cherries, especially on festival days.[131] By the seventeenth century, middle-range urban families in southern Spain regularly consumed figs, grapefruit, oranges, and cherries, suggesting that these products were easily within their reach and perhaps even a symbol of their financial success.[132] A seventeenth-century fictional dialogue among students suggests that fruit had become more common. These young men certainly would not have been included among the elite and wealthy, but when a prospective student asks about the culinary customs of his companions, their response includes a listing of pears, apples, cherries, plums, grapes, and peaches, incorporated into any meal of the day.[133]

FOOD AND THE URBAN COMMUNITY

Given the powerful associations between food and social status, it is not surprising that the provision and consumption of food was closely interwoven with ideas of urban community and the practice of local authority. Different categories of people and an enormous variety of foodstuffs shared public space in the urban context, generating endless possibilities for social performance and the need for a certain degree of administrative control. We usually envision meals as being shared by a family around a domestic table, but for early modern Europeans this was probably the exception. For elites, the distinction between dining privately at home or publicly with companions was not necessarily clear, as such households were staffed with large numbers of servants and other dependents, and meals frequently could include dozens of guests.[134] Urban residents also had a wide range of beyond-the-home dining options: one could purchase prepared food at any number of lively street stands, pastry shops, and marketplaces as well as from strolling vendors. Indeed, many urban dwellings did not include kitchens, so many residents bought their meals on the street rather than preparing them at home. There were also several kinds of places to sit down for a meal, from inns to taverns, though formal restaurants as we think of them did not begin to appear until the late eighteenth century. Although conduct books and social expectations dictated that aristocrats should not partake of food in such public areas, these sites brought together a wide range of people together from the rest of society. Lope de Vega's plays and poems are full of references to the variety of people and food that came together in the streets of Madrid. The servant Martín in *La moza de cántaro* marvels that "the court sustains so many things, I do not know how it is possible. Who could imagine so many different people and professions selling different things? Cakes, buns, biscuits, nougat, chestnuts, marmalade treats, electuaries and preserves, a thousand sugar figurines, flowers, rosaries, rosettes, doughnuts and marzipan, spirits and cinnamon-waters."[135] Quevedo's description of the marketplace of Salamanca promises a similar wealth of culinary delights: "Here you will find the kid goat and the spotted calf; here the lamb; here the honey in its comb, and the trout in its trap; here the firm chestnut, guarded by its hedgehog armor; the walnut, imprisoned in its shell; and here, with the brown pear, you will find the golden pippin. Stay, and state what you lack."[136] Sharing food in a public context, as it is today, was an important form of social and political connection. Merchants in Valencia in the fourteenth and fifteenth centuries met in taverns over meals to discuss business.[137] Food and drink even played an important role at the *corrales de comedias*, open-air theatrical playhouses that proliferated in the sixteenth and seventeenth centuries. Their principal attraction was the latest works of Lope de Vega or Calderón de la Barca, but an important element of the experience was the chance to partake in aloja, wine, fruits and confections.[138]

By the early fourteenth century, increased regional specialization, the gradual reduction of transport costs, urban growth, and growing consumer markets all led to a greater volume of trade and a wider variety of products from which city dwellers could choose. The increased mobility of groups such as soldiers, merchants, officials, scholars, and pilgrims also led to greater demand for foods that could be purchased and consumed on the go. The preparation and sale of certain foods was designated to corresponding urban spaces. One could construct a food map of any early modern city, the details of which would be shaped by practical issues of supply and public access, municipal authorities' need to maintain quality control, and cultural associations with space. In Madrid, for example, a typical seventeenth-century resident might begin his day in the Puerta del Sol on the eastern edge of the city with a shot of aguardiente and a serving of letuario, a sweet confection of honey and orange peel. During the course of the day, he could pick up fruit, small cakes, savory pastries, and other treats from street vendors or have a quick plate of prepared food from a *bodegón*, especially in the neighborhood around the Plaza de Santa Cruz. If he wanted to enjoy a glass of wine at a tavern, the options were nearly limitless. At the beginning of the seventeenth century, Madrid boasted nearly four hundred of them, including public taverns established in the monasteries of San Jerónimo and the Jesuits.[139] Given the range of dining options, people of every social rank could partake of street food in one form or another.

In spite of this mix of different foods, dining establishments, and customers, most of these eateries reflected and reinforced the social hierarchy. There were small bodegones, informal cantinas that prepared simple and cheap meals for a clientele of mostly urban workers, sometimes in established buildings with an assortment of tables, sometimes hardly more than temporary street stands (*bodegoncillos de puntapié*). In the minds of contemporary Spaniards, such businesses were defined by their customers rather than their products: the 1726 dictionary of the Real Academia describes a bodegón as "the cellar or entryway where food is prepared for poor and ordinary folk."[140] Their offerings included pork rinds, sausages, pig feet, and mutton tongue, mostly meat products but all of them ranked on the low end of the perceived food hierarchy. In Barcelona, street vendors sold a stew called *malcuinat*, cooked over small portable stoves, that was often the only hot meal available to those with limited resources.[141] *Empanados* (fried breaded foods) were common street food, usually worth four or eight maravedís (roughly the same price as a loaf of bread) and also associated with the working poor. For more elegant and expensive fare than that offered in the street stands, both in terms of food and wine, there were the *figones*, which were allowed to sell foods like partridge and venison that were considered more appropriate to the upper classes. Later we will see how municipal authorities actively reinforced these social differences via food regulations.

While Spanish cities and towns offered a remarkable variety of prepared foods, for those who cooked at home, meat and produce were available in open-air markets. While Seville had been known as the gastronomic capital of Spain, Madrid, with its dramatic growth after becoming the permanent seat of the court in the 1560s, soon gained a reputation for providing extraordinary variety (and we will discuss later the negative side of the city's growing reputation for gluttony). Of the sixteen public plazas in Madrid in the seventeenth century, nearly all of them were dedicated at least some days of the week to the provision of food. In spite of the city's location in the geographic center of the peninsula, two hundred miles from the nearest coast, fresh fish and seafood were always available. For preparing meals at home, nearly every main ingredient could be found in the market of the Plaza Mayor, which, according to a seventeenth-century chronicler, "seems to enjoy the privileges of Paradise, in that against the laws of nature it is a garden that is always fruitful."[142] The same chronicler boasted that "there was no bird so fleet nor fish so hidden that if it existed in any land, Madrid could not get hold of it."[143] Walking clockwise around the plaza, one would have passed stands for beer, sweets, bread, frogs, wine, pastries, fruit, fish, aguardiente and let-uario, chicken, eggs, more bread, vegetables, tripe, mutton, and goat.[144] Secondary food markets were set up in the plaza of San Martín, the Puerta de Santo Domingo, and the Red de San Luis, all around the edges of the seventeenth-century city. More specialized sites included the streets of Postas and Mayor for chocolate vendors, the plazas of San Salvador and Arrabal for fish, the Plaza de la Cebada where grains and vegetables were sold, and the plazas of Puerta Nueva and Santa Luisa for butchers who provided beef, mutton, and goat. Animals were provided for in the Plaza de la Madera's marketplace for grain and hay.

As cities and their food supplies grew, the provision, maintenance, and quality control of markets and eating establishments became a significant responsibility for local authorities. Cities by their very nature relied on imports of food from the surrounding region and from greater distances; even a town with three thousand residents required 4,500 acres of land to produce enough grain for its needs.[145] Municipal grain policies began to develop in earnest in the thirteenth century, seeking to guarantee a supply of grain, control prices, maintain quality, and avoid popular upris-ings.[146] During the conquest of the Muslim kingdom of Granada in the late fifteenth century, Ferdinand and Isabella (as well as local authorities) were concerned about maintaining the stability of the food supply in the newly conquered regions. The town of Alhama surrendered on February 28, 1482, and on the next day Seville was ordered to provide it with seven thousand animals, seven thousand sacks of grain, and over a hundred thousand liters of wine.[147] In the context of the Reconquest, armies were careful to protect and maintain ovens, mills, and marketplaces in good

condition, so that conquered towns could return to self-sufficiency as soon
as possible. This was for practical reasons, but also meant as an expression
of "princely paternalism," through which rulers followed a moral imperative to protect their subjects. Nascent capitalism still operated within a
framework where market forces were not allowed to endanger the body
politic when it came to the supply and price of food.[148] Subjects may
have understood droughts and disease to be acts of God, but they were
also aware that food shortages were at least in part the responsibility of
city officials. In times of dearth or crisis, local authorities acted to protect
local interests, and this could lead to conflicts between different territories over scarce resources. In 1470, the city of Toledo was so short of
grain that it sent a delegation to Córdoba, some 180 miles to the south,
asking its permission to purchase grain from their stores. The officials
of Córdoba not only denied their request but also issued a decree that
the Toledans could not travel through their territory in possession of
any grain purchased from any other region. Toledo in turn protested to
King Enrique IV, with the plea that such a denial went "against all charity,
humanity, and divine and human law," but it is not clear whether the king
was able to take any action.[149] During the food crisis of the late 1640s,
there were hunger-related uprisings in southern Granada, Córdoba, and
Seville; Madrid refused to send grain in fear that its own citizens might
riot as well.[150]

Concerns over the availability of food also marked the relationship
between urban populations and the surrounding countryside; in every
case, the city had the upper hand. In times of dearth, city authorities
could requisition grain from the surrounding area, prohibit the removal
of grain from the region, control how much was milled, manipulate prices,
provide rations to city residents, and even demand forced loans of money
or grain. Municipal food regulations also reflected a degree of concern
about maintaining sustainable food supplies, by placing restrictions on
the depletion of fish stocks, limiting hunting to certain seasons, and
other such cautionary measures. As we have seen earlier, city authorities
were deeply concerned about maintaining bread supplies in the interest
of public order. Meat supplies were less crucial, and they merited only a

brief note in the Madrid regulations: "If on any day there is a shortage of meat, the contracted providers shall be fined, so that they shall be aware that they need to provide enough or face greater penalties. . . . In the worst case, someone trustworthy should be sent to purchase more from the regional fairs."[151] The privileged position of the court was reflected in the fact that city regulations dictated that in times of bread shortages, the royal household was to be supplied first and hospitals and convents afterward, at the aldermen's discretion.[152] Regulations and decrees regarding the production, sale, and price of bread number in the hundreds in the records of Madrid's alcaldes de casa y corte, more than those concerning any other foodstuff. City authorities kept careful track of the production of wheat in areas within sixteen leagues of the city and the amounts that each region was obliged to provide each week. In 1630, facing concerns about maintaining the supply of bread for a growing population, local officials decided to extend the wheat obligation to a broader geographical range.[153] Barcelona, meanwhile, had less authority over its surrounding areas and depended more on imports of grain from Sicily and Provence; its poor were therefore more susceptible to fluctuations in price and supply. In early 1334, following a year of poor harvests, city councilors wrote that citizens were "perishing from hunger" and that they feared the city was on the verge of "tearing itself apart," foreshadowing a spate of riots and violence that broke out later that year in response to rumors of grain-hoarding.[154] While this was essentially a practical and political issue, one curious side effect was that after the fourteenth century, hagiographies came to record a new form of miracle along the Mediterranean coast of Spain: the providential arrival of ships loaded with grain.[155]

With growing urban populations, municipal governments came to take an increasingly active role in inspecting and guaranteeing, to the best of their ability, the quality of the food supply as well as its quantity. Far from being a trivial duty, this was perceived as an important contribution to maintaining social order. The Augustinian Juan de Soto's recommendations to King Philip III on the proper role of all "estates and offices" included a chapter on local magistrates and governors, emphasizing that an important part of their role was the supervision of marketplaces to guarantee fair prices, quality supplies of meat, wine, and bread, and accurate measurements.[156] (Curiously, Soto's chapter on merchants and grocers tends to assume the opposite, that their natural behavior will be to cut corners: "although certainly some of them must do their job well, there is such temptation in it, to not give each customer what he is owed, or to not be content with modest earnings, that it will be necessary to admonish them in the Lord and advise them as to what they ought to do."[157]) In Madrid, the records of the alcaldes de casa y corte are replete with licenses, price lists, quality checks, and other indications of the ongoing concern that alcaldes had with guaranteeing the safety and availability of food. These officials granted licenses for, and supervised the sale of, items as minute and diverse as olives, sugar, sausages, biscuits, asparagus, eggs, and paprika.[158]

Beyond the guarantee of quality and quantity, municipal authorities played a role in the public reinforcement of social hierarchy by determining what kinds of people had access to certain kinds of food. Even at the low end of the social scale, while bodegones and taverns sold food and drink to humbler folk, they were instructed not to sell food to slaves and blacks. Officials in the Andalusian town of Baeza, for example, complained that "the taverns and inns and other houses are providing food and drink to the slaves of this city, with the result that they leave their masters and lords to go out and eat and drink."[159] City ordinances in Madrid included directions in 1596 to the owners of bodegones to not provide food to slaves and blacks, and in 1617 tavern owners were prohibited from selling alcohol to slaves or even letting them enter the taverns.[160] Madrid authorities also expressed repeated criticisms of elites who did not impose distinct forms of dress and hairstyle on their Muslim slaves and servants. This may have reflected fears that if slaves and blacks socialized freely with Christian Spaniards, eating and drinking in public places, it could be too challenging to tell them apart, and the former would be too inclined to think of themselves as equal.

On the higher end of the social scale, local authorities sought to guarantee certain foodstuffs for their most important citizens. Cities established yearly contracts with people who provided basic items such as meat and bread for the city, and quantities of the best fruit, meat, fish, and grain were set aside from those supplies for certain elites. The wealthy of course had access to superior foods because of their greater purchasing power, but these basic divisions were inscribed into local government as well. The municipal ordinances of the Andalusian town of Loja in the late fifteenth century, for example, directed that butchers and fishwives should reserve their choicest products for the mayor, clerics, and aldermen. Similarly, the town's aldermen were guaranteed a regular supply of mutton, with the promised slaughter of three animals per day for themselves and the sick.[161] In Toledo, the guardians of the chapel of don Sancho (the first king of Castile) in the cathedral had the privilege of keeping the equivalent of ten pounds of meat from each cow and one pound for each sheep that was butchered in the city, in spite of complaints that this drove up the price of beef and mutton.[162] In Madrid, once the court was established there, these decrees included special supplies for the royal household and those of ambassadors. City officials kept lists of what each ambassador's household was allowed to have, both in terms of provisions from the marketplace as well as hunting rights in the Casa de Campo. For example, the official supplier of meat to the court was instructed to provide one veal calf each week and one kid goat each day to the house of every ambassador, and a 1617 decree established that the ambassador of the Holy Roman Emperor could augment his own pantry with up to 160 doves and 80 partridges a day and 450 rabbits a week. At the same time, as we have seen, these decrees reserved tripe, giblets, and heads for hospitals and the poor.[163]

The basic food practices of early modern Spaniards were shaped by a range of beliefs and practical realities, from the daily challenges of acquiring and preparing food to the importance of consuming foodstuffs appropriate to their status and nature. Their choices reflected a careful adherence to Galenic medical beliefs related to the bodily humors as well as popular ideas about the qualities of foods and their relationship to human society. The kind of bread people baked, the amount of wine they drank, the spices with which they seasoned their dishes, and their choices of meats and vegetables were shaped by both legal frameworks and informal social pressures. For monarchs at the national level and city officials at the local level, policing these hierarchies and guaranteeing a sufficient and healthy food supply was part of their political and moral responsibility. This chapter has served to provide a general overview of early modern Spanish culinary customs and the most important connections between food and the social hierarchy, particularly in the urban context. The following one will examine groups and collective identity, to show how food worked to solidify connections between members of certain social categories and to define their boundaries in relation to others.

2

Social Groups and Collective Identity

IN 1407, A GLASSWORKER FROM THE VILLAGE OF BIGUES petitioned the city council of nearby Barcelona to be accepted as a legal resident of that city. The councilmen discussed the issue and decided in his favor, not because of his wealth or length of residence but because he had participated in all the city's festivals with his wife and children.[1] Sharing food, ritual, and entertainment with other members of a community formed an important element of the performance of collective identity. This identity, as it was perceived in early modern Europe, could be inherent and immutable, as in the case of gender, or elective and temporary, as in the case of students or confraternity members.[2] One's participation in a collective could be performed by one's association with its activities, such as sharing an exclusive dinner with other members. Or it could be determined by outside judgment, as in the case of Christians' belief that those who did not eat pork must be secretly Muslim or Jewish. There also existed powerful associations between certain social categories and food customs. Women in the marketplace were expected to deal in fruits and vegetables but not meat or wine; rulers had to follow elaborate ceremonies in their dining habits. Early modern Spaniards believed that if you were a certain kind of person (royal, male or female, student) you had

49

to make the food choices that corresponded to that kind of person and, conversely, that if you followed certain food practices (such as fasting on particular days), those practices revealed the sort of person you were. This chapter examines a variety of groups, categories, and institutions (people defined by their hereditary/political role, gender, occupation, religion, or religious dedication) to show how early modern Spaniards used food practices to categorize themselves and others and how society associated certain kinds of food, preparation, and customs with particular groups or categories of people.

ROYALTY AND FOOD AT COURT

While monarchs may compose a small social category, their influence is undeniably significant, and public displays were an important part of their performance of power. The relationship between royalty and food was weighted with issues of wealth, power, display, self-discipline, and the negotiation of relationships. Rulers needed to negotiate a delicate balance between, on the one hand, presenting a certain distance between themselves and their subjects to maintain respect and authority and, on the other, maintaining a sense of connection with the people to inspire their loyalty and service. Over the early modern period, the way in which Spanish kings publicly presented themselves shifted from an emphasis on generosity and mutual dedication to greater distance and limited access to the monarch's person. Both changes can be perceived in patterns of dining and commensality.

Late medieval courts were itinerant; kings and their retinues traveled throughout their territories rather than remaining in one place. Madrid was not fixed as the court of Spain until 1561, and even then the court briefly moved to Valladolid in the early 1600s. Therefore one obligation of high-ranking subjects was to provide food and lodging for the ruler and his or her household during their travels. *Yantar*, a verb that in the early modern period was synonymous with feasting or dining, has its origin in a term referring to the tribute or fee paid by subjects to satisfy the obligation of hosting and feeding a monarch who traveled through their territories.[3] This constituted a substantial expense but also carried the advantage of guaranteeing privileged and personal access to the ruler and presumably a sense of reciprocal debt. In the early fifteenth century the archbishop of Toledo made a reputation for himself as a staunch and loyal subject to the queen of Castile because of the "sumptuous dishes" that he offered her. A few decades later the archbishop's nephew, don Álvaro de Luna, was criticized for having prepared a poor table for John II of Castile (even though he possessed one of the most admired cooks in the land), and in fact he was later arrested for intrigues against the king and was executed in 1453. When the archbishop of Toledo hosted Rodrigo de Borgia, the papal legate, he sought to gain the legate's support through an impressive feast, purchasing whole flocks of sheep and calves, gallons of wine, and "so many hens from the surrounding towns and villages that the next morning there was not a rooster left that didn't look around in astonishment at the deserted rungs of the henhouse."[4] Contemporary chronicles delighted in describing the details of such encounters between significant people, always including notes on the quality and amount of food prepared for the occasion. Their descriptions may not be entirely reliable in terms of such details, but they do convey the importance of food as signifier of generosity, patronage, loyalty, or supplication.

In the fifteenth century, as royal households grew in size and complexity, they became less peripatetic and began to settle in fixed locations for greater lengths of time. This meant a shift in the burden of hosting, from elites providing food and housing for their monarch to the monarch entertaining elites who came to the court. Such a shift led to a corresponding change in the symbolism of sharing food with kings. While generosity at the table was most frequently associated in medieval chronicles with bonding, association, and concord, by the sixteenth century, as the ruler came to be the principal host, it came to represent power and supremacy. Royal banquets became "elaborate acts of political theater," including not just guests but spectators, in a kind of visual spectacle that could win over the people and be written about afterwards.[5] The Portuguese king Dom Pedro I in the fourteenth century celebrated the knighting of one of his followers by providing a public feast in the Rossio Square of Lisbon, set up in giant tents with "great mountains of bread and as many tubs full of wine ready to drink, and outside there were whole cows roasting on spits, and all who wanted to partake were allowed, and nothing was denied to anyone, and the tents remained throughout the festivities."[6] There was always a tension between the intangible benefits and the practical cost of such meals. As early as the thirteenth century, the Cortes of Valladolid asked King Alfonso X of Castile to moderate the consumption of those who shared his table and to limit the number of servants and squires that accompanied them.[7] A century later, as King Henry IV of Castile continued to provide his guests with rich banquets, his treasurer complained about the expense; Henry responded, "I feed them so they will serve me."[8] Commensality was an important source of connection and patronage: in the fourteenth and fifteenth centuries, the rulers of Aragon always shared their meals with relatives and representatives of the noble and ecclesiastical estates.[9] As we shall see, this generosity gradually shifted toward restricting the access that guests had to the king and court. Charles V was the last of the Spanish kings to be famous for his munificence at the table, to the extent that the humanist Francisco de Monzón complained that "half the court eats from his kitchen." Monzón went on to note that the representative assembly of the Cortes had sternly requested that Charles provide only what was necessary for his own meals and those of whatever palace officials were absolutely required to dine with him.[10]

There was also a sort of trickle-down effect of royal generosity, for servants and other inferiors. Monarchs were always attended by a substantial group of servants and courtiers, though there was some uncertainty as to their proper position at the table. On one hand, for a king to be surrounded by a coterie of attendants was a powerful reminder of both his position and their loyalty. On the other, a ruler's regality could be enhanced by a certain distance and not allowing others to share his table. The ordinances of Pedro el Ceremonioso of Aragón decreed that servants should never be allowed to eat in front of royalty.[11] Servants in the royal household nevertheless received a substantial part of their payment in daily *raciones*, or food supplies, which also served to communicate their relative status.[12] A series of letters between royal secretaries in 1562 addressed Philip II's efforts to regularize some of these payments, specifically to make sure that the servants of the household of his son Prince Carlos were receiving the same *raciones* that the servants in Philip's household in Flanders had received. These in turn were carefully structured according to the position of the servant: the majordomo received daily rations of over 5.6 kilos (12 pounds) of bread and thirteen jugs of wine, while the baker received 2.4 kilos of bread and two jugs of wine, and the seamstress's share was just under a pound of bread and one jug of wine.[13] Sharing a meal with the king was also a valuable symbolic reward for service. In the Habsburg court, if a queen's lady-in-waiting were to marry, her nuptials were celebrated by allowing her to share her first meal after the wedding with the king and queen. One such dinner, acknowledging the marriage of doña Juana de Silva, involved fourteen dishes of meat, principally poultry and game, white wine, and a range of flavored drinks (lemonade, hippocras, and cinnamon water).[14]

During and after the sixteenth century, the royal table became increasingly select and exclusive. Banquets still brought together important people on a regular basis, but the king's ordinary meals took place in greater isolation. The arrival of Charles of Ghent in Spain (who became King Charles I of Spain in 1516 and Charles V of the Holy Roman Empire in 1519) marked a significant change in royal food habits. He was responsible for the introduction of more ceremonial forms of dining, drawn from the protocols of the late fifteenth-century court of his great-grandfather Charles the Bold in the famed duchy of Burgundy, admired throughout Europe for its elegance and taste. The advent of the Burgundian protocol, with its particular emphasis on dining rituals, required a complex set of rules, laid out in no fewer than 153 pages in the *Etiquetas de palacio*, as well as a greater number of household servants.[15] While late medieval kitchens already had an array of specialized positions, such as baker, wine steward, and saucier, Charles V's household under the new system added several pages responsible for the rituals of setting the table and serving the ruler. These included separate roles for those who handled the salt, bread, drinks, and the ruler's personal napkin as well as a head steward (*mayordomo mayor*) to supervise them all. There was a corresponding shift in emphasis from the quantity of the food served to its sophistication, quality, and the level of service at the table. The seventeenth-century court chef Martínez Montiño argued that when it came to royal banquets, "the important touch is the presentation; regardless of how much money is spent, if it is not well served, it does not shine."[16]

With greater emphasis on ceremony came greater insistence on limiting the king's dining companions. Monzón, author of one of the best-known advice books for princes, warned that rulers needed to take great caution in choosing their dining companions. He acknowledged the importance of impressing grandees with the style and quality of the royal table and rather reluctantly admitted that kings and emperors occasionally needed to dine with others, especially foreign visitors, whose effort in traveling to the court should be honored and recognized with a meal. Nevertheless, royal dining companions absolutely had to be "people of status and nobility who are deserving of being seated with [the king] to eat," and the king should choose them carefully and in limited numbers. Otherwise, Monzón cautioned, the rare privilege of dining with the monarch would be devalued and royal majesty would be diminished.[17] Spanish rulers took this advice to heart: combined with the strict regulation of behavior advocated by the Burgundian etiquette, it led to the increasing distance between the monarch and his subjects that became a hallmark of Spanish Habsburg rule. This distance corresponded to the broader early modern European pattern of centering political power in courts, to which the nobility were lured in pursuit of opportunity and prestige. The development of court culture, perhaps best represented in Castiglione's famous conduct book *The Book of the Courtier*, led to a growing emphasis on sophistication in behavior and a concern with personal appearance and self-control.[18]

Sir John Elliott and others have demonstrated the extent to which the Spanish Habsburg kings cultivated more symbolic distance between themselves and their subjects than did their French and English counterparts. In Versailles, which became the center of French court culture in the seventeenth century, King Louis XIV's bedroom was the architectural and cultural focal point of the entire building. His *lever* and *coucher*, the rituals of getting dressed in the morning and preparing for bed at night, far from being private moments, were virtually public ceremonies attended by the elites of the court.[19] In contrast, in the Spanish palace in Madrid, Philip IV's bedroom was reached only at the end of a long series of antechambers to which one had access to according to one's status. The only individuals who were allowed to penetrate as far as the royal apartments were the papal nuncio, cardinals, the president of the Council of Castile, and a select few others.[20] The same pattern held for meals: the monarchs of France and England generally dined with those who sought their patronage and influence, while Spanish kings in the seventeenth century usually dined alone. They were not truly alone, of course. Palace records from the 1620s, the early years of the reign of Philip IV, show that there were forty-seven gentlemen and ten valets whose jobs centered on waiting on the royal table. But no one actually accompanied the king at his meals, not even his wife and family. Even during royal banquets, which were offered as often as once a week, the king and queen ate separately from the rest of the guests (and from each other; the queen generally ate apart with a small group of ladies-in-waiting).[21] In fact, the queen had a separate household staff including her own cook and her own kitchen accounts. While the medieval royal table served as a site of connection and reunion around the king, the early modern table, at least in the Spanish case, came to represent separation and exclusion, except for a very select few.

In spite of the emphasis on kings eating alone, such meals were meant to be observed. In the seventeenth century it was customary to allow an audience once a week where people could gather behind a sort of railing or balcony and watch the king dine.[22] In these cases the meals were more abundant than if the monarch ate in his private quarters, and the ceremony was more extensive.[23] The Burgundian protocol has twelve pages describing how the king was to be served in such circumstances: for the moments when he wished to drink, for example, the cup-bearer who stood just to one side would approach, drop to one knee, uncover the cup, hand it to His Majesty, wait for him to drink, and receive the cup again. A second servant would then step up with a napkin that he kept folded over his left shoulder.[24] The ritual of these dining occasions was much admired: the scholar and court official Pedro González de Salcedo commented that "nothing is more lovely, delightful, and worthy of veneration than to watch a Prince eat with cleanliness, refinement, gravity, and composure, through which he inspires respect in those who view him."[25] A Portuguese traveler in Valladolid in 1605, Pinheiro da Veiga, noted that one of the most important events of his visit was having seen Queen Margarita de Austria eat in public on a Sunday in June. The queen was seated at a table on a platform, under a brocade canopy, with three ladies-in-waiting standing at each side of the table to serve the food, with a fourth to provide water, and other gentlemen and the queen's majordomo standing to the back.[26] Pinheiro also recounted, later that month, chatting with a group of noblewomen on the street during the Corpus Christi celebrations, who suggested as the day's entertainment going to watch the visiting English ambassador at dinner. Pinheiro joined them, and he noted with some astonishment that there were more than 700 dinner guests, with 62 English noblemen at the center table, being served by several of the Spanish king's manservants. He counted at least 24 different dishes served on 260 great plates, including beef and mutton stew; doves; roast beef, chicken, and mutton; tortes, puff pastries, rice with milk, olives, fruits, cheeses, and nuts. It is not clear just how (or which) outsiders were able to observe such a banquet, but Pinheiro's companions' proposal clearly suggests that it was an acceptable form of entertainment, at least for elites, and the frequency of such descriptions indicates that a host may well have expected an audience to observe and indeed to record their observations, as Pinheiro did.

The growing ritual and complexity around public events involving the king were also part of a post-Reformation effort to emphasize the sacred character of the king and reinforce the linked authority of church and state by demanding greater participation. For example, when Charles V (I of Spain) celebrated the birth of his son Philip in 1527, he sent an announcement of the event to the local governments throughout the empire but did not suggest any specific response or action on their part. Two generations later, Philip III's announcement in 1605 of the birth of his heir included a demand to local officials that they celebrate and give thanks to God through a series of festivities. On the day after the baptism, when the prince was presented at the church of Our Lady of San Llorente, the Condestable of Castile hosted a dinner for the visiting English guests. This banquet was staged "with open doors for all men and women to watch" the three hundred invitees enjoying their array of different dishes of meat and fish (the latter brought from the various ports of Spain by relays of mules so that it would arrive as fresh as possible).[27] The arrival of Philip IV's son Balthasar Carlos in 1629 was celebrated with fireworks and bells, and urban residents who did not participate in decorating their houses with luminaries were threatened with a fine of twelve reales each.[28] Following the same logic, the ceremonies that accompanied the crowning of a new king became more elaborate and theatrical through the sixteenth and seventeenth centuries, as did their funerals. In both cases this was true not only of the court but also of the rituals that were imposed upon cities and towns throughout the empire. In Santander, for example, fairly off the beaten path from the centers of political power, the exequies for Philip II in 1598, Philip III in 1621, and Philip IV in 1665 were celebrated with increasing grandeur and expense.[29] From such national ceremonies to the king's own table, food was an important element of a ruler's performance of power. The rituals surrounding a king's consumption of food, the theatrical element of having an audience, and the limited access to his table were all meant to convey the impression of superiority and exclusivity.[30]

GENDER AND FOOD

Rulers were expected to follow particular food practices because of their position, though they were also able to choose the performative elements of their dining customs to enhance their power and encourage the loyalty and service of their subjects. In the case of social categories such as gender, certain foods and eating behaviors were associated with the inherent nature of being male or female. Early modern men and women faced powerful social expectations to follow the behavior that corresponded to their gender. In general, connections between food, gender, and the domestic sphere followed the same patterns in early modern Spain that they have for much of European civilization. The preparation of food and related responsibilities such as the tending of vegetable plots and domestic poultry were an important component of women's responsibilities toward the household and family. The knowledge and skills relevant to this task were generally passed down by example and oral tradition from one generation to the next, rather than following any pattern of formal education. The particular nature of these tasks depended a great deal upon social status, but even in households where servants carried out most of the purchases and preparation of food, they were at least supervised by the female head of household. Men, meanwhile, were more likely to take on the tending of large domestic animals (cows, sheep, and goats) and the public and economic role of going to the marketplace for household food purchases.[31]

Such associations are visible in records that reflect gender differences in the context of labor. For example, in agreements related to agricultural labor in late medieval Mallorca, most manual labor was paid in coin with a supplement of *forment e vianda*, meaning rations of wheat and oil, and a meal on Sundays. In the case of day laborers, who were hired as needed, women earned a salary that was only 39 percent that of men's, but the payment for women's work never included food.[32] One possible explanation for this is that the jobs that earned food in addition to coin were usually the ones involving the greatest physical strength, meaning that they were likely to be held by men, and the food was a logical part of that compensation. However, it also suggests that women were expected to prepare and bring their own meals. Curiously, contracts for rural household servants reveal a similar gender division regarding food: male servants were paid in coin and foodstuffs, while female servants were only paid in coin.[33] The predominance of women in household maintenance and food preparation is also noticeable in the management of *posadas*, or boarding-houses. In university cities such as Valladolid, where there was a substantial student population looking to rent rooms, the majority of posadas were run by women. Those managed by men were much less likely than the women's to include meals and cleaning services.[34]

These expectations of women's domestic and culinary responsibilities were supported by scholarly writing on gender, human nature, and social expectations. Early modern treatises on education generally suggested that men were inherently equal among themselves, because they were all shaped by the four principal humors, and thus depended on education to form them best according to their status and purpose. These writers also assumed that men and women were inherently different, so that particular roles and duties were much more fixed for women than they were for men. Women, regardless of status or personal inclination, were suited to domestic care and food production, and education was much less recommendable for them than it was for men. Those scholars who did support the concept of women's education thought it should be carefully directed toward gender-appropriate activities. Juan Luis Vives, author of the influential 1524 treatise *Instrucción de la mujer cristiana* (*The Education of a Christian Woman*), argued that all women, even princesses, should learn to spin thread, embroider, and cook. Other writers consistently emphasized the same themes of women producing textiles and food. Antonio de Guevara touched on this in several of his letters, including one giving advice to the recently married, which insisted that women of all ranks should occupy themselves principally with cooking for their husbands: "What a pleasure it is to see a woman . . . sift the wheat, knead the dough, bake the bread, sweep the house, light the fire, and prepare the cooking pot. . . . There is not a husband in the world who would not find his wife more beautiful on Saturday when she makes bread than on Sunday when she dresses up."[35] Similarly, Francisco de Osuna wrote that it was acceptable for a husband to physically punish his wife for errors in these fundamental duties, such as not sweeping the house or failing to have meals prepared on time. These writers shared the assumption that the natural condition of women was to be married. Those who remained single were expected to take on the role of serving in a relative's household, if they did not take religious orders.[36]

In spite of this powerful association between women and domestic food production, several factors emerged that may have affected women's involvement in this area in the sixteenth and seventeenth centuries, especially in urban areas. One is the rise of prepared food sold on the street, which made it easier for men to purchase their own meals rather than eating at home.[37] For some contemporary critics, these opportunities were perhaps too attractive. Francisco de Santos's *Día y noche de Madrid* (Day and night in Madrid), a gently satiric overview of the city, includes several scenes that criticize men who spent all their money on eating out with friends, those who bragged that they never ate at home with their families, and those who ate out and then returned home only to criticize everything that their wives prepared.[38] Another factor was the combination of rising unemployment and the growth of urban elites who hoped to imitate the nobility. The resultant cheap labor, especially in urban areas, meant that domestic staff was much easier to acquire and more households took on servants to do household work and prepare meals. Such domestic work generally remained the purview of women but was no longer undertaken by the female head of household.[39] Married urban women still supervised cooking, preserving, distilling, and other domestic work but no longer were likely to do it themselves. (This in turn led to increased social concern about women giving themselves over to idleness and luxury, which we will discuss at greater length in chapter 4.)

The most important exception to the rule of women and food preparation, however, is related to social status and the performative element of cooking. In humble households or those with no public or political role, cooking was less of a performance and more of a domestic responsibility and thus a feminine task. For example, in cloistered convents, where the preparation of food did not serve to publicly demonstrate status, taste, or wealth, cooking was usually done by servants and never by the senior nuns. It was considered to be such a humble task that the Carmelite nuns of Córdoba praised their prioress Catalina de Jesús for repeatedly asking, as part of her regular exercise of humility and self-negation, to help out in the kitchen.[40] If one looks at cooking in elite households, however, the different skills and greater public visibility of such work led it to be considered more professional and thus more masculine.[41] Palace cooks and those in noble households were responsible for maintaining part of the appearance and impressiveness of the household through the food they prepared, so these posts were most often held by skilled men. The fourteenth-century *Ordinacions de Cort* (Court rules) of Pedro IV of Aragón assume that the royal family's kitchen staff would be male, and as a rule, in early modern Spanish court kitchens, this continued to hold true.[42] Antonio de Guevara, the author of several advice books for courtiers, noted that lords took more pride in having a talented cook serving their household than in having a brave warden defending their fortress.[43] There even seemed to be an international network of chefs. One of the head cooks for King João II of Portugal came from Burgundy, and he brought other well-known chefs from across Europe to assist in the preparations for particularly grand festivals.[44] As urban elites sought to impress their peers, they emulated the court and hired male cooks for their kitchens; even comfortable bourgeois households would have a hired cook and perhaps an assistant or two.[45] Ana Guerrero Maylló's research on Madrid city councilmen in the sixteenth century shows that their families employed on average four servants each (for an average household of nine), including cooks who were always male.[46] One of the only semipublic cooking positions held by a woman was that of cook to the prisoners in the court jail in Madrid in the 1630s, hardly a prestigious job.[47]

By the seventeenth century, this had become standard enough that the lack of a male cook in a high-ranking household was a sign of deprivation. When the parents of Ana de Mendoza (later the princess of Eboli) quarreled during their stay in the court at Valladolid, her father departed for their home territory of Pastrana and left them without funding. Ana's mother made a point of living with extreme frugality, partly out of necessity and partly to demonstrate to the members of the court the direness and injustice of her situation. The best way to accomplish the latter was for her to spend as little as possible on her meals, and so she dismissed her male cooks and "made a pantry of her bedchamber and cooks of her maids"; the most powerful symbol of her indignity was to have to make do with female servants as her cooks.[48] In the sixteenth and seventeenth centuries, with growing numbers of household staff, such gendered divisions grew. More specialized service positions were taken on by men, while the female servants in charge of table service such as napkins and handwashing evolved into chambermaids, less skilled and less respected.[49] While all of the "official" cooking in noble kitchens, particularly for guests and banquets, was likely to have been done by men, some evidence suggests that elite women maintained a more active role in their own kitchens than we have given them credit for. Doña Estefanía Requesens, the wife of the viceroy of Naples, regularly corresponded with her mother in Barcelona in the 1530s. The two exchanged gifts of cheese, oil, fruit, and honey and discussed recipes and cooking techniques; doña Estefanía mentioned things she had learned from her mother and took pride in her own abilities as a cook. She even remarked on having prepared special dishes for the young prince Philip (later King Philip II) when he was ill.[50]

MEN'S AND WOMEN'S ROLES ALSO DIFFERED IN THE CRE-ation of recipe books and collections. Male chefs in elite households enjoyed a certain degree of public recognition as individuals. Their names are sometimes known to us; with the advent of printing in the fifteenth century, we have the first published and reproduced recipe collections, and these were exclusively written by men. These elite cooks also enjoyed a degree of rivalry with their competitors. Diego Granado Maldonado, for example, wrote the *Libro del arte de cozina* (Book of the art of cooking), which pulled together several bits of earlier works, as was common at the time, and reflected the strong Italian influence that then predominated in Spanish cuisine. Published in three editions between 1599 and 1614, Granado's work was more traditional than innovative; it is now best known for compiling the tastes and techniques that were most common to its time. His contemporary, Francisco Martínez Montiño, who became the head chef to Philip III, then published his *Arte de cozina* (Art of cooking) for the first time in 1611. Montiño claimed in its prologue that what had moved him to write was the complete lack of previous guides for those who dedicated themselves to cooking, "except for one that I have seen, so full of mistakes that it could only confuse those who consult it, and written by one who is hardly known in the Court." After that pointed reference to Granado, Montiño went on to emphasize his individual accomplishments and authorship: "All of these [recipes] are mine, and none have I copied from anyone else, and many of them are my own invention."[51] This phrasing emphasizes the individual and public elements of skill and creativity associated with elite male chefs. So too do their titles: cookbooks written by men often emphasized that cooking is an "art" (as opposed to a mechanical skill), associating it with other markers of elite status and sophistication such as dance, chess, and fencing. The fourteenth-century chef known as Taillevent (Guillaume Tirel), who served Kings Charles V and VI of France, published a renowned recipe collection and for his efforts was "ennobled and given a coat of arms with three stewpots."[52]

Despite their popularity, such recipe collections were not necessarily useful in guiding someone with little cooking experience. In keeping with their authors' roles as symbols of the wealth and taste of the elite households they served, these books were intended more to showcase the art of cooking than to share expertise. Given the difficulties in calculating time and the absence of conventional measurements, one would still need a good deal of practice in the kitchen to know how to prepare any given dish, even with written instructions. Cooking times, if they were given at all, were described in comparison to familiar tasks or events (saying an Our Father, or walking the length of a field) or in reference to accomplishing a particular state in the recipe: heat until it boils, stir until it thickens, or most frequently, the simple instruction to "cook until it is done." The weight and volume of ingredients could be stated in relative proportions (a sauce with three parts cinnamon, two parts cloves and one part ginger) or using comparisons (cut the meat into pieces the size of walnuts, slice cheese a finger-width thick). As early as the fifteenth century, Spanish recipes made reference to quantities in ounces and pounds, but as these varied between regions (a Galician pound was slightly heavier than a Castilian pound, which in turn outweighed a Navarrese pound) this may have been useful more to maintain relative proportions than to judge absolute amounts. In any case, recipe books published by men seem to be more about establishing the reputation and legacy of the writer than about teaching particular practices. Actual cooks, both male and female, were much more likely to learn from experience and oral tradition than from books.

The relationship among women, food, and print culture was quite different from that among men. None of the Spanish recipe books published before 1800 was authored by a woman, and since the published books were presumably written for chefs in other elite kitchens, women were not their principal audience. (This represents a curious difference from England and Germany, which had a much richer tradition of housewife manuals written by and for women.[53]) There was a small genre of Spanish household books written by men for women, such as Eiximenis's *Llibre de les dones*, Manuel Dies de Calatayud's *Flor del tesoro de la belleza*, and fray Luis de León's *La perfecta casada*. These were concerned with men's views of morals, domestic life, beauty, and the proper behavior of women. None of them had anything to say about recipes or food preparation, about which the authors presumably knew little.[54] While they did not participate in the creation of published works, elite Iberian women were certainly involved in the informal, unwritten traditions of passing down knowledge and skills related to cooking. The few of their written works that survive are usually anonymous, sometimes with several authors, manuscript rather than print, and meant for the female head of household's own use rather than as a public performance of knowledge. When recipes from women's collections did make it into print, it was through the channel of a male author. Both Ruperto de Nola and Martino da Como in their published work seem to have copied recipes for sweets and conserves from the *Manual de mugeres*, a women's collection of recipes, medical remedies, and other domestic guidelines compiled around 1500 that otherwise remained unpublished until the late twentieth century.[55]

The earliest Portuguese recipe book, the *Livro de cozinha da Infanta D. Maria de Portugal*, is a good example of women's cookery writing. This was a manuscript, probably from the late fifteenth century, that Maria (the granddaughter of King Manuel I of Portugal) brought to Italy on the occasion of her marriage to Alessandro Farnese, the Duke of Parma, in 1565. It was composed of four sections that may originally have been separate, and written in at least two different hands; this quiltlike composition suggests the work of women over more than one generation.[56] None of the existing manuscripts identifies any of its authors by name, but as in the case of the *Livro de cozinha*, they bore hints of female ownership and readership; the sixteenth-century *Receptas de pivetes, pastilhas e aguas perfumadas y conserbas* bears the note, "This book belongs to Joana Fernandez."[57] Other women's manuscripts display similar characteristics that suggest cooperation and a degree of social networking, alongside possible attempts to imitate the style and accomplishments of elite women. The seventeenth-century *Receptas experimentadas para diversas cosas*, which contains sections in several different hands, includes recipes with titles such as "doña María de Mendoza's hand cream," "Isabel Vazquez's aromatic plant oil," "how to prepare oranges in the manner of the countess of Modica," "a recipe for pastries sent to me by doña Felipa," and "eau de toilette used by the princess of Salerno."[58]

Unlike the recipe collections compiled by men, these manuscripts represented a wider range of household interests, demonstrating that issues of food, medicine, preservation, beauty, and cleanliness closely overlapped in women's domestic knowledge. These manuscripts included recipes for food as well as instructions for preparing medicines, cosmetics, and cleaning products, items that never appeared in recipe books written by men. While the formal practice of medicine was a profession exclusive to men, household treatments for mild ailments such as coughs, toothaches, and earaches were clearly still the domain of women across social levels, at least through the sixteenth century.[59] Juan Luis Vives' *Instrucción de la mujer cristiana* and other prescriptive literature for women indicated that taking care of minor injuries and illnesses was part of what women were expected to know.[60] The sixteenth-century manuscript *Recetas y memorias para guisados* includes recipes for meats, vegetables, pastries, and sauces, then fruit conserves and mustards, then a set of household remedies such as how to prepare perfumes and scents and remedies to strengthen teeth and encourage hair growth. Even the princess María of Portugal's *Livro de cozinha* includes a section on remedies for ailments such as toothache, sore throat, and burns. More unusually, one manuscript includes a remedy for madness, based on nettle seed taken with aged white wine. If that proved insufficient, "ivy and rue and fennel, boiled in this wine and then drunk, brings one back to one's senses. If the sufferer takes rue seed while reciting an Our Father and an Ave Maria and then drinks, he will be healed."[61]

Outside of the home, women's medical knowledge was also essential to caring for the imprisoned and those in poorhouses. Most women in these positions were salaried workers or religious volunteers, often *beatas*, women who dedicated themselves to lives of charity and religious work without formally taking orders. Their knowledge came from experience and the aforementioned household remedy books rather than any formal training. Few were formally recognized for their work, though the contemporary lists of "illustrious sons of Seville" include several nuns who were well-known for curing the ill. A rare example of an elite woman taking on this role was doña Catalina de Ribera, the mother of the Duke of Medina Sidonia, who established a hospital for poor women in Seville in the early sixteenth century, and attended to the women's medical needs herself. In spite of this rich tradition of female healing, the seventeenth century saw increasing pressure from men to define medicine and medical practice as a formal (and therefore masculine) course of study, following a 1593 decree by King Philip II that barred women from practicing medicine and established a set of examinations and standards for men's medical study. The Inquisition, in turn, came to view women's healing activities as increasingly suspicious and indicative of witchcraft. Women continued to treat family members and assist in hospitals and prisons, but only if they worked as volunteers.[62] The connection between food, medicine, and women's work was accepted as long as it was private and informal, but the public and professional realms were reserved for men.

WOMEN'S TRADITIONAL ASSOCIATION WITH DOMESTICITY and food production carried over to salaried jobs, such as cook, waitress, innkeeper, and bartender, in the thriving food industry of the cities. Strong gender associations determined expectations in these jobs as well as in agriculture, animal husbandry, and various levels of commerce. In the realm of bread, the most important early modern food, the sale and supply of grain was the province of men, though the preparation of dough at home and its baking in a communal oven were likely to be managed by women. Seventeenth-century city ordinances in Seville tended to refer to *panaderas*, the feminine plural, for those who prepared, baked, and sold bread.[63] The same was true of municipal regulations in other principal seventeenth-century cities such as Santander and Toledo.[64] In 1798, a woman, Manuela Chueca, held the contract for the oven of the village of Alcalá de Ebro for two years. In return for paying the local duke a certain amount of grain a year and baking his bread for free, she was required to operate the oven at least four days a week. The residents of the town were required to use her oven, as it was the only one, and she kept a percentage of the grain that was brought to her.[65] In spite of the dominant role of bread in the early modern diet, the position of bakers was not very powerful. The women who baked and sold bread did not control the networks of supply and were less likely to be organized in guilds (which tended to be male-oriented organizations). Unlike other occupations, they had no representation in the city assembly.

In the realm of meat production, it was women's work to raise and sell chickens and their eggs and other small domestic animals such as rabbits and ducks, while men tended to the larger animals.[66] The yearly contracts that cities established to guarantee the provision of basic supplies of meat animals, wine, and oil were always made with men, but more informal transactions in taverns, markets, and street stands were often the province of women. Madrid in particular offered many possibilities for women in such positions, given its rapid growth in the sixteenth and seventeenth centuries and the large immigrant population of young men who were not in a position to keep their own houses. Such job opportunities also were likely to have increased as agricultural production dropped and more people went to cities to search for service work. In the marketplaces, women were most commonly involved in retail, buying food supplies from peasants who brought them to the city and reselling them in the urban markets.[67] Madrid drew most of its vegetables from gardens along the Manzanares River, and the *verduleras*, those who raised these vegetables and brought them to market, were most commonly women. During the late medieval period, accounts of food purchases for the Navarrese court put lettuce and radishes in the same accounting category as bread.

This was perhaps because such produce was grown by women along the riverside where grain mills and ovens were also located, so those who came to purchase flour and bread would buy their greens at the same time.[68] River and ocean fish were generally caught and brought to urban centers by men, but fishmongering (the selection, preparation, and sale of fish) was traditionally the province of women, perhaps because of the low rank of fish in the cultural food hierarchy.[69] Notarial records showed that women frequently managed fruit and fish stands in the main plaza of Madrid, either on their own, by renting a stand, or as salaried workers for the owner.[70] These women shared social connections as well as economic roles. The women who sold wine and sweet buns in front of the royal palace in Madrid, for example, all knew and supported each other.[71] Research on the land registry (*catastro*) of the northern Spanish town of Oviedo from 1753 shows that substantially more women than men worked in sales and service (269 women to 175 men); most of these were breadmakers and innkeepers. Their work may have been more than just supplementary income, since this registry also shows that 25 percent of the households of Oviedo were headed by women, and a good 10 percent were composed of single women living alone.[72] Women were able to take on these tasks in part because such work was not regulated by guilds, which meant that they were not subject to formal regulations or obliged to abandon their work upon the death of a husband. Instead, women doing marketplace work seem to have relied on extensive social networks with their peers, combining resources to purchase stock, intermarrying between families, and recognizing each other in wills.[73]

This relative independence made women's role in public food sales an area where different gender expectations often came into conflict with each other. Cultural norms accepted women as producers of food but were not as comfortable with women occupying public space and engaging in business transactions. Despite this being common practice, city authorities found it discomfiting and frequently tried to minimize women's business activity. This was especially true in Madrid, perhaps because the city's dramatic growth implied a large number of recent immigrants, and there was greater concern than elsewhere about *vagamundas* or vagrant women. As women increasingly took on the role of *revendedoras* (resellers), purchasing food from the main markets to sell it in streets and plazas throughout the city, civil authorities perceived dangers in their work and even in the products themselves that were not associated with men partaking in the same activity:

> The merchants' boys used to sell their wares in the streets, and this was enough to provide for the court. . . . There was great abundance of everything and at appropriate prices. But now everything has gone up and is of worse quality, because these vagabond women have come in, buying and reselling everything in the street, of lower quality and at a higher price. . . . Some sell oranges and limes, others toasted seeds, chestnuts and cheese curds, all things that have no value whatsoever for common sustenance, and are no more than unhealthy treats. . . . An additional problem is that there are more than two thousand women occupied in this way, so that there are not enough washerwomen or servants, and these vagabond women avoid work and service and make a profession of their vice.[74]

The alcaldes went on to suggest that the solution was to keep women out of the streets and plazas and not allow them to participate in such activities (apparently forgetting for the moment their complaints about the unhealthfulness of the products themselves). In their view, if food sales on the street were returned to the control of market owners and their (male) employees, the prices, quality, and availability of their goods would all improve.

City authorities were concerned about the independent sales activities of women even when they were contributing to family food-oriented businesses. In 1585, for example, Madrid decreed that women could not operate taverns in the city and that male tavern owners were obliged to go in person to purchase the wine for their taverns. The men protested that if they had to leave their taverns to make purchases and their wives weren't able to run the tavern in their absence, how could they maintain their businesses? In response, the city created individual licenses for female *medidoras*, or "measurers," to allow women married to tavern owners to

serve wine in their husbands' absence.[75] A few decades later, city authorities tried to ban women from selling fish and pork in the markets. The
women in question protested and requested that they be given formal
licenses to continue their sales. Those whose husbands were deceased or
absent argued that they needed to work to support their families. As in
the case of the taverns, those who were the wives of men who worked
in the markets were supported in this plea by their husbands. The men
complained to city officials that they needed to travel to local fairs and
markets to purchase animals to bring to the city, and that it only made
sense for their wives to manage sales at their stalls while they were away.
The Sala grudgingly allowed the women in this second group, the wives,
to weigh and sell meat and fish in the markets but only if they were dealing
in the products owned by their husbands.[76] Similarly, a decree from 1608
allowed women to sell roasted chestnuts on the street but only if they
were married, and the following year the sale of chestnuts was restricted
to men and women over the age of fifty.[77] These cases reveal that women
were clearly active in public marketplaces and that their spouses saw them
as essential partners in business. Municipal authorities, meanwhile, were
wary of allowing them such freedom and clearly would have preferred
these women to pursue domestic work out of the public eye. Overall,
social expectations related to men and women's food activities clearly
corresponded to collective beliefs about their fundamental nature as well
as their appropriate private and public roles.

CHRISTIANS, JEWS, AND MUSLIMS

Just as gender carried powerful associations with food habits, so did early
modern Spaniards' expectations about religious conformity. While today
we think of religious identity as individual and personal, in early modern
Europe religion was an important part of communal identity; one person's
proper or improper religious behavior affected the community to which
he or she belonged. Food practices were an important and visible part
of religious identity, and majority Christians demonstrated their own
collective identity through common food habits as well as identifying and
denigrating culinary practices that seemed to suggest non-Christian belief.

From their earliest years, the preference of Christian communities for bread, wine, oil, fish, and lamb set them apart culinarily from the surrounding Roman culture.[78] After the fall of Rome, most of Europe blended these traditions with the distinctive food culture of the Germanic tribes, who favored meat and butter over the cultivation of grains and olives. Spain's sixth-century Germanic invaders, the Visigoths, quickly adopted many elements of Roman culture, but some tensions remained between these different culinary heritages. Christian Spaniards found it challenging to maintain all of the church's requirements for fasting, particularly those related to the use of fish and olive oil over meat and lard.[79] Nevertheless, food customs became particularly valuable in Spain for underlining religious identity in the early modern period. One driving force behind this was the Protestant Reformation, which divided Christians throughout Europe. Protestants rejected many of the Catholic practices that they believed to be unfounded in Scripture, including the dietary restrictions of fasting and abstinence. In the sixteenth and seventeenth centuries, many Protestant treatises argued against the traditional restrictions on meat, and indeed fish consumption dropped noticeably in Protestant areas once it became optional.[80] The Catholic church responded to these challenges by reinforcing Lenten and fasting rules and defending the significance of the Eucharist and the Last Supper as more than just commemorative. The Inquisition, charged with supervising the proper behavior of Catholics, was alert for those who did not properly observe the fasts. As we shall see, many of its efforts focused on people who were suspected of secretly maintaining Jewish or Muslim practices, but proper food habits were required of old Christians as well.[81] Pedro Calvo of the province of Avila and some of his companions were accused in 1556 of eating roasted pork skin on the eve of a religious holiday, when Christians were meant to abstain from meat. They insisted that they had done so only because that was the only food they had, besides some bread and a few prunes. In 1625, a group of friends were on their way to Madrid when (as they explained) one of them threw a rock at a piglet and accidentally killed it, so they took it to a nearby inn to roast and eat the animal so that the meat would not go to waste. These events happened on St. Joseph's Day, when the men were supposed to be abstaining from meat. In both cases, the offenders were investigated and given penance by Inquisition officials for endangering the Christian community by not following proper food practices.[82]

One unique challenge Spain faced in its attempts to create a common cultural identity centered on Catholic belief and practice was how best to incorporate its substantial population of Jews and Muslims. Spain's urban population had included communities of Jews ever since the first century CE, when they were established by refugees from Judea who made their way to the peninsula following the Romans' destruction of the Second Temple of Jerusalem. Thus the Sephardic branch of Jews was established in Spain at around the same time as Christianity itself, though the latter gained a distinct advantage once Christianity was recognized as a legal religion throughout the Roman Empire in the early fourth century. By the early modern period, Sephardic Jews constituted at least five percent of Spain's population. Historically they were more influential than that number would suggest. As a well-educated and mostly urban population, they often worked as merchants, royal officials, and diplomats, especially in the courts of Ferdinand III and Alfonso X of Castile. The process of the Reconquest incorporated substantial numbers of Muslims into the Spanish population, as the Christian kingdoms of Castile and Aragon extended their reach southward into formerly Muslim territory in the thirteenth through fifteenth centuries. While the medieval period saw a remarkable degree of cultural mixing and tolerance between Muslims and Christians in the peninsula, by the end of the fifteenth century, the pressure on Spaniards to become Christian rose to a peak. In 1492, Jews in Castile and Aragon were forced to convert or go into exile, and Christian forces conquered Granada, the last Muslim kingdom in Spain. At that point, Muslims (who were a majority of the population in many regions of southern Spain) were allowed to remain but faced increasing pressure to convert and adopt Christian Spanish cultural habits. By the beginning of the seventeenth century, they, too, were forced into either conversion or exile; those who remained and converted were known as moriscos.

While both groups were eventually targeted for their different food practices, perceived as signs of religious difference, they were also both responsible for introducing important elements of cuisine into Spanish cooking. Jewish cuisine in Spain relied heavily on soups, especially those based on chickpeas with meat and spices.[83] Catalan bread soups with garlic and thyme are also of Jewish origin, as are milk-based sweets.[84] For the most part, though, Sephardic communities worked hard to blend in with their neighbors (keeping in mind that they had been established in Spain for centuries), and except for the specific dietary restrictions of their religion, the foods they ate were not recognizably distinctive. Muslims, meanwhile, had a significant impact on Spanish agriculture and cuisine. They introduced to southern Spain the cultivation of artichokes, spinach, eggplant, pistachios, rice, almonds, citrus fruits, and sugar cane as well as the techniques of irrigation that made these sustainable. Many of these were wholeheartedly adopted into Spanish cuisine during the centuries of Muslim occupation and ceased to be perceived as foreign. Even the quintessentially Spanish olla podrida may have had its origin in the Arab technique of slow-cooking meats and vegetables in terra-cotta pots. Muslim cuisine increased the use of cinnamon, ginger, and saffron; these, along with the earlier-mentioned fruits and vegetables, became key elements in Renaissance cooking in Spain and southern Italy.[85] Ruperto de Nola's *Llibre del coch* and Martínez Montiño's *Arte de cocina* both incorporated traditionally Muslim ingredients and techniques, from acidic marinades to almond sauces, couscous, and thin noodles. Most Spanish recipe collections included preparations designated "morisco," from the "olla morisca" in the *Manual de mugeres* to the "gallina a la morisca" in Martínez Montiño (the latter, ironically, prepared with diced bacon).

These ingredients in and of themselves were not perceived as different or threatening, but Jewish and Muslim food practices were strongly associated with their religious identity. By the sixteenth century, in a Europe divided by doctrinal differences within Christianity and threatened (in Christian eyes) by corruption from Muslim and Jewish influences, Spaniards were concerned about defending themselves and their spiritual community. Since doctrinal errors were believed to threaten not just the soul of the sinner but the entire community, church officials and ordinary neighbors alike strove to promote proper belief and behavior. As Sara Nalle notes, "the surest way to achieve a common understanding of religion was to make sure that everyone knew a basic minimum about the tenets of their faith *and* performed a minimum of actions that signified belief."[86] All three religions included food practices as important elements of religion, so after the sixteenth century, when all Spaniards were ostensibly Christian, old Christians viewed the continuation of any of the former Jewish and Muslim food habits as signs of heresy. It was also easier for neighbors and church officials to observe someone's cooking than it was to know their inner thoughts, so authorities targeted those practices as shorthand for belief.

The most visible actions that stereotyped religious groups were those related to fasting, dietary restrictions, and food preparation. For Jews, the yearly celebration of Yom Kippur was the principal fast (known in Spanish as the *ayuno mayor*, major fast, or "the fast of the great day"), during which believers abstained from all food and drink from sunset to sunset. Women also celebrated the fast of Queen Esther from dawn to dusk on the eve of the Purim holiday. For Muslims, fasting was one of the five pillars of Islam, to be kept through the month of Ramadan, commemorating the revelation of the Qur'an to Mohammed. This fast required abstention from food and drink from dawn to dusk, though it included festive meals every evening after sunset. Dietary restrictions were rather more complicated for Jews than for Muslims. Neither was allowed to eat pork, and while most of the Islamic world took the Qur'an's injunction against the excess consumption of intoxicants to a mean a complete prohibition of alcohol, on the whole Hispanic Muslims accepted the consumption of wine, though probably not to the degree that Christians did.[87] Jewish dietary restrictions, drawn from the biblical books of Leviticus and Deuteronomy, prohibited a wider range of animals and fish (land creatures other than those with cloven hooves that chew their cud as well as water creatures without fins and scales). Pork and blood products were particularly to be avoided, as was leavened bread during Passover. Both Jews and Muslims followed strict slaughtering practices for the animals they consumed. Jewish custom included restrictions on work done on the Sabbath. In early modern practice, this meant that those who wanted to maintain Jewish practices in the household washed their clothes, put out clean table linens, and made other preparations on Friday to keep the Sabbath on Saturday. Sabbath food often included *adafina*—a pot of legumes, vegetables, eggs, and meat that could be prepared on Friday night and kept warm to avoid the necessity of cooking on Saturday.

In the medieval period, in Christian-dominated regions these were simply perceived as different practices and respected in local law and custom. In Aragon, until the early fifteenth century, Christians, Jews, and Muslims often shared slaughterhouses, although each group had its own butcher and separate slaughtering block and even separate pasturing areas for its animals.[88] In the Christian court of Charles III of Navarre in the fifteenth century, the distribution of food to Jewish and Muslim markets seems to have respected their dietary practices and forms of butchering, since they were provided with live animals.[89] While the earlier-mentioned condestable of Jaén did offer wine to his guests, his chronicler wrote that pork lard and bacon never appeared in the food at his receptions when Muslim guests were present, despite the ubiquitous role they played in most Castilian dishes.[90] Even so, the three religious communities tended to maintain careful separation of their food supplies, and the preparation and supply of meat and wine was an ongoing theme in local legislation. Jews in Christian territories were generally not allowed to make or sell wine, cheese, or meat to Christians. Wine was important to both Christian and Jewish tables, but to avoid religious cross-contamination, as it were, the use of wine made by non-Jews was not permitted to Jews under the laws of *kashrut*. Questions presented to the fourteenth-century Zaragoza rabbi Ishaq ben Shéshet Perfet included whether it was possible for a Jew to use a wine jug that formerly belonged to a Christian, how to deal with wine that may have been touched by a Christian while it was aging, and how to handle the presence of a Gentile passing through a Jewish wine cellar to gain access to a well.[91] Individuals were also cautious about sharing food across religious boundaries. Martín Pérez's 1316 treatise *Libro de las Confesiones* included a section on status and social position, in which he warned that Christians who worked for Jews or Muslims should never share their food.[92] In Toledo, which had had a substantial population of both Muslims and Jews before 1492, the decades before the expulsion of these populations saw increasing attempts by city authorities to limit their interactions with Christians, especially those involving food. A proclamation of 1480 stated that Christians were not allowed to purchase meat from Muslim or Jewish butchers, with penalties of 300 maravedís for the first offense, 600 the second, and 1,200 or fifty public lashes for the third.[93]

Such developments foreshadowed the emphasis on food practices that accompanied the movement toward conversion and religious conformity following the completion of the Christian Reconquest. Food became one of the most visible signifiers of religious identity, to the extent that it became more a metaphor than a simile—food *was* religion. As Jesús Contreras reminds us, an awareness of one's own cuisine only fully develops when this cuisine can be compared with someone else's, at which point food becomes a symbol of belonging to one group or another. One had to dress like a Christian and to consume food in a Christian manner—or at least, following the habits of the majority of Spanish Christians—to be acknowledged as a member of the Christian community. (Following the same logic, Muslims and Jews who had been forced to convert but sought to preserve their customs and beliefs in secret were likely to hold fast to their traditional food customs, which could be maintained privately in the home.) Both patterns are clear in early modern Spain, as majority Catholics increasingly relied on foods such as bread, wine, and pork to be indicators of true Catholicism, and ostensibly converted Jews and Muslims clung to their fasts and traditional foods as ways of privately preserving their identities and heritages. The principal work of policing proper Catholic behavior fell, of course, to the Spanish Inquisition. While this institution had jurisdiction only over baptized Catholics, by the sixteenth century all Spaniards were essentially required to be Catholic, and one of the principal concerns of the Inquisition was that converted Jews and Muslims (now known as *conversos* and moriscos) were not fully or convincingly Christian. The clearest sign of this danger was their adherence to the fasting, food preparation, and dietary practices described previously.

Since Jewish food and fasting practices were more extensive and visible, they appear far more often in Inquisition records than similar denunciations of suspected Muslims. Accusations of continuing to practice Islam were sometimes based on fasting practices or a refusal to eat pork, but Muslims were more frequently identified by their practice of daily prayer. Jews might be suspected on the basis of cleaning the house and wearing clean clothes on Friday in preparation for the Sabbath and keeping lamps lit on Friday nights, but the predominant theme in such investigations was culinary.[94] Inquisition officials and ordinary neighbors became sharply attentive to the practices that were the most visible and the most religiously meaningful: the avoidance of pork, fasting on days that were not Christian fasts, the consumption of dishes such as adafina, the preparation of food on Friday nights, and the slaughter of chickens in a particular form. This concern also carried an important gendered element: women played an important role in transmitting religious values in a household, and the preparation of food was an essential element of that transmission. In cases relating to purported practices of Judaism or Islam, men were often questioned in relation to their travels and their commercial contacts, while women were most frequently described in terms of their role in food preparation. Since the rules of food preparation were more distinctive for Jews than for Muslims, it was more common for Jewish women to be denounced based on their culinary practices and for Muslim men to be denounced for having followed the fasts of Ramadan.[95]

Christians were particularly attentive to fasting practices that differed from their own. For Jewish men, maintaining the proper fasts was a challenge, given the powerful social expectation of eating with companions and business partners. Many were merchants, and the trade fair season in the fall often coincided with Yom Kippur, and so it was hard to avoid observation. Many alleged Judaizers were denounced at the September fair of Daroca, near Zaragoza, because of their fasting.[96] The extent of Spaniards' association between fasting and Judaism is evident in the case of Beatriz Navarro, who confessed that she had been curious about Jewish customs, after her landlady's family tried to persuade her "that the law of Moses was better than that of Jesus." They advised her to fast on Mondays, Wednesdays, and Thursdays, not eating or drinking anything from sundown to sundown, and to keep Saturdays as holy days. In the course of her questioning, no other issues of practice or belief were engaged. It seems as though the whole of Beatriz's understanding of Judaism, and of the Inquisition officials' concern, centered on the issue of fasting.[97] Similarly, the trial of Beatriz Arias in 1651 focused on fasting: a young neighbor testified that she had told him that the law of Moses meant fasting certain days without eating or drinking anything during the day, and Beatriz herself confessed that her mother had taught her to keep the fast.[98]

Pork became the most significant culinary marker of Catholicism, since it was so definitively prohibited to both Jews and Muslims. Anyone who has traveled to contemporary Spain, where rows of cured hams are on prominent display in every bar and market and where every city features branches of chain restaurants with names such as *Don Jamón* (Mr. Ham) and *El Museo del Jamón* (The Museum of Ham), will not be surprised to find that ham has a history as an important marker of Spanish Catholic identity. The enthusiastic and ostentatious consumption of pork in its various forms—particularly ham, bacon, and lard—has its origin in this period of religious tension, and Spaniards regularly eyed each other's tables to confirm its presence. Cervantes himself noted that the best safe-conduct for a foreigner traveling in Spain was to carry a chunk of ham.[99] Even the *matanza*, the traditional late-fall slaughter of pigs, developed more ceremonial and folkloric elements as an exhibition of Christian faith than the slaughter of any other animal.[100] As we have seen, pork ranked relatively low in the cultural food hierarchy. Before the fifteenth century and in the rest of Europe it was largely associated with peasants and the poor, but in Spain its consumption took on greater symbolic value as a proof of Catholic identity. For Inquisition investigations, the mere avoidance of pork or lard was enough to support an accusation of harboring Muslim or Jewish beliefs. Even if they did not have direct evidence of cooking practices, many denunciations took note of families who kept separate sets of frying pans, one used by the household servants to prepare their own meals that were likely to include pork and another for cooking only with olive oil.

Offerings of food, usually a benevolent sign of generosity and friendship, could be intended as a religious challenge. Beatriz Álvarez, of the village of Barajas near Madrid, was condemned by the Inquisition following a visit from a neighbor who offered Beatriz and her daughters a bit of blood sausage (*morcilla*). A visitor to their house observed that although they warmly thanked the neighbor for her gift, as soon as she departed, they debated where to throw the sausage out, saying that it would defile their house and that "eating such a thing would mark their souls."[101] The sausage incident became a central point in the investigation of Beatriz and was confirmed via the questioning of several other witnesses, though Beatriz and her daughters insisted that they had tasted the sausage and threw it out after realizing that it was dirty. Many denunciations came from such spurned gifts. The choice not to include non-kosher foods in one's own meals was suspicious enough, but rejecting an offering from a friend or neighbor was even more telling. A suspected Judaizer could be convicted on these things alone. The shorthand version that appears in most Inquisition investigations, whether in the accounts of those who confess to maintaining Jewish practices or in the denunciations of accusers, was generally expressed as "not eating bacon or blood sausage or anything including blood," which was synonymous with being guilty of Judaizing.[102]

The use of lard as a cooking fat was as significant as the consumption of pork in determining religious affiliation. In spite of today's identification of the "Mediterranean diet" with the consumption of heart-healthy olive oil, early modern Spaniards used pork lard as their preferred cooking fat, resorting to olive oil only on church-directed fast days.[103] Lard was valued over oil to the extent that even Benedictine communities, whose original dietary regulations were explicit in their exclusion of meat, by the fifteenth century had come to allow the use of pig fat in their cooking even on fast days (though it was still prohibited during Lent).[104] Avoiding the use of *manteca* (a term for a variety of animal fats, generally meaning rendered pork fat, though it could also refer to other animal fats or butter) was one of the most common grounds for accusations of Judaizing. Eighteen-year-old Ana González, who along with her friend Ana Francisca had worked for a few years in the household of Mariana de la Paz and Alfonso

Álvarez in Madrid, offered her testimony to Inquisition officials in 1654. She said that her erstwhile employers, as well as their next-door neighbors Diego Enríquez and Luisa Rodríguez, "cooked meat with olive oil and not with lard, and they [Mariana and Luisa] instructed us to cook for them always with oil. . . . Their husbands knew perfectly well that their meat was cooked with oil and not with anything else." Ana also noted that if she and her friend ever tried to keep the blood from butchered chickens (as was common among Christian families, to prepare blood sausage or other dishes) their masters scolded them harshly and made them clean out the sullied dishes with particular care and lots of hot water. Such observations were more than enough to generate suspicion of Judaizing.[105] The performance of food customs was a visible way for Catholics to identify themselves as a community and to stigmatize those they suspected of harboring other religious identities. While these collective identities were perceived as fixed and homogeneous groups (one was or was not Jewish, or one was or was not part of the Catholic community), members of other kinds of groups used food to display or negotiate their position within a group and to display that group's purpose within the larger society, as we shall see later.

MONASTIC LIFE

Collective religious identity was performed by a particular subset of Christians through the taking of holy orders. Food consumption in a monastic context followed its own unique pattern, since it was part of the monks' visible commitment to poverty, austerity, and the virtues of abstinence. The earliest Christian monasteries, established in the fourth century, embraced the strict regulation of diet as a means to spiritual purity; the consumption of flesh was thought to lead to greater worldly temptations. In the Galenic view, sexual activity and red meat were associated with an excess of heat and damp, and therefore with each other. Both were things that holy people should avoid. The guidelines of St. Benedict, developed for religious brotherhoods in the sixth century and still used in many monastic communities (not only those of the Benedictine order), emphasized obedience and the renunciation of individual will and provided instructions for the practical organization and management of a religious community, with a schedule of reading, prayers, and labor. These instructions also included recommendations about the quality and quantity of meals, meant to support both the practical and spiritual goals of the community. The original rule allowed for a maximum of two cooked meals a day, prioritizing bread and vegetables. Benedictine practice also limited the consumption of the meat of all quadrupeds, except in the case of monks who were ailing and weak. Benedict reluctantly acknowledged the necessity of wine—"Although we read that wine is not at all proper for monks, yet, because monks in our times cannot be persuaded of this, let us agree to this, at least, that we do not drink to satiety, but sparingly"—and allowed for the consumption of one *hemina* of wine per day, about a third of a liter.[106] Saint Vincent Ferrer's guidelines, written for a young Dominican friend, show how the monks' demeanor at the table echoed the obedience and austerity of their religious practice. Ferrer warned that the young monk needed to eat only what was necessary for his sustenance, "and if at any point you indulge in excess, do not let it pass without the proper penitence." He and his companions had to come to the table properly dressed, seating themselves with their robes neatly folded about their knees, without crossing their legs, never putting their elbows on the table, and eating only what the others ate, without taking extra servings.[107]

Monastic communities underwent several phases of transition through the medieval period, as they found that time, habit, and the acquisition of wealth gradually worked to soften their strict practices, including those related to diet. As this happened, they either went through phases of renewal or were challenged by newer, more energetic groups. Such was the origin of the Cistercian order in the eleventh century, dedicated to reviving the strict observance of the rule of St. Benedict, and the thirteenth-century Dominican and Franciscan orders. Castile in the fourteenth century saw a period of particularly vigorous religious revival with the support of the crown, resulting in the establishment of the royal convent of the Poor Clares in Tordesillas, the Hieronymite monks of the Royal Monastery of Guadalupe, the Carthusian monastery of Santa María de El Paular, and the Benedictine monastery of Valladolid. While they belonged to different religious orders, these shared the goal of reaffirming the basic principles of the Benedictine rule, and the last, San Benito of Valladolid, was confirmed in 1431 as a "center of renewal" and leadership for the Benedictine order in Castile.[108]

In spite of this emphasis on going back to the basics, monasteries tended to develop their own food-related practices, and their determination to hold firm to the original Benedictine principles did not always last. The ideal of limiting the consumption of meat was the one most frequently abandoned. By the twelfth century, eating fowl had become generally acceptable in religious communities, especially those that drew their novices from elite families. By the fifteenth century, with the expansion of pasture land, more meat was consumed by the general population, and monastic communities began to follow suit, also increasing their consumption of other forms of protein such as eggs and cheese.[109] Carthusian communities, generally the strictest in holding to dietary regulations, began to allow meat for their servants and members who were sick.[110] Financial accounts from the Cistercians and other convents of Toledo record regular purchases of pork, partridges, hens, and mutton for the nuns' tables.[111] In the fifteenth century, the regulations of the monastery of Santa Anna of Barcelona allowed the monks to slaughter a pig between Christmas and Lent, sharing the meat among the community and salting the rest to eat during the rest of the year.[112]

These changes reflect the tensions between the negative associations of meat held by Christian theologians and the high value placed on it in the Galenic and informal food hierarchies. While many monasteries were poor and relied heavily on donations of money and food, others possessed great wealth and drew many of their novices from noble families. It was logical for the latter to seek to maintain some of the practices that identified their family's social privilege even as they sought to renounce worldly temptations.[113] The nuns of San Payo, generally from privileged families, ate white bread "of the best quality possible" while their servants ate rye. Their regular rations suggest that they ate food of substantially higher quality than their secular Aragonese counterparts;

when they consumed meat, it was lamb and hen, with no mention of lowly beef.[114] Some convents and monasteries possessed special privileges related to the control of food by city authorities, receiving the same kinds of distributions of valued foods such as veal and partridge as did ambassadors and other high-ranking officials. In Madrid, the convent of Discalced Trinitarians was guaranteed ten mutton heads and *asaduras* each week.[115] Monasteries also played a role in hosting travelers, from pilgrims to high-status diplomats or members of the royal family, and had to be prepared to set an appropriate table. Serving impressive meals was therefore a way to demonstrate the wealth and social importance of the church as an institution as well as to maintain the aura of the elite origins of many of its members.

By the early seventeenth century, even the rules of San Benito of Valladolid, meant to govern all of the Benedictine communities in Spain (collectively referred to as "the Congregation"), gave in to the allure of meat. The revised regulations of 1612 reflect this struggle, echoing the helpless shrug of St. Benedict centuries earlier over the issue of wine: "According to the holy rule and ancient practice of our saintly Fathers, the eating of meat should be prohibited to our members. But keeping in mind human debility and weakness . . . and the poor health and strict confinement of our monks, it is necessary for them to eat meat during much of the year." The new regulations went on to suggest that all of communities of the Congregation be given a full pound of mutton (or three quarters, for those who were under eighteen years of age) at their main meal on Sundays, Mondays, Tuesdays, and Thursdays each week except for the seasons of Advent and Lent, and that they also be allowed to enjoy beef or mutton tripe as part of their secondary meal.[116] How these rules were carried out in practice probably varied among different monasteries. The Madrid monastery of Monserrat remained strict, choosing to refuse all meat.[117] The late seventeenth-century account books of the Benedictine monastery of San Martín in Madrid, probably more representative, show that the monks consumed a little over one thousand pounds of mutton per month (probably close to the revised recommendation of a pound each per day) as well as occasional meals of finer meats such as rabbit, partridge, and kid goat. They also made daily purchases of bacon, even on fast days.[118] Meat was also featured prominently in the seventeenth-century recipe collection of Antonio de Salsete, who cooked for a Navarrese monastery; his recipes include dozens of preparations of pork, mutton, beef, and rabbit.[119]

The celebration of festival days also led the members of convents and monasteries to temporarily abandon their commitment to alimentary austerity. The emphasis on the absence of meat for religious fast days meant that in turn it came to be strongly associated with special feasts. The Beguine religious communities of Valencia, for example, celebrated key events in the festival calendar with the slaughter of particular animals: young goats for Carnival and Easter; a goose for Saint John, lamb for the beginning of Advent, a pair of hens or capons for Christmas Eve, and another kid goat for Christmas.[120] The nuns of San Clemente in Toledo during Holy Week provided meals to the poor consisting of beans, leeks, garbanzos, and fish, and they ate the same foods themselves as a gesture of sacrifice. Nevertheless, they celebrated the religious holidays of the Ascension, Pentecost, and Holy Trinity with feasts of mutton, eggs, and fritters with milk and honey. On the feast day of Saint Bernard, they slaughtered a pig, and for their biggest festival, honoring their patron saint San Clemente, they ate pork, *rosquillas* (similar to doughnuts), rice, fruit, and nuts with candied ginger.[121] On July 11, the feast day of St. Benedict, the Benedictine monks of the monastery of San Martín celebrated with a feast of veal, pullets, hens, rabbit, and a variety of fruit.[122] Early modern monasteries were also more relaxed about wine than were their medieval counterparts. Wine was the principal drink in nearly all religious communities, as it was for the rest of the populace, and normal rations in the early modern period went well beyond the small amount permitted by St. Benedict.[123] The Barcelonan monks of Santa Anna by the fifteenth century were drinking a liter each per day.[124] The 1612 constitutions of the Congregation of Saint Benedict did not specify any restrictions on the amount of wine but stated that bread and wine should be provided to each monk "according to his need."[125] The Benedictine monks of San Martín in Madrid made regular substantial purchases of wine: 136 arrobas (over two thousand liters) for the month of February 1679, for example, as well as nine and a half arrobas of fine white wine from Esquibias for their father superior.[126]

During the rest of the year, religious communities maintained their commitment to simple, humble food. Nevertheless, they often developed a reputation for excellent cooking, perhaps precisely because of the need to satisfy human appetites while following the restrictions of their order.[127] The monastery cook Antonio de Salsete wrote in the introduction to his recipe collection that servants of Christ must eat simply but that this did not preclude eating well, and he emphasized cooking with as much variety as possible with limited ingredients.[128] In fact, the two principal cookbooks that emerged from the monastic context were both quite similar to their courtly counterparts. Salsete's work borrows substantially from the court chef Martínez Montiño, while the recipe collection of Domingo Hernández de Maceras, oriented toward the predominantly ecclesiastical population of one of the colleges of the University of Salamanca, nevertheless echoed the kinds of dishes commonly prepared in the household of the Dukes of Gandía.[129] In spite of their relative isolation, convents and monasteries sometimes led the way in introducing new foods or innovative preparations. Chocolate made its first appearance in Spain in the southern city of Jerez via the convent of the nuns of the Holy Spirit, and its use seems to have spread via connections between religious communities.[130] Salsete's *El cocinero religioso* includes some of the earliest European culinary references to potatoes, tomatoes, and paprika (which was made from peppers brought from the Americas).[131] The account books of the monastery of San Clodio de Leiro show mutton, sugar, spices, and chocolate among its regular purchases, along with the more ordinary lentils and garbanzos.[132] Certain monasteries, such as those of Irache (in Navarre) and Guadalupe (Extremadura) became known as centers of culinary expertise, and others hired their own professional cooks rather than relying on the skills of their own members.[133] As a result, Rachel Laudan has credited such institutions with spreading a kind of "Catholic high cuisine" to rural areas throughout Europe.[134] Many convents also gained (and still maintain) a particular reputation for producing excellent pastries and confectionery.

Although the monastic communities emphasized the humility and spiritual equality of all their members, the organization and distribution of food functioned to display the internal hierarchy of the group. The regulations of most monastic groups and seminaries included clear instructions about the order in which everyone was to sit at meals. At the first table was the rector or vicerector, and then the priests or seminarians, followed by their servants, each group ordered by seniority.[135] Novitiates had to take their meals apart from the rest, an important sign that they were not fully incorporated into the group. The Benedictine regulations suggested that they eat in a separate area, and if such were not available that they eat in the refectory but at a separate table with their master.[136] The content of their meals was different according to rank: in many monasteries, the rations of the established monks were twice as big as those of the novices, and three times those of the other residents of the monastery.[137] The prelate and those who ate with him at the monastery's first table always received an extra ration.[138] In the convents of Toledo, all the nuns enjoyed the appearance of mutton and chicken on their tables, but their abbess was occasionally able to partake of partridge as well.[139] There were even separate cooking areas for different groups: one for the abbot and any high-status visitors, one for the sick, and one for the community of monks.[140] The Benedictine rule suggested that it was appropriate for the abbot to eat with any distinguished guests, which meant eating the same fine foods that were prepared for them. In San Martín, a separate line in the account book listed extraordinary food expenses for guests, including chicken, squab, and testicles (probably calf or lamb) for the visiting abbots of San Millan and Santo Domingo de Silos, and purchases of ice in the summer were recorded in the category related to guests hosted at the monastery.[141] The regulations of the convent of San Payo de Antealtares in Galicia included different rations of wine according to the relative status of the nun. The abbess was to receive twenty-four *cañados* (a little over two liters) a day, the nuns who had been longest in residence twelve cañados, the younger ones nine, and the vicars' servants three. The nuns were also instructed to distribute the better wines first, to those who had seniority.

The amounts, however, were more likely symbolic than real, since in practice the nuns could drink whatever part of their ration they wished and receive the value of the rest in coin; the wine proportions served more to recognize their relative status than to control the amount they actually drank.[142] The revised Benedictine guidelines of the seventeenth century made some attempt to circumvent these hierarchical tiers of rations, by emphasizing that former abbesses were not to receive double rations and that no nun was to be allowed to maintain her own kitchen to prepare her own food; all were to eat equally from the communal pot.[143] These guidelines also stated that any monk who tarried in his work or in arriving to the table was punished by being made to eat alone, give up his ration of wine, or both.[144]

Customs of commensality in the monastic environment were designed to create a sense of community, establish order within that community, and perform the humility and austerity that formed an important part of the identity of its members. Just as Christians abstained from certain foods during certain periods in the liturgical calendar, monks and nuns indicated their commitment to a completely religious life by following a more restricted diet throughout their monastic lives. These dietary practices formed a significant part of their collective identity, setting them apart from the rest of society. The Benedictine rules of the early seventeenth century identified eight affiliated colleges under the administration of the congregation and noted that they were obliged to follow all of the rules set out in the Benedictine constitution except for those related to food. Students in the colleges were given a special dispensation to eat meat, particularly mutton, at both daily meals except during Lent.[145] This practice recognized the more worldly and secular dedications of the students while highlighting the greater religious identity of those who belonged fully to the order. Food was also a means through which monks and nuns symbolically surrendered their individuality and demonstrated their dedication to the collective. The early eighteenth century friar and scholar Benito Feijóo noted that monks and nuns usually ate food of roughly the same quality as would a family of average means but with a crucial difference: while the layman was free to follow his appetite and individual preference, the monk must follow his community, eating what and when they ate.[146] Even as most monasteries seemed to gradually lessen their emphasis on asceticism over the sixteenth and seventeenth centuries, they still used distinctive dietary practices to emphasize their collective identity and distinguish themselves from the rest of society.

UNIVERSITY LIFE

Royalty, gender, and religion were relatively fixed categories of collective identity, all of which were associated with particular food customs that visibly distinguished royals from non-royals, men from women, Christians from Jews and Muslims, and monks from laymen. Spaniards could also belong to any number of chosen communities and institutions, from their neighborhood to an occupational guild to a religious confraternity. Whether formal or casual, these groups also strove to define their internal structure and distinguish themselves from the rest of society.[147] Shared meals emphasized the connection and mutual support between members of a group, and the rejection or avoidance of such meals threatened its stability. In the annual dinners celebrated by guilds, for example, the absence of any member would be interpreted as an expression of defiance or enmity and punished by a fine.[148] One group whose internal relationships are particularly well illustrated by food is that of university students. These young men shared a culture based on circumstance more than social status, as they came to Spanish universities from a wide range of social, economic, and geographic backgrounds. They did have gender in common, as women could be privately educated but generally did not have access to higher education. Most students came from the regions surrounding the principal universities of Alcalá, Salamanca, and Valladolid, but others came from across the country and from abroad. Children of noble families did not predominate; they were more likely to receive their education via private tutoring, though younger sons were often encouraged to pursue the study of law. By the early seventeenth century titled families increasingly relied on formal study to gain access to high juridical and administrative positions connected to the court.[149] Students who wanted to pursue their studies at the university level needed to have a basic educational foundation, including Latin. While this favored the access of urban families with relative wealth, it did not preclude the presence of students from rural or even peasant backgrounds, who were able to prepare themselves through the charitable support of others or via work as servants to more established scholars.[150]

Whether they came from the families of elites, small landowners, poor hidalgos, urban merchants, professionals and bureaucrats, or rural laborers, all hoped to improve their situation in the increasingly fluid society of early modern Spain. With the rise of humanism in the fourteenth century, education was increasingly perceived to play a key role in individual development and to have greater practical value, especially for those of lower social status. Francisco de Monzón and others who wrote on education in the sixteenth century argued that the formative power of education was more important than one's inherent nature. Monzón suggested that man was the only creature born without inherently knowing any skill but that through free will and innate ability he could perfect himself: "no matter how rough and rustic a human mind [*ingenio*] may be, if it is shaped and taught well, it may be made wise and discerning [*discreto*]." He followed this with a long list of historical examples of men who, through effort and education, were able to rise to the highest levels of power.[151] The process of education that Monzón recommended to achieve these levels of success included the usual subjects of philosophy, languages, science, and Scripture but also chapters on developing the proper manners and self-control in relation to food and drink. Such recommendations suggested that one's behavior was as important as one's knowledge in the proper formation of a student.

While writers such as Monzón generally focused their didactic efforts on advice for ruling families, they also emphasized the importance of educating the poor (and financially subsidizing that education) instead of reserving wisdom and learning for the rich and powerful.[152] Such goals were supported in practice as well as in rhetoric, at least to some degree. Many seminary regulations included a clause stipulating that leftovers should always be given to poor students, and the Colegio of the archbishopric of Toledo, one of the secular colleges that supported the

University of Salamanca, supported twelve poor students each year.[153] The *colegios mayores*, the principal institutions of higher education in Spain, were originally designed to facilitate access to poorer students by providing housing, food, books, and clothing, though after the sixteenth century they became more exclusive.[154] The Franciscan scholar Francesc Eiximenis commented favorably on the transformative power of education, noting that the sons of peasants were "taking command of the study of wisdom that the nobles have forsaken. . . . What's more, they have taken their profits, for a learned man is immediately wealthy and a nobleman almost never or rarely."[155] By the sixteenth century, with the growth of state bureaucracies, education served as a gateway to important official positions as well as the usual specializations in theology, law, and medicine. University studies were pursued by sons of families who wanted to maintain their privileged position as well as by those who hoped to gain status in a society that offered few other possibilities to rise. One of the dialogues in an anonymous seventeenth-century conduct book includes a riddle posed to a son by his father, "How are you different from a dog?" with the answer, "Because you can become a man, and the dog can't, provided you go to school, where beasts go to become men."[156] The sixteenth century saw the greatest rise in enrollments and the greatest possibilities for social advancement through university study.[157] Some of course were uncomfortable with this, perceiving a threat to the dominance of old landed families but ostensibly worrying that university study would draw too many people away from agriculture and mechanical labor.[158]

In principle, having been brought together for the same purpose put students on an equal basis as members of a privileged community. Having left their families and probably having engaged in some days' travel and able to bring only limited possessions, they embarked on a new phase of life, living together in shared houses or pensions, dressing in the same scholastic robes, and sharing the same course of academic study.[159] University regulations tried to limit ostentation in students' dress and behavior (particularly via clothing and the use of servants and carriages). Most students entered university life around the age of eighteen, and of course all were men. The rhetoric of proper dedication to university life emphasized sobriety, humility, and dedication to life of the mind. The university was a protected space outside of the trials of ordinary life, even to the extent of having a separate legal jurisdiction, to which students could flee if they found themselves (as they often did) in trouble with the law after a bout of drinking or a brawl.[160]

The purported equality of students within the sphere of university life was reflected in the regulations regarding the food with which they were provided. Scenes from literary works such as *Don Quixote*, *Guzmán de Alfarache*, and *El Buscón* have contributed to the picaresque image of starving students, and many scholars have taken these descriptions at face value, concluding that "hunger and university life have been constant companions," but this may have been more a literary tradition than reality.[161] The rations offered in residential programs were substantial and meant to smooth over social differences and maintain a sense of common ground among students. The kitchen account books of the colegios mayores give us an idea of the kinds of meals that were regularly offered, which register a level of quality far better than that suggested by the literary stereotype of the starving student: meat, including mutton, with every meal except for fast days; fish, eggs, and the chicken-based *manjar blanco*; more inexpensive fare such as lentils and garbanzos; regular servings of fruits and vegetables; and a variety of spices.[162] The meals served on special occasions included chicken, rabbit, and *pastel en bote*, a kind of potted pastry.

Even for students who lived outside of university residences, one of the most common forms of lodging was the *pupilaje*. In this system, a small group of students would live with a *bachiller*, a student who had completed the first level of university study, roughly corresponding to today's undergraduate degree. Even though these were private residences off university grounds, students were required to follow certain guidelines. Regulations at the University of Salamanca included attention to food as well as tutelage, stipulating that the bachiller had the responsibility to supervise his pupils' study, make sure they did not engage in the immoral hobbies of cards or dice, and provide them with basic rations of one pound of mutton each day as well as extra delicacies six times a year for special occasions. The students were to take their meals together each day in the company of their bachiller and were not allowed to supplement their rations with any personal purchases. Similarly, the regulations of the *colegios menores* associated with the University of Salamanca expressed concern for the eating habits of their students: the twelve poor students subsidized by the university were all meant to sit together with their rector, eating at the same time as the other students. If any of them came late enough to miss the blessing that began the meal, they were to pay one maravedí; if they missed the entire lesson read at dinner, they had to reimburse the cost of the meal. The section on meals concludes with a stern warning that "each is to be content with the rations served on his plate, without murmur or complaint."[163] While university records reveal occasional conflicts and complaints over food, mostly the system seemed to work well. Typical is the case of the students who lived with their bachiller Francisco de Fermoselle, who reported in 1602 that "there is always leftover food on the table and no restrictions; each one eats as much as he wants."[164] Information from the *libros de visitas*, records of supervisory visits made by university officials, suggests that students were regularly and well fed. The average daily cost of the food provided to students at Salamanca ranged from eighty-three maravedís per student on fast days to ninety-five maravedís on meat days, substantially more than the value of the meals of the average laborer. Meals on festival days included highly valued foods such as rabbit, kid goat, poultry, and a variety of sweets.[165]

While food was part of the common academic culture that united students, it also helped to mark the inevitable differences between them as well as the larger hierarchy of the institution. Relative age and experience were one source of differentiation: students came to share a common culture and set of daily habits, but the gateway to that culture was often marked by rituals of initiation. One of the first tests a student faced was the *patente*, a custom by which new students were expected to invite a group of more established students to dinner, in order to be fully integrated into the group.[166] In the pupilaje run by the bachiller Juan Fernández de Aguila, new students were obliged to pay patentes of chestnuts and wine to their companions.[167] Newer students were also expected to finish their meals before their more senior classmates, out of respect.[168] Food could function as a reward or a punishment: misbehaving students could be denied food or their ration of wine. A particularly embarrassing punishment for a student was to be sent to the *mesilla* or little table, where he would be allowed to enter the common dining room but had to take his meal at a separate table from the rest.[169]

The internal structure of the university was also reflected in food rations, as university officials generally received special rations above and beyond the standard fare of the students. In the episcopal seminary of Montalegre, the rector and master each received the same rations as the students, with an added daily supplement of pork or lamb and a larger portion of wine.[170] At the other end of the hierarchy, while the food provided at San Ildefonso and the other colegios mayores corresponded to a fairly comfortable social status, the colegios mayores were initially designed to help students with limited economic resources, and many students received various levels of financial aid. San Ildefonso provided for thirteen each year who, without residing in the colegio, received bread and the leftovers of the other students' meals. Such a distribution made clear their inferior and dependent status.[171] In contrast, the Jesuit school of Cordelles, dedicated to the education of children of noble families, instructed its students that taking the leftovers of others was discourteous, sinful, and an indication of baseness—clearly it was more "noble" to give than to receive.[172]

CONFRATERNITIES

Another important form of early modern collective identity may be found in the cofradías, voluntary lay associations with an emphasis on providing social services. The first of these were formed in the late fourteenth century, and the majority developed following the Council of Trent (1545–1563), which actively encouraged a variety of forms of community-based religious activism. In the sixteenth and seventeenth centuries cofradías made up the majority of such local organizations, and even by the late eighteenth century, as their influence declined, there were still twenty-five thousand of them across Spain.[173] Their duties included providing assistance to the sick and poor, praying for souls in purgatory, maintaining devotion to particular saints, sponsoring festivals, processions, and other public entertainments, and occasionally providing social support for their own members such as covering funeral expenses.[174] In urban areas, these brotherhoods often took on the responsibility of establishing hospitals, such as the Hospital de la Pasión in Madrid, the Hospital de Pobres Sacerdotes de Valencia, the Hospital de la Concepción in Toledo, and the Hospital de las Misericordias in Seville. Such institutions in early modern Europe were far from the sites of professionalized medical care that we think of today. They simply provided food, shelter, and a range of religious and welfare assistance to those who had no other resources, whether these were pilgrims, orphans, or the sick and destitute; in other words, *hospitality*, to evoke the origin of their name. While some attempted to provide medical treatment, in most cases, their greatest practical impact came simply from their provision of food. Such hospitals were generally funded by local governments or charitable organizations such as the cofradías, and while they were often small, insufficient, and overburdened, they served as one of the few institutional sources of support for the urban poor of early modern Europe.

These brotherhoods were always established on the principle that everyone is equal in the eyes of God, but their membership structure and activities reflected a keen sense of social hierarchy. As an important and visible social institution (similar in many ways to the early modern guild), the cofradía in many cases was only open to those who met the proper genealogical and occupational requirements (such as not having any Jewish or Muslim heritage, or not having worked at any mechanical trade) and thus served to display that position to the community. One particularly exclusive group was the brotherhood of the Dulce Nombre de Jesús, founded in the small Mediterranean town of Vélez-Málaga in the early seventeenth century. The town was too small (just over one thousand residents) to have an established titled nobility, so its aristocracy was defined more by political power and social reputation than by lineage. The Dulce Nombre de Jesús confraternity accepted members only from this group of self-established elites, and thus served to reinforce its boundaries, to the extent that membership in the cofradía eventually came to serve as proof of nobility. While those who aspired to join had to be accepted by a vote of existing members, the latter were also allowed to preserve their position by passing on automatic membership to their own family members, thus guaranteeing their position despite economic or social changes. Its activities, like those of other brotherhoods, centered on providing charitable support for the poor, especially widows and orphans. However, its single largest yearly expenditure was on its patron-day procession, a public display of its position and status in the community.[175] At the very least, membership identified *cofrades* as people who possessed enough wealth and position to dedicate themselves to charity. Cofradías had a clear position within their community, communicated via their participation in religious festivals and the prominent place they held in public processions.

Food was always an important element in the activities of cofradías, whether this involved a light collation at meetings, the rich banquets with which they celebrated their patron saint day and other holidays, or the meals they prepared for the poor. Each brotherhood upon its founding generated a book of regulations to guide its governance and operation. The symbolic and practical importance of food is clearly inscribed in these books, as typically over a third of the chapters directly address the organization and provision of various kinds of meals.[176] Their regulations and account books generally describe two kinds of meals: those where the table was shared by the members of the cofradía itself, which served to identify it as a group and define its internal structure, and those meals prepared by the cofradía for others, which displayed its social role in assisting the poor and established a line of differentiation between members and nonmembers. Like university students and monasteries, cofradía members used food to make visible their internal hierarchy, determined by the social status of individual members and their relative position of authority within the cofradía, as well as the chronological seniority of their membership. Food could be used to regulate these relationships and resolve tensions within the group, as when members who committed infractions against the brotherhood's rules did their penance by providing a meal for its officials or the entire group, depending on the severity of the offense.[177] Members could also be punished by being made to eat apart from the group at their celebratory banquets, partaking of only bread and water at a separate table until their superiors allowed them to rejoin the festivities.[178]

When confraternities provided food for others, these meals could indicate either solidarity between peers or superiority over the less fortunate. Mantecón Movellán argues that the sharing of food represented the collective hospitality of the group's parish and neighborhood, not just that of the members themselves. These meals they provided for others at or near their same social level—such as the refreshments of wine, bread, and fruit traditionally served on Holy Thursday under the portico of the parish church, or the collations they provided for meetings between cofradía officials and representatives of the town and parish—could therefore serve as a form of community integration.[179] Similarly, along the eastern Mediterranean coast of Spain, brotherhoods would host communal meals in the countryside to celebrate the end of the harvest or other collective projects.[180] Such offerings reinforced the connections between the cofradía and its community and helped to enhance the relative position of the cofradía through the symbolism of its generosity.

More central to the charitable purposes of these brotherhoods were the offerings they made to the poor. In a few cases, confraternities kept their charitable activities to those within their own ranks. The charter of the small Cofradía de San Onofre in Seville, run by members of the silk guild, dictated that its donations were available only to the wives and widows of its own members and that they "would not receive any other poor except those of the guild."[181] Such efforts helped to reinforce the cofradía's identity and the advantages of belonging. More frequently, such offerings were more widely distributed to the needy of the community, and making presentations of food to the poor became a statement to the community of the wealth and status of the cofradía itself, as well as of its charitable Christian raison d'être. Brotherhoods would often invite a symbolic group of thirteen poor guests to the banquets at which they celebrated their patron saint day. The poor were to receive the leftovers, in a kind of microcosmic rendition of society's wealthy providing for its needy. This well-intentioned goal was occasionally marred by the members' practice of bringing along their servants to take advantage of any excess food, as recorded by additions to the regulations of several brotherhoods reminding them that the purpose was to have enough leftovers to share with the poor.[182]

In addition to this sharing of food at banquets, the brotherhoods also provided meals exclusively dedicated to the needy. The rulebook for the Cofradía de San Antonio Abad, established in Benavente in 1535, dictated that a meal consisting of beef, pork fat, cabbage, bread, and wine be provided "to the poor of the town" on St. Martin's Day, November 11. In the same town, the Cofradía de las Animas del Purgatorio provided a yearly feast of bread and meat and wine on November 1. Even though their regulations emphasized quantity and generosity in these meals, specifying that food was to be provided "abundantly" and "to all the poor men and women who are able to come," such once-a-year feasts would have hardly been enough to sustain those who could not support themselves.[183] Among the most generous donors were several of the brotherhoods of Toledo who distributed substantial numbers of meals with an average serving of meat of over 750 grams (worth nearly half of an average worker's daily salary), but even in this case the brotherhoods' festive meals were provided only on eleven feast days throughout the year.[184] For their daily needs, the poor were more likely to rely on begging, handouts from the parish, or the hospitals (these patterns of charity and poor relief will be discussed at greater length in chapter 4). Therefore these brotherhoods provided food to the poor both in a regular, sustained manner via the hospitals they funded and through festive meals on special occasions. The latter served as a symbolic gesture to publicly establish the members' role as charitable benefactors and to confirm the economic and social distance between themselves and the recipients of their generosity more than as a practical tactic for feeding the destitute.

In some circumstances, however, the cofradías' efforts may have provided better nutrition for their needy than similar organizations across

Europe. Mediterranean countries in general tended to consume proportionately less animal protein than those of northern Europe, and Spain was no exception. Nevertheless, for those who were fortunate enough to receive regular distributions of food from the brotherhoods (admittedly a small fraction of the poor), meals were more substantial, balanced, and healthy than those of much of the population.[185] Such meals also corresponded to the marginalized social status of the poor, consisting of bread, fish, vegetables, and beans, but as such, by today's nutritional standards, they were probably healthier than the rich food the donors kept for themselves. In the hospital of Santa María la Real in Burgos, the founder's will specified that those who had taken ill among the hospital's indigent residents should be given extra food beyond the standard poor rations until they were fully recovered.[186] That same hospital also developed the tradition of providing meals of fish, vegetables, bread, and wine to thirteen poor people during the entire forty days of Lent. While this was not written down in the brotherhood's original regulations, it came to be the most substantial and costly of their charitable activities.[187]

Several cofradías across Spain were founded specifically in the interest of caring for those who were held in the public prisons and could not afford to feed themselves.[188] One such group, the Cofradía de Nuestra Señora de la Misericordia in Zamora, provided the poor of its jails with rations of over a pound of bread daily and half a pound of cooked meat, with double rations at Easter and the cofradía's festival days. To those in prison who were about to undergo torture in the course of their trials, the brotherhood provided them succor in the form of small cakes or soft biscuits.[189] Most confraternities preferred to feed the poor within some sort of controlled institutional context (prisons or their own hospitals), but a few took their charity to the streets. In Madrid, the Hermandad del Refugio, a Jesuit charitable brotherhood organized in 1615, included among its principal activities the "Rounds of Bread and Egg" (Ronda de Pan y Huevo), in which members went out every night through the streets of the city to provide basic sustenance in the form of bread and boiled eggs to the hungry.[190] At the same time, the lower quality of these charitable foods in the perceived hierarchy of value (beef or ox meat instead of mutton, turnips and cabbage instead of fruit, an absence of spices and seasonings) reiterated the relative social position of donors and recipients.

While the meals provided by cofradías to the poor were often substantial and nutritious, the banquets they provided for themselves were, as one might expect, finer and more elaborate. Brotherhoods held festive meals for standard religious holidays, for their patron saint days, to celebrate the admission of new members, or any number of other reasons. The Cofradía de San Antonio Abad in Benavente saved the fines paid by its members for minor transgressions throughout the year to fund a special meal the day after its patron saint day, consisting of mutton *torreznos*, bacon, white wine, oranges, and "good bread."[191] The brotherhood that maintained the Hospital de San Pedro in Toledo celebrated the festival of Candlemas with a feast for its members consisting of partridge, hens, rice, lamb, seasonings including honey and saffron, a wide variety of fresh and dried fruits, and abundant wine.[192] In 1511, the same Burgos confraternity that provided Lenten meals to the poor spent a total of 1,416 maravedís on those meals over the course of the year, while in the same year it spent more than that amount on only two banquets for its own members.[193] Such differences served to reinforce the identity and purpose of these organizations as well as their social position: the brotherhoods demonstrated their Christian charity by serving the poor at the same time that they performed their wealth and relative social superiority through their festival and banquets. This kind of emphasis on collective identity echoes the patterns we have seen throughout this chapter. Early modern Spaniards categorized themselves and others in a variety of ways, some voluntary, some according to their perceived nature. Whether these categories were defined by royal blood, gender, religion, or voluntary association, food was fundamental to displaying, imposing, and reinforcing collective identity and social relationships.

3

Status and Change

PEOPLE USED FOOD TO DEMONSTRATE WHO THEY WERE, but they could also use it to project an image of who they aspired to be. While the previous chapter explored the ways in which early modern Spaniards used food to reinforce their own collective identity and impose their expectations on others, this section will show how individuals used food customs to negotiate their position in society and how such efforts led to changes in food practices over the early modern period. This was a time of transition, with the demographic and economic instability following the fourteenth-century Black Death coupled with the beginnings of capitalism and the rise of urban elites. Across Europe, the social hierarchies of the Middle Ages were giving way to more fluid and negotiated ways of defining status. The traditional nobility (based on inherited titles, wealth based on land, and military service) found itself weakened, a shift that found its best expression in Cervantes's *Don Quixote*, whose hero clung to the faded trappings of his noble ancestry even while his material resources and influence were severely diminished. At the same time, those with new wealth (but lacking land and hereditary title) sought to establish a place for themselves in a society that believed that one's outward appearance indicated one's true nature. As those with new wealth increasingly rubbed elbows with both titled traditional elites and ordinary townspeople, each group struggled to distinguish itself through outward signs such as clothing, carriages, servants, and food consumption. The new social fluidity engendered both fresh possibilities for upward (and downward) mobility and anxiety about maintaining one's place, and food was one of the mechanisms that Spaniards could use both to support and to contain these changes.

The traditional social organization of early modern Europe was based on estates (essentially clergy, nobles, and peasants), each with its own distinct legal identity. We tend to think of these groups as fixed and clearly distinct from one another, although the reality, especially in Spain, was not so rigid. Spanish titled nobles largely derived their origin from their military service during the Reconquest, meaning both that their titles were relatively recent and that they were based on accomplishment rather than heritage (though of course over the generations following their establishment they would emphasize the importance of heritage). Below the titled families in the social hierarchy—but still in the noble estate—were the *hidalgos*, a term that loosely translates to "son of something," where the "something" could be anything from wealth to ancestry to royal favor. In Spain, the law recognized the status of hidalgos as "favored by kings, since they carry out their conquests, and are useful in times of peace and war, and for this they have been given privileges and liberties. . . . They may not be interrogated under torture; their arms and horses may not be confiscated for debt, nor may they be arrested for debt."[1] As armies became increasingly professionalized and less associated with noble obligation, and as the crown came to seek more varied sources of funding, titles of nobility and *hidalguía* were far more likely to come as royal grants in return for payment. After the end of the Reconquest in the late fifteenth century, with the exception of those who simply shifted their historic tasks of conquest to the new empire of the Indies, traditional Spanish nobles found they had to redefine themselves. Many turned their attention to politics, throwing their lot in with the growing nation-state, particularly with the establishment of the first fixed court in Madrid in 1561. The court was particularly well suited to performative displays of status, as it attracted the ambitious. In a place where most of the population was new and looking to establish itself, it was all the more important to display one's networks and status (or ideally to manipulate and improve them). With the increased possibility of purchasing titles in the seventeenth century, traditional titled nobles were virtually outnumbered by their more recently appointed peers. Philip IV insisted that the latter had to be at least hidalgos already and with seigniorial incomes, but by the reign of Charles II in the later seventeenth century, the crown was willing to sell titles to virtually anyone who could afford them.[2] Consequently the definition of nobility was rather hazy by this point, and subject to much debate; this made it all the more important for nobles (or those who aspired to be) to convincingly act the part.

As the boundaries between nobles and non-nobles (and between the various ranks of nobility) grew increasingly fluid, factors such as wealth, education, and talent came to be important mechanisms in improving one's status. A foreshadowing of this change may be seen in Martín Pérez's fourteenth-century *Libro de las Confesiones*, part of a broader tradition of late medieval confessors' manuals, which includes in its discussion of Christian doctrine a vision of society based on clear categorical divisions. Pérez addressed sin, penitence, and confession in terms of the needs and interests of particular groups. However, instead of following the custom of his time of identifying people by estate (peasant, cleric, or noble), he argued that his audience's thoughts, behaviors, and need for spiritual guidance could best be addressed in the context of their professions, from bishops to tailors to prostitutes. He then broke down professions in terms of their usefulness, which reflects a growing emphasis on practicality and ability rather than social status based on birth.[3] Wealth, however obtained, became increasingly acceptable as a measure of social value. Even Saint Teresa acknowledged wryly that "honor and money almost always go together; he who desires honor does not disdain money, and he who disdains money is given little honor. . . . It would be a marvel to find an honored man in this world if he were poor."[4] Sometimes this exchange was quite literal; not only were noble titles available for purchase, but in many cities, so were significant public offices. Such positions were only within reach of those with substantial wealth, which had formerly kept them in the hands of the traditional nobility. In the mid-sixteenth century, one could purchase an office in Segovia for 1,500 *ducados*, or for 2,000 a position in Burgos.[5] (For comparison, a day laborer at that time might earn 70 ducados in a year.) Technically, one had to already belong to the noble estate to purchase such a position, which would have been confirmed by a formal genealogical investigation. But by the late sixteenth century, the barrier to nobility had become more permeable. Juan de Cuéllar, a wool merchant from Segovia who amassed a substantial fortune, is a case in point. In spite of his social position as a merchant, he aspired to join the city government of Segovia. While his genealogy was not sufficiently noble, it seems his pockets were sufficiently deep, and he was able to purchase the office of *regidor* in 1605.[6] The famous painter Diego Velázquez is a similar example. Though his family origins included only a few connections to lesser nobility, he applied for membership in the noble Order of Santiago based on his accomplishments and the position he had achieved as official court painter to Philip IV. He clearly fell short of the requirements of the genealogical test, and his petition was rejected by the order. Nevertheless, the king intervened on his behalf to obtain a papal dispensation, and he was finally accepted as a member, an indication that accomplishments and royal favor could trump bloodlines.

Cuéllar, Velázquez, and others who became "hidalgos of convenience" were to some degree accepted by the existing nobility, as long as they were perceived to bring something to their new social peer group rather than demeaning it. The secret was to take on the appropriate appearance. In Spanish Baroque society, appearance was expected to be a faithful reflection of reality; social prestige and the elegance of one's appearance could be sufficient to verify one's hidalguía. As we saw in chapter 2, the religious brotherhood of the Dulce Nombre de Jesús in Vélez-Málaga pursued this same strategy with great success. This group represented what was essentially a self-created nobility, based on the reputation and influence of its members rather than their inherited titles or bloodlines. Membership in this group was exclusive enough that it alone came to be considered as proof of noble status. Such status had to be reinforced by the brotherhood's visible acts of charity and, in particular, the wealth they expended in their yearly patron-day festivities.[7] Similarly, Ana Guerrero Mayllo notes in her study of the lives and possessions of Madrid elites that the pomp and style they embraced in their dress, food, and tableware was even more important than their wealth in determining their position in the hierarchical order of status.[8] As long as these pseudo-nobles took houses in the proper neighborhoods, carried swords, dined on the proper foods with the right people, and did not call overt attention to their mercantile dealings or humble occupations, they were accepted. Juan de Cuéllar, the Segovian merchant, followed these guidelines: he invested in land (one of the most important symbols of noble status) and began to use a horse instead of a mule, especially for public processions.[9] In many regions, such members of the wealthy bourgeoisie became virtually indistinguishable in their appearance and economic behavior from the lower nobility. Both groups purchased land that produced for the urban marketplace (principally wine, grains, fruits, and vegetables), participated in local politics, and dedicated their sons to legal studies.

While the expression of individual taste and cultural protagonism via food, clothing, and furniture was first mastered by Italian urban elites during the Renaissance, such patterns were quickly adopted in Spain in the sixteenth and seventeenth centuries. Ken Albala has noted that food carries more than its usual cultural weight during periods of uncertainty, and this period of greater social mobility seems to bear out his argument.[10] So for the estate of traditional nobles, the boundaries to which had always been more permeable than they probably would have admitted to, and for those who wanted to make their way into it, food became an ideal mechanism with which to negotiate their position. With better transportation networks and more regional specialization in agriculture, a greater variety of foodstuffs was available to those with the wealth to pursue it. Indeed, as Yolanda Guerrero Navarrete notes, urban growth had a substantial influence on food culture, not only because the urban context brought together a richer variety of food habits but also because "cities do not consume what they produce; rather, they make others produce what they wish to consume."[11] Across early modern Europe, old aristocracies and urban elites both vied for superiority in supplying their tables, a competition that resulted in a greater gap than ever before between the quotidian diets of elites and those of the rest of the population.[12] Venetian merchants in the fourteenth century sought to demonstrate their new commercial power by pursuing costly sugar imports, driving a dramatic rise in recipes for sweets, and Spaniards followed suit in their quest for spices such as cinnamon, cloves, and pepper. The humanist and gastronomist Bartolomeo Sacchi (known as Platina) proudly noted that there is "no reason why the gourmandism of the ancients should be preferred to ours. . . . There is nothing in the whole world that has not been employed by our culinary masters, and everyone rigorously debates the seasoning of dishes."[13]

In Spain, a well-provided table was an effective way to demonstrate merchants' ability to hold their own with traditional elites, and they used their commercial networks to pursue unusual foodstuffs, spices, and treats with which to set a fine table and impress their guests.[14] Recipe books and household account books show a notable change from the sixteenth to the seventeenth centuries in the variety of foods and seasonings that were available, and urban diets became substantially more varied. (From these developments came the rhapsodic descriptions of the variety of delicacies found in urban markets, discussed in chapter 1.) Spaniards therefore began to demonstrate a greater sophistication in choosing the best available ingredients: recipe books and other sources proudly specify elements such as cheese from Mallorca, almonds from Catalonia, dates from the Maghreb, or white wine from Aragon.[15] The fifteenth-century bishop and scholar Alfonso de Cartagena commented in his *Doctrinal de Cavalleros* on this growing obsession with obtaining spices and other ingredients from Asia and overseas, noting that status-conscious hosts prioritized these rare ingredients over even high-quality local ones, since "the flavor is less sweet when the price is low."[16] García Marsilla's study of Valencian businessmen in the 1400s suggests that they were cautious with their money, eating far less meat and purchasing fewer spices than typical noble families but that for festivals or hosting important banquets their food expenditures rose to the same level as that of nobles.[17] Antoni

Pallarés, the head of a wealthy (but not noble) rural Catalan family in the early seventeenth century, offered a full day of feasting on the occasion of his son's marriage. The midday meal consisted of five courses, each with its own corresponding wine, including a main dish of roasted meats and stew (olla). Later, at dinner, his guests were offered chicken soup, partridge, kid goat in sauce, mutton, cheeses, and sweets. Noble families, not to be outdone, often had wedding ceremonies and accompanying meals that lasted up to three days.[18] In matters of appearance, their attempts to maintain their superiority could easily engender fierce competition. As early as 1544, the writer Francisco de Monzón worried about how nobles had "invented a new genre of grandeur at the table," adding more variety and more courses to every meal in the interest of impressing their guests in what Monzón perceived as the "new arts of gluttony."[19] Both groups of elites, new and traditional, sought to maintain a clear separation from the masses via their greater sophistication and purchasing power as demonstrated by the food they ate and served to their guests. In turn, food for the first time became clearly associated with class and status. Before the fifteenth century, wealthy and poor Europeans had eaten fairly similar diets, except that the wealthy simply had access to much greater quantities. Now, food became a way to visibly demonstrate status and wealth.[20]

One of the clearest examples of this phenomenon came with the growth of the sugar trade in the sixteenth century. Sugar was known to Europeans in the medieval period, as it was produced in the Middle East and Egypt and brought to Europe via Venetian traders. Being rare and difficult to acquire, it was used as a medicine more than as a seasoning; honey was the principal sweetener. As the Portuguese established their own production in Madeira by the mid-fifteenth century and in Brazil by the mid-sixteenth, sugar production increased dramatically; by 1600 Brazil was exporting thousands of tons annually. Europeans adopted Islamic techniques for cooking with sugar, incorporating it into sorbets and iced drinks, fruit pastes and marmalades, pastries, and even main-dish recipes for meats and vegetables.[21] Martínez Montiño's recipes called for sugar in the preparation of roasted suckling pig, poultry, and veal.[22] Its fortuitous combination with chocolate led to the increased consumption of that product as well, as we shall see later. Sugar's ultimate marker of success was to join the list of foodstuffs whose provision was guaranteed by yearly contract to the court in Madrid in the early seventeenth century. Especially in its early decades, sugar was clearly the province of elites: after a dinner with the visiting Cardinal Barberini in Madrid, the Countess of Olivares sent him a gift of "some sugared things," and some months later, following his arrival in Valencia, the cardinal was welcomed with "a gift of various sweet things, sent by the Duchess of Gandía, made of sugar that is refined nearby, fourteen leagues from Valencia[:] . . . conserves, a variety of sweets, pomegranate and quince jellies . . . and other various delights of this sort."[23] Queen María Luisa, wife of Charles II, was particularly enamored of sweetened lemon and cinnamon drinks, the production of which required thirty-two pounds of sugar each day.[24] The substance came to be so valuable that a Spanish diplomat in 1582 complained about having to deal with the problem of several tons of sugar having been seized by pirates.[25]

As sugar production increased, the price dropped, and it became no longer exclusively the province of elite kitchens. The same was true of other rare or expensive seasonings and ingredients; it was not difficult for urban elites with new wealth to acquire these ingredients and use them with as much enthusiasm as their erstwhile social superiors. As trade in these items expanded and they became more widely available, they began to lose their cultural cachet. One signature Spanish dish that worked its way down the social scale from exclusive to popular was manjar blanco. Prepared with boiled and finely shredded chicken breast, rice flour, almond milk, and sugar, it was cooked until thick and eaten as a room-temperature pudding.[26] The earliest descriptions of this dish come from fourteenth-century Aragon, in the *Sent Soví* cookbook and Vilanova's *De regimine sanitatis*, in which it received particular recommendation as something that could be eaten frequently in the pursuit of good health. Its popularity grew in the 1550s, and it was known to be a particular favorite of King Philip II. Its presence in the menus of banquets such as that held for Philip II during his visit to Valencia in 1586, in Francisco Martínez Montiño's royal cookbook of 1611, and in the memoirs of the

French noblewoman Madame d'Aulnoy of her travels to Spain in the late 1670s has often led scholars to conclude that manjar blanco was a delicacy reserved exclusively for the upper classes. Yelgo de Vazquez's detailed seventeenth-century instructions on maintaining a royal household confidently include frequent references to the variety of ways in which a cook should be able to prepare the dish.[27] Such associations are logical, given the nature of both chicken and sugar as highly valued ingredients in the food hierarchy. Nevertheless, manjar blanco may have had a wider base of popularity than previously believed, as non-elites sought to profit from its aristocratic associations. The dish began to appear frequently on the winter menus of the students of the University of Alcalá de Henares, and it was occasionally provided as a treat to the students of Salamanca.[28] The account books of the Benedictine monastery of San Martín show that the monks purchased it already prepared, for their guests.[29] In Madrid, by the early seventeenth century, the dish seemed to be widely available to the general populace. Municipal records note the existence of several street vendors who sold manjar blanco, made of chicken on meat days and fish for fast days.[30]

Curiously, in spite of the potential transformation inherent in the "Columbian exchange" of new plants, animals, and cooking styles across the Atlantic, and in spite of Spaniards' eagerness to acquire unusual and expensive foodstuffs, they were remarkably resistant to New World cuisines. As their empire expanded into the Americas, they refused to adopt most of the native foodstuffs, even the fruits that grew in such abundance in the tropics. Instead, they transplanted from Europe to the Americas the foods that were most significant to them (wheat, grapes for wine, sheep and cattle for meat) and constructed bench stoves, ovens, and mills that would let them prepare these foods in familiar ways.[31] Very few foods or cooking techniques were brought back from the Americas to Europe, at least in the century or two after the conquest. Spaniards did fairly quickly incorporate turkey, peppers, common (Phaseolus) beans, and corn into their diets, though none of these was considered to be particularly exclusive or elite. Of these, corn had the biggest effect on the peasant population, especially in northern Spain, where it bore a resemblance to the millet that was commonly used. By the late seventeenth century, Galician peasants were eating bread made from cornmeal and reducing their meat consumption as more land was given over to corn.[32] Corn was also adopted in the Basque country more than in central and southern Spain, largely because it grew well in areas where wheat did not, but in both cases it was used for animal feed at least as much as for human consumption.[33] Europeans overall were suspicious of the potato, though Spaniards seemed to have consumed it as early as the mid-sixteenth century, and indeed Saint Teresa of Avila thanked the abbess of a neighboring convent for her gift of potatoes.[34] Given the enormous variety of foods native to the Americas, though, the transfer of American cuisines to Europe was "restricted, lop-sided, long-delayed and to this day radically incomplete," a situation that probably reveals the power dynamics inherent in the colonial relationship.[35]

Chocolate is worthy of particular mention, because it was entirely unknown to Europeans until the conquest of the Americas, and it is one of the few products that Spaniards did enthusiastically incorporate into their own culinary and social habits.[36] The first treatise dedicated entirely to chocolate was written by Antonio Colmenero de Ledesma, a doctor from Écija, who (with the approval of the king's personal physician) argued that cocoa beans were cool and dry (and therefore astringent) in character, but that once ground and prepared as a drink, or made into a paste with sugar, chocolate was healthy, balanced in terms of its humoral characteristics, and highly recommendable.[37] King Charles II, whose entire life was plagued by physical difficulties including ongoing digestive problems, took chocolate every morning upon the recommendation of his doctors, who found that it was one of the few things that "quieted the stomach of His Majesty."[38]

More telling, though, is the cultural response to chocolate and the meaning invested in it by early modern Spaniards. Historians have generally assumed that Spaniards accepted chocolate only by incorporating it into their existing palate of flavors, adding sugar and removing the unfamiliar spices with which Mesoamericans were accustomed to blend it. Marcy Norton argues instead that the influence of cultural transmission ran in the other direction, that Spanish colonizers recognized the cultural value of chocolate as a tribute item within the Aztec empire and accepted it in part because of their dependence on the Aztec social and economic framework. Norton's argument is supported by the way in which Spaniards incorporated chocolate into their social practices, as it quickly became a symbol of the proper reception of friends and favored guests. Its elite associations were supported both by its origins (Aztecs welcomed Spanish governors and priests by serving them chocolate) and by the nature of its preparation, which required familiarity with the proper techniques. At the highest social levels, the careful preparation and presentation of chocolate was a sign of cultivation and generosity as early as the sixteenth century. Colmenero notes that chocolate was most commonly served with sugar, cinnamon, chile or other peppers, cloves, vanilla or anise, achiote for color, and hazelnuts or almonds.[39] The French baroness Marie-Catherine d'Aulnoy described the presentation of chocolate in her visit to the household of the Duchess of Terranova, head chambermaid of Queen María Luisa: after games of cards and treats of dried fruit, "they present you with Chocolate, every one a China Cup full, upon a little dish of Agate set in Gold, with Sugar in a Box of the same. There was Chocolate ordered with Ice, and some hot, and some made with Milk and Eggs; one drinks it with Bisket, or else with some thin Bread as hard as if it were toasted, which they make so on purpose."[40]

Sharing chocolate thus became an important element of social display in the receiving of guests. In a 1691 treatise on the multitude of sins related to vanity and luxury in elite women's dress, the preacher Antonio de Ezcaray wrote to the wives of ministers and nobles that "I will not visit your palaces, or drink your chocolate, or take your confessions, because you cannot be absolved until with God's help you rid yourselves of such profanity," suggesting the importance of taking chocolate with someone as a form of social recognition and approval.[41] The beans themselves, unprepared, were valuable enough to be a highly appreciated gift; those from Oaxaca were prized as of the highest quality.[42] When the disgraced royal favorite Fernando de Valenzuela fled the court in early 1677, officials took inventory of his house in Madrid and found "such immensity of riches that it seems impossible not to have known" that he had stashed so much away: these riches included diamonds, rich tapestries, and a large closet full of chocolate.[43] Chocolate's popularity continued to increase through the eighteenth and nineteenth centuries, and it retained its role as a facilitator of social interaction. The whirl of dances, salons, and *tertulias* that occupied eighteenth-century social life nearly always included chocolate, and elegant presentations of chocolate such as that described by Madame d'Aulnoy could still be found in the early nineteenth-century household of the Cervera family of Almagro. Part of the lesser nobility, the Cerveras spent 6 percent of their substantial food budget on chocolate, which was always served as part of social occasions with friends and guests.[44]

As with manjar blanco, while chocolate after its introduction in the sixteenth century was a product favored by the Spanish elite, as others strove to emulate their customs, it became gradually less exclusive, at least in urban areas. The first license granted in Madrid to produce chocolate was issued in 1634, and it became a common breakfast drink by midcentury.[45] Street vendors appear ever more frequently in city regulations through the rest of the seventeenth century, and Madrid municipal records listing the basic duties of city officials included a whole chapter on the proper supervision of these stands, noting that "chocolate has introduced itself in such a way . . . that there is hardly a shop on the streets of Postas and Mayor where it isn't sold."[46] A chronicler in Jerez in 1658 noted that "this year chocolate from the Indies came to Jerez. . . . It is a drink of the heavens and not very expensive."[47] By the late eighteenth century, it was common enough that families with domestic servants occasionally included chocolate as part of their wages, and chocolate grinders gathered to form their own guild.[48] The offer of chocolate to visitors, especially in the morning, became so standard a practice that to reject it was cause for suspicion. In the 1650s, two brothers of the Enríquez family were accused and convicted of secretly maintaining Jewish practices; part of the evidence against them was that they had appeared one morning at the house of their aunt and refused her customary offer of chocolate, allegedly because they were observing a religious fast.[49] The chocolate that was so popular on the streets of Madrid, of course, was probably of a much lesser quality than that of the elegant drink in china cups enjoyed by Madame d'Aulnoy. In the late seventeenth century, Madrid city officials worried that it was hard to maintain any level of quality control over the chocolate sold in street stands. It was difficult to confirm the ingredients, and they feared that a substantial amount of what was being sold as chocolate was actually cut with bread crumbs, cornmeal, or dried and ground orange peel.[50]

GUESTS, CONDUCT BOOKS, AND TABLE MANNERS

In addition to the acquisition and presentation of high-quality foods, two crucial parts of the performative aspect of competition over social ascent were the form in which such foods were consumed and the people with whom they were shared. As spices such as cloves and cinnamon and condiments such as sugar became more accessible and "common," those who wanted to display their social superiority turned increasingly toward behavior rather than possessions to distinguish themselves. Table manners, place settings, the order of seating guests, and the form of serving food all took on an increasingly performative element in the sixteenth and seventeenth centuries as techniques that could be acquired to demonstrate sophistication and status. Early modern Spanish culture was rich with protocol surrounding all kinds of personal interactions, especially those that expressed differing levels of power and authority. In the regulations guiding Madrid's aldermen, following the briefer sections on maintaining hospitals and prisons and how to deal with the plague, there are a full two pages on the protocol of visiting the president of the Council of Castile, the presidents of other royal councils, and other high-ranking figures such as cardinals and ambassadors. The instructions clarified before whom the aldermen should remove their hats, whether they should enter with their staffs of office raised or lowered, and whether they should let the other party introduce new topics of conversation.[51] Antonio de Guevara, the writer of courtly advice, described the difficulty (and importance) of navigating such relationships in the court: "You must take your hat off to everyone, call the official "Your Honor," give up your seat to the courtier, leave the head of the table to the royal favorite."[52] Such protocols governed virtually all interactions; they involved a careful calculus of relative position, and the sharing and consumption of food was well suited to such negotiations.

The relationship between host and guests at the table was a particularly important site of negotiation. Shared meals could be used to establish a group's internal hierarchy, to celebrate the role or accomplishment of a person or group, or to demonstrate support for a host or guest. At late medieval tables, the most important quality to demonstrate was generosity when dining with others; this spoke to a power relationship that (if performed properly) worked to the advantage of the host. The medieval emperor Charlemagne had an excellent reputation for his hospitality at the table, but according to his biographer Einhard, the enormous expense was justified since "in exchange for these immense nuisances, this attention provided him with a reputation for generosity and good standing."[53] Such generosity, politically speaking, translated into power and influence, as one who provided food was one who could expect loyalty and service in return.[54] As the growth of the state and the establishment of a fixed court in Madrid in the mid-sixteenth century created new and complex opportunities for developing social networks, many writers gave advice on how to navigate the opportunities and pitfalls of sharing a table. For a host, the challenge was to be sufficiently generous in the frequency of one's banquets to cultivate a proper following but not so much that the effect was diluted. As we saw in chapter 2, Francisco de Monzón's recommendation to kings was that one should not share one's table too freely with others, lest that honor be diminished. Monzón made the same recommendation to all elites, that they should invite only carefully chosen and respected guests to sit with them for a meal. Inviting others too frequently, he admonished, was merely a sign of following one's appetite and desire, rather than maintaining the proper gravity and reverence appropriate to one's status.[55]

As hosts sought to provide a fine table and carefully chosen foods, these excellent meals could provide their own challenge to guests, who were easily tempted to give in to their appetites. One of the most frequent concerns expressed in advice books was to make the best use of the possibilities for social networking but to choose wisely and not to give way to greed. Guevara cautioned that "the gentleman should not go to where he will eat best, but to where he will most be esteemed. There are sons of gentlemen and lords who shamelessly go to eat at the houses of their parents' enemies, and they do this not for the sake of their conscience [to smooth over the differences], but simply out of greed for a fine meal."[56] Juan de Vega, president of the Council of Castile, sent his son Hernando to Spanish Flanders in the mid-sixteenth century with the advice to not eat alone in his lodgings but to eat with others as often as possible, to establish good connections. Sharing meals, especially with one's superiors, seems to have been a key element of a young courtier's education. The Count of Portalegre, who collected Vega's advice to his son along with several other letters from fathers to sons, commented that Vega did not send his son to be a guest at the table of the Duke of Alba for the friendship that they already had but for what he could learn from the Duke and the grand company that could always be found there.[57] Guevara, though, also added a tongue-in-cheek warning about the consequences of committing oneself to too many such meals, "because no man can eat at another man's table without losing his liberty. . . . The day one bends down to eat at another's table, he obliges himself to become the other's servant."[58]

Even as sharing meals became an important mechanism of social connection between established superiors and those who hoped to gain from their patronage, such fraternization between people at different social levels had its limits. Early modern Spanish households often had domestic servants, who often resided in the household where they served. Even though these servants were likely to spend many years with the same family, and notarial records suggest that they often developed close relationships, one of the key markers of distinction between master and servant was their separation at meals.[59] Generally, if a servant's wages included food, they were provided with meals prepared in the house but were obliged to eat them in a separate room apart from the principal family.[60] In the seventeenth-century picaresque novel about Teresa de Manzanares, the main character's employer says, "I have brought Teresa to my house out of my great love for her, to have her here as a daughter, not a servant," but Teresa in turn notes dryly that such maternal love did not mean they were allowed to eat together.[61] One also had to be cautious of the connections implied by sharing food with others in public: in a case in sixteenth-century Germany, a flayer entered a tavern and wanted to join two boiler-makers in having a drink, but they sent him away. The flayer's occupation was considered distasteful, and to share a glass with him would have been damaging to the honor of his companions.[62]

When people did choose to eat together, a principal issue was the proper role and position of guests, as the relationship between members of a dinner party could be publicly communicated by their position at the table. An important distinction among guests was the difference between those seated at the "first table" and the "second table." As we saw in the introduction, Antonio Moreno de la Torre, the Zamoran merchant, mentioned in his diary a particular meal that he attended in May 1675. His description notes that he, along with the priests and aldermen of the town, were seated at the "first table."[63] This reflects a pattern common among early modern Spaniards at formal meals of establishing (whether literally or figuratively) one table at which would be seated the guest or guests of honor, the host, and the highest-ranking members of the group. The "second table," or tables if there were more than two, were for the rest of the guests in descending order of importance. The experiences of the cardinal Francesco Barberini are suggestive of how important this division was perceived to be. During his travels in Spain, the cardinal and his retinue encountered a wide range of accommodations from simple inns to noble estates. They did not complain even when on more than one occasion they arrived at their lodgings late at night and had to go without dinner. What did matter to them was the appropriateness of their seating arrangements and table settings. At one meal where Barberini was joined by two other cardinals, they were concerned that there was only a single table with identical chairs. Fortunately it was possible to have them arranged "so that those who served us understood the hierarchy of the table." The diners were also able to simulate the first table/second table division by providing the three cardinals with *paneras* (a separate small plate for their bread) and plates of silver, while the other guests were given porcelain dishes and a folded napkin on which to place their bread.[64]

This division was not exclusive to the highest social ranks. Instructions for the refectory of the San Fulgencio seminary in Murcia directed that bread left over from the seminarians' first table, if it consisted of pieces large enough to be useful, was to be passed along to the second table, and whatever was left over from that could be saved for the poor.[65] In the context of established groups of cohabitants such as universities, convents, and monasteries, as we have seen, residents seated themselves in order of status and then by seniority among those of equal status. Similarly, in meals at court, protocol demanded that guests be carefully organized by rank and position. In cases where people who did not ordinarily live together were gathered for a meal, one of the host's most important obligations was to determine the proper seating order. Miguel Yelgo de Vazquez's instructions for maintaining a noble household, influential in the seventeenth century, counseled that "if the lord should invite another noble to eat . . . one of the table settings must be placed at the head of the table, and another to the right, so that the lord may give his guest the best place."[66] Juan Francisco Guevara, author of a prominent treatise on elite childrearing, provided extensive guidance to children of noble households regarding their proper place at the table:

> [At home,] once the child's hands are washed and he arrives at table, he must wait for his parents to seat themselves first, so that he seats himself last, and at the humblest part of the table. . . . This is not the case of public meals or gatherings. There, if he is among others of his own status, he should not take the humblest and lowest place; instead he should wait to follow the guidance of the master of ceremonies, who will put him in the appropriate seat. If by chance he is not shown the seat appropriate to his status, whether by oversight or malice, he must dissemble with much prudence and wisdom.[67]

In other settings, the meaning of the hierarchy was adjusted appropriately: in the Hospice for Poor Beggars in Madrid, which provided regular meals for the indigent, those who were most ill and weak were seated first, in recognition of being most in need of the charitable services of the hospice.[68]

Another element of behavior that allowed urban elites to imitate the behavior of nobles was their comportment at the table. The seemingly innocuous topic of table manners has been the subject of much analysis in the context of early modern Europe.[69] The very idea of civilization presupposes an artificial construct in which people abandon their "natural" or "wild" state and create a system of rules of conduct that allow them to live together and control their natural environment. Amid the social fluidity of the early modern period, aspiring elites began to place increasing emphasis on monitoring and calibrating their behavior in a shift from "heterocontrol" to self-control.[70] This change echoed the change in food choices, as the expansive eating associated with late medieval banquets began to be associated with gluttony rather than generosity and court culture shifted toward temperance and self-restraint.[71] Catalonia seems to have led the way here; in an early foreshadowing of the arguments of Max Weber, Eiximenis attributed the fourteenth-century economic growth of Barcelona to the bourgeois virtues of sobriety, thrift, and foresight. These habits translated to the table in the form of a greater austerity in the amount of food served at banquets and a reduction in the number of guests, though hosts put an increasing emphasis on the quality and presentation of their meals.[72] The next step was to develop new forms of table etiquette, focusing on cleanliness, presentation, and control of one's body and appetite. Such a process held some advantage for traditional elites, since it shifted the burden from readily available wealth, which they did not always possess, to knowledge and sophistication, to which they could presumably lay greater claim. However, it also allowed those of lower ranks to argue for the transformative power of education and the conscious cultivation of habits, elements much more within their reach. Table manners, like spices and luxury foods, therefore migrated from the highest court circles favored by the traditional aristocracy down through the social ranks, eventually to be embraced by humanists who favored universalized principles of civic virtue—as Capitán Díaz puts it, from *cortesía* to *urbanitas*.[73]

In response to this interest there arose the genre of the conduct book, providing advice to those who wished instruction in proper behavior, particularly in the competitive context of the Renaissance court. The most famous of these were Italian, Baldassare Castiglione's *The Courtier* (1528) and Giovanni della Casa's *Galateo* (1558), though they quickly caught on in Spain as well.[74] These "books of education and good habits" were purchased and read by noble families and those of the rising urban bourgeoisie who wanted to learn the best rhetorical techniques, how to entertain guests, and above all how to cultivate an appearance of natural ease and confidence. Table manners occupied a substantial portion of such discussions. The emphasis on proper behavior at table was not new, but the idea that such behavior could be taught, rather than being inherent in noble heritage, made its first appearance in the early sixteenth century. This idea, reproduced thousands of times over with the help of the printing press, made such knowledge more broadly accessible, rather than limiting it to the things one learned within one's family or from observation of one's peers. Conduct writers themselves emphasized the value of such education: Lucas Gracián Dantisco's *Galateo Español* (an adaptation of della Casa's *Galateo*) argued that "no one is born educated or instructed; a good nature without guidance is like a wing without air."[75]

Conduct books' encouragement of certain behaviors rested on the assumption that the capacity for self-improvement was the most important characteristic that distinguished man from beast, and that such improvement depended on control and restraint of one's animal nature. This was particularly evident in discussions of food behavior. Writers, especially in the earliest conduct books, advised their readers not to spit, sneeze, or cough at the table, not to chew audibly or talk with their mouths full, and not to wipe their mouths on their hands or sleeves. Although late medieval and Renaissance dining customs featured shared platters of food rather than individual servings, early modern courtly advice leaned toward a greater physical separation between diners, with individual place settings and utensils rather than shared vessels. The use of the individual fork, one of the key developments in early modern table manners, was encouraged in the court of Philip III (1598–1621). Gracián emphasized that one should not touch items that others might eat, "nor should [one] give another to drink from a glass from which [one has] drunk, unless he is a close friend or a servant."[76] Diners should display control of their bodies as well as their appetites: one should not "sit with his elbows on the table, nor with his chair tipped back, because such things are only done among people not worthy of respect"; "one should not do anything to indicate to others that he has greatly enjoyed the food or the wine; these are customs of taverns and garrulous drunks."[77] Such recommendations hint at the idea that one's customs reveal one's true identity—one who uses his own glass is a respectable courtier, while one who belches in satisfaction is a garrulous drunk. Yet they also leave room for the role of artifice, as the boor could presumably control himself, modify his behavior, and present himself convincingly as a decent dining companion. While the earliest conduct books were directed at adults, because of this emphasis on training and learned behavior, they increasingly came to focus on students and children, who were presumably more malleable.[78] The constitutions of the Jesuit college of Cordelles in Barcelona included a full chapter on table manners for students, which instructed them "to attend mass properly combed and dressed, and to go to meals with the same formality. . . . In this way they will accustom themselves to eating with the same decency and decorum that is required at the tables of noble families. If they follow the rules of civility at the table of the Seminary, they will appear well at any other."[79]

Since improved behavior at the table was accompanied by an emphasis on each person consuming food on their own plate rather than sharing common bowls, one could also display one's sophistication and superior taste by developing increasingly specialized and elegant table settings. Renaissance tableware was relatively simple; even in elite houses such as that of the Dukes of Alba, the basic table setting for each diner consisted of a piece of bread, a cloth napkin, and a knife. The lord's setting was the same except that it would be kissed by the servant setting the table, and it would include a bowl with perfumed water in which the lord could wash his hands.[80] Forks were not common until the mid-seventeenth century, and then only in elite houses. Soup was eaten out of a common tureen until the sixteenth century, when prevailing manners began to encourage the use of spoons (though these may also have been shared). A preference for each diner having his own soup bowl did not emerge until the seventeenth century.[81] The law code of the Siete Partidas, compiled by Alfonso X of Castile in the thirteenth century, included the commentary that eating with five fingers was impolite, as the proper style was to use three. His words were echoed as late as 1599 in Ledesma's instructions for children: "Bread, meat, and fruits should be picked up with two fingers, or with three; it is rude to grab with all five."[82] Eating with specialized utensils rather than the hands became more common in the seventeenth century, as the individual knife and shared bowls gave way to separate individual forks and knives for meat, fish, and dessert, as well as individual drinking glasses.[83] The Spanish and Italian courts in the sixteenth century were pioneers in developing the individual table setting, in which each diner had his own spoon, knife, and occasionally a fork. During Cardinal Francesco Barberini's travels in Spain in 1626, he dined with the brother of the Duke of Braganza and several others and was upset because the guests at the first table were being served at the same time as those of the second table, without spoons and forks, and with only two or three glasses to be shared by the group, "to the great discomfort of the gentlemen." The majordomo was summoned and firmly instructed to prepare the first table only for the gentlemen, with spoons and forks and other appropriate tableware; only then could the dinner proceed.[84] This gradually became the precedent for elite tables and became more common over the next two centuries. All of these developments reflected an emphasis on the personal cleanliness, individuality, and self-restraint that were associated with good breeding and education.

The performance of good conduct at the table needed an appropriate stage, and so the sixteenth and seventeenth centuries saw the gradual establishment of separate dining areas and increasingly intricate tableware. Typical European houses of the late medieval period had very little differentiation in terms of how their space was allocated; the concept of distinct areas for dining, sleeping, and socializing did not develop until the modern period. The appearance of a separate dining area was the first step in this process. Already in the early fifteenth century in Valencia, elites were expected to maintain a separate dining room for their meals, rather than a multipurpose great hall.[85] Wills and other valuations of household items show that the dining table became a showcase of the household's wealth and sophistication. The household possessions of the Segovian merchant Juan de Cuéllar around 1600 reflected his social aspirations: a large walnut dining table and two dozen chairs, with several silver serving bowls, fine tablecloths, and napkins. In keeping with the times, his tableware included dozens of knives, thirteen spoons, and only three forks, in all likelihood the larger kind for serving rather than for individual diners.[86] A study of the possessions of Madrid's aldermen in the sixteenth century shows that interior decoration (not including clothing and jewels) represented over 10 percent of the total value of their possessions, with particular emphasis on silver and porcelain dinnerware and serveware, as well as a dazzling variety of accoutrements such as spice dishes, marrow spoons, toothpick holders, flasks for vinegar and oil, marmalade jars, sugar bowls, and salt cellars. Plates for daily use were usually made of fine porcelain from Talavera, Seville, or Portugal, while special occasions called for silver marked with the family crest. The quantity of tableware seemed to matter as much as its quality and variety; the collection of Pedro Franqueza, for example, included forty-eight pitchers, thirty-seven cups, thirty-two glasses, four hundred plates, and no fewer than fifty salt cellars.[87]

RESISTANCE TO SOCIAL CHANGE

While a degree of social fluidity was advantageous to those who could work the system by acquiring valuable spices, setting an elegant table, and learning the finest points of etiquette, such changes were of course threatening to those who had always benefited from unquestioned hereditary privilege. Urban elites might successfully copy the appearance of nobility, but many found this artifice troubling; how was one to know who was truly noble? It was one thing for well-established men like Juan de Cuéllar or Diego Velázquez to penetrate the ranks of nobility but quite another for anyone to be able to perform the part. Writers began to complain in the 1530s that it was no longer possible to distinguish rank by appearance; similar protests appeared in the Cortes of Valladolid in 1537 and the Cortes of Madrid in 1551. The philosopher fray Alonso de la Cruz warned that "the merchant should be humble, not desiring to be the equal of the gentleman who has dukes for ancestors while he himself has only ducats," while the doctor and philosopher Pedro de Mercado complained that "there is no one left who knows and moderates himself, in accordance with his potential and quality of person, but all men attempt to present themselves as if they were lords."[88] Mercado went on to narrate an example in which a finely dressed young student passed through the territories of the Count of Ureña and encountered the count himself three or four times but did not directly address him (as one of lower status was expected to do when meeting his superiors). The count finally stopped him to ask who he was and why he had not presented himself. The young man, embarrassed, begged the count's forgiveness. The count replied that the young man was not at fault for his poor upbringing; rather, his camel-hair jacket was to blame for making him feel so superior. He demanded that the young man surrender his fine jacket, threw it on the ground, and trampled it under his horse's hooves. The commentary in Mercado's treatise following this example expressed great satisfaction at this outcome and agreed that justice like that of the count's should be applied to everyone who tried to adopt an appearance that did not match his origins.[89]

Many early modern scholars (as well as traditional nobles) shared this view that status, as well as the dining habits that corresponded to it, should remain fixed. Not only should the socially ambitious be prevented from obtaining noble titles, but their behavior and appearance needed to be contained as well. The fourteenth-century Franciscan writer Eiximenis maintained the traditional Christian position that those with means were obliged to provide charity to the poor, especially in the form of food. Yet at the same time he warned that one should not reward one's servants with food of high quality, lest they be tempted with the desire to rise above their station and become rebellious.[90] And just as we have seen food work as a form of symbolic connection between individuals and groups, so its denial functioned to separate them. Juan de Soto's guide to the proper behavior of people in different social categories included a recommendation to priests that they not eat and drink frequently with laymen, because such familiarity would cause them to lose all respect for the clergy.[91] Enea Silvio Piccolomini (who later became Pope Pius II) wrote a treatise in the early sixteenth century about the challenges of serving great men in the court, which included a good deal of wry commentary about the ties between food and social status. Those who flocked to the court hoping to share the fine meals of princes and courtiers, Piccolomini warned, would be disappointed, as they would only be able to eat according to their rank, and that meant monotonous foods not well prepared.

> Great is the envy you will feel . . . when you see placed before the insatiable lord plates of venison, hare, boar, roe deer, beaver, pheasant, partridge, crane, duck, hen, thrush, all well prepared with their sauces and gravies. . . . Even if you wanted to eat leeks or onion or garlic, you will not be able to, because Horace called them noxious; nor will you be able to eat what the lords eat, because such delicacies are too honorable to enter into your stomach; nor will they allow you to partake of the workers' meals, since this would make you malodorous and bothersome to the lord.[92]

The only option for the courtier, according to Piccolomini, was to suffer through the cold meat, half-cooked vegetables, and wormy cheese that was their lot, while watching the parade of fine dishes go toward the lord's table. While Piccolomini's account was certainly written with tongue in cheek, it emphasized that the food as well as the status and influence of those in power was meant to remain out of reach of most who aspired to it.

In the first stages of this competition for appearance, principally in the fifteenth and sixteenth centuries when elites of all kinds were striving to outdo each other in terms of banquets, extravagant food purchases, and the pursuit of other luxury goods such as clothing and carriages, opposition to these developments was phrased principally in economic terms.[93] Sumptuary laws began to appear in the thirteenth century, in an attempt by the state to restrict excessive spending on appearance (particularly food and clothing) on the part of elites and those who aspired to elite status. As early as 1286, the Cortes of Castile suggested limits on the number of godparents that could be invited the feast in celebration of a baptism, because such meals had grown so large that the baptisms themselves were delayed when the family could not provide enough food.[94] By the first half of the sixteenth century, such laws had become more frequent and more insistent. In the 1560s, the records of the Cortes of Madrid indicate extensive discussion over the "notorious excess and disorder caused by dinners and banquets." These were identified to be the cause of sickness in body and soul and the financial ruin of great families and ordinary citizens alike, as well as an offense to God and the source of many other vices and sins.[95] The solution, which its proponents hoped would be "one of the most important things to be dealt with in this kingdom," ended up being a limit of no more than two kinds of fruit at the beginning of a meal, two kinds at the end, and four different dishes over the course of the meal.[96] Weddings were the most frequent targets of sumptuary laws, as they were also the best occasions for public display. Those who married in the Catalan town of Bagà were not allowed to have more than seven guests on each side, not counting children under fourteen and those coming from outside the town; in Barcelona the limit was twenty. In neither case were the bride and groom allowed to serve poultry as part of the wedding dinner. Barcelona city councilors ordered that no one could celebrate within a week of their wedding by feasting on capons, hens, partridges, or any other fowl, nor could they serve more than two different dishes or serve veal prepared in more than one way.[97] The final years of the reign of Philip III (d. 1621) were marked by his summoning of a general Reformation Council (Junta de Reformación), which continued into the early reign of his son Philip IV. This ten-man council, staffed by representatives from the royal administration, aristocracy, and church, was designed to address the various problems of the kingdom, from a declining population and excess expenditures in the court to low agricultural production and overpopulated monasteries. A particular interest of the Junta was the perceived excess in spending on luxury goods, particularly clothing and food. This excess not only made Spaniards effeminate, the

Junta warned, but it also drained budgets, endangered good customs, and was "damaging and indecent to a politic and Christian government."[98]

Historians have generally interpreted the role of sumptuary laws, especially in the fifteenth and sixteenth centuries, as an attempt on the part of traditional elites to place restrictions on the social mobility and ambitions of wealthy townspeople. Maria Giuseppina Muzzarelli argues that such laws provided a way "to control who held elevated, intermediate, and marginal places in society" and to "maintain and reinforce social barriers."[99] In many cases this was true, especially in England, where Elizabethan sumptuary laws articulated precisely what sorts of clothing and ornamentation could be worn by people at different social ranks. However, in the case of Spain, these laws emphasized limitations on excess spending by those at all social levels, rather than reserving certain displays for titled elites. The Council of Castile's discussion of sumptuary laws restricting food expenses frequently pointed at the tables of grandees and lords, though they acknowledged such excesses were widely practiced. This attitude suggests they were not attempting to reserve the ability to serve a fine banquet to certain elites. The restrictions on Barcelona weddings mentioned earlier were meant to apply to everyone, regardless of rank. If, as the debates surrounding them suggest, these efforts were aimed at avoiding economic overindulgence, their goal was to limit excessive spending at all levels, on the part of titled nobles as much as urban elites. Such laws can also be understood alongside the shift in emphasis from quantity to quality in dining, from the enormous banquets of the early Renaissance to the carefully chosen foods and limited numbers of guests that prevailed in the seventeenth century. If traditional nobles were trying to defend their status and appearance through limiting expense on food and clothing, this effort only served to move the battlefield of social mobility to the realm of manners and taste, where the urban sophisticate could compete just as well as he formerly could with his pocketbook.

While sumptuary laws attempted to rein in excessive spending on banquets and other festive performances, they were not able to have an effect on the attempts of those who were simply trying to keep up the appearances expected of their rank. Most of the concern about social mobility was to keep social upstarts from climbing too high, but downward mobility was also an issue, and elite Spanish families found that food was one of the most accessible ways for them to maintain at least the image of their position if not the reality. When Philip II's former secretary Antonio Pérez was imprisoned in the castle of Turégano in April 1585, under suspicion of corruption and the murder of a political rival, he still managed to supply himself with food that corresponded to his elite social standing rather than his circumstances of temporary disgrace. His cook's records for that period show that Pérez's retinue was well provisioned with daily purchases of fish, eggs, fruit, vegetables, and wine, while the imprisoned Pérez himself dined on the elite-appropriate foods of partridge, chicken, snails, sweetbreads, and kid goat.[100] In the court of Madrid around the same time, Isabel Sánchez Coello, the widow of a Madrid city councilman, requested permission from the king to withdraw for herself the substantial sum of five hundred ducados from the inheritance that was meant to pass on to her son. She argued that the funds were necessary for her to maintain, among other things, the level of food quality and table decoration "appropriate to her status."[101] A more typical struggle was that of the family of the Marchioness of Cervera in La Mancha, which for generations had been at the top of the social hierarchy but by the early nineteenth century had fallen into significant debt. Their household expenses, carefully monitored by judicial decree, showed that in spite of their financial difficulties, food was the one area where they did not reduce their expenditures. In fact, they shifted nearly all of their available resources into maintaining their traditional patterns of consumption, dedicating a full 95 percent of their household expenses to the purchase of mutton (over three pounds per day), white bread, and other delicacies such as partridges and turtledoves.[102]

While traditional nobles struggled to preserve their distinctive social position in the face of encroachment by businessmen and others wielding their new wealth, one advantage they did preserve was their privileged access to certain foods via the *despensa*. This was a kind of private pantry or food store maintained by ambassadors, princes, and titled nobles in the seventeenth century. It seems to have been a development particular to Madrid once the court was established there, emerging out of the unique circumstances of many powerful families competing for social and political position and the ability of court authorities to marshal nearly infinite supplies of all varieties of food. By the middle of the seventeenth century, there were over eighty such despensas in Madrid.[103] As we saw in chapter 1, the accessibility of different kinds of foods depended not exclusively on wealth but also on one's social position, and the despensas became a mechanism for elite families to preserve their access to highly valued foods. In theory these families were obliged to make their food purchases from the public markets like everyone else, following certain limits of access. For example, in some cities, veal was to be made available in the marketplace at least two days each week, but one could not purchase more than a certain amount until after midday, to guarantee fair access.[104] In practice, however, they were allowed larger shares of finer foods—for example in the case of shortages of veal or rabbits or other delicacies, these households were provisioned first, and without having to pay full taxes on their purchases.

The despensas conferred even greater advantages when these families regularly used their privilege to acquire more of these foods than they needed for their own consumption, so that in turn they controlled access and could provide such delicacies for others. Possessing these caches of fine food became such a powerful symbol of status that Madrid city authorities complained that "one is not held to be a lord, even if he is an important nobleman, if he lacks one."[105] This practice did not give noble families exclusive access to such foods; as we have seen earlier, those with purchasing power and access to trade networks could acquire virtually any kind of food they wanted. Holding a despensa simply gave these elites greater control over the supply, which they in turn used to reward their friends, garner support from their social networks, and often turn a profit along the way. This was a creative response to losing the competition with urban elites over the content of what was served at their tables—if nobles could not maintain exclusive access to certain foods, they instead shared access to privileged foods with those who otherwise would have found it more challenging to acquire them and used this access as a form of manipulation. Ironically, such negotiations helped those farther down the social scale to acquire precisely the foods that helped them compete in the social arena.

Despensas quickly became a point of conflict between elites for whom their possession was a point of pride and local authorities who feared the manipulation of food supplies beyond their control. In theory such redistribution of food was illegal; repeated municipal decrees were issued from 1573 through 1708 attempting to restrict their stores to what could be used by the proprietary family and to prohibit the families from reselling their contents.[106] A series of attempts to close them altogether in the mid-seventeenth century was followed by a list of existing despensas in 1662 and further bans in 1683 and 1698, suggesting that these attempts were less than successful.[107] City authorities feared that they would not be able to maintain their responsibility to control the quality and price of food, as some families gathered so many supplies as to have a virtual monopoly on the dearest foods. This separate channel of supply also damaged the interests of those who held public contracts to provision the city with food. As those who sought certain delicacies gathered at the despensas of noble families, the sites took on (in the view of officials) the worst characteristics of places like public taverns. Authorities complained of men and women socializing together, and large groups of people eating, drinking, and gambling at the despensas.[108] The situation became so uncontrolled that Philip IV's Junta de Reformación in the 1620s targeted the despensas as a particular problem, both because people who visited them tended to "behave with liberty" and because of the potential for the owners to use them to manipulate large numbers of followers.[109] With this, as with so many of the other social and economic issues that the Junta tried to address, no real change took place.

Hunting was another area in which traditional nobles were able to maintain certain visible privileges. As we saw in chapter 1, game animals such as boar, deer, pheasants, and hare were highly ranked in the food hierarchy. This did not necessarily reflect the characteristics they were believed to possess according to the Galenic model; rather, their value was more closely associated with their exclusivity. The availability and presence of game on early modern tables depended on two key factors: whether there was a physical environment suitable to maintaining them, and social legislation or custom that dictated who was allowed to consume them. In the late medieval period it had been common and accepted for the rural peasant population to supplement its diet with hunting and fishing. But the twelfth and thirteenth centuries saw a significant expansion in cultivated land, which reduced both pasture land and forest and led to a decline in the availability of meat, especially of animals that could be raised or hunted by peasants. Those centuries, especially in Castile, also saw the greatest advancements of the Reconquest, and as Castilian kings granted land to their nobles in return for their military victories, the nobles in turn established increasing control over that land, including the restriction of hunting rights.[110] The lands of the Counts of Niebla and Cabra and the Dukes of Arcos in southern Spain, for example, were all entirely off limits to their own residents in terms of hunting rights. Others, such as the Dukes of Osuna, allowed some hunting for the residents of their territories as long as they paid the appropriate fees, but they also maintained certain lands as private game preserves for themselves or to make available to the royal family.

Transitions in hunting rights came to separate small game from larger animals such as deer and boar. The former remained to some degree available to non-elites, while the latter were restricted to aristocrats. When peasants did retain hunting rights, they were only allowed to pursue small animals such as rabbits and birds, using techniques such as traps and snares that were not considered appropriate to elites.[111] In a few cases, peasant hunting was even encouraged and considered beneficial. Legislation in Córdoba and Lorca in the sixteenth century encouraged the capture of birds such as thrushes and sparrows, which were potentially damaging to seed crops.[112] During the hunting season (which in Castile generally lasted from Saint Michael through the end of Carnival, or late September through late February), those who hunted legally on the outskirts of Toledo could bring their meat to sell in the city markets. This served as one of the principal sources of meat for the city; in the municipal records of Toledo, 12 percent of the references to meat provision are to rabbits, hares, and other small game animals brought in from outside the city walls.[113] Madrid city regulations regarding inns, hoping to keep them economically accessible to travelers of all kinds, included the provision that such establishments should not charge too much for preparing food supplied by the traveler, such as roasting partridges or rabbits. This implies that travelers could, and indeed were expected to, hunt their own small game on the road.[114] Hunting for the non-elite population remained a possibility in the early modern period, but only of small animals and only insofar as it served the purposes of survival or practicality. These limitations still stung; the perception in early modern literature that peasants were not able to consume meat may not reflect actual limits on their access to protein but rather the fact that they no longer had hunting rights and thus did not consume as much game as they had in previous centuries. (One nostalgic element in the Robin Hood stories is that they reflect a "utopian image of a world in which one could freely hunt and eat meat," as peasants had formerly been able to do.[115])

Curiously, this left small game animals such as rabbits and partridges holding an unusual role in the cultural food hierarchy. At least in the limited circumstances noted earlier, they remained accessible to peasants and ordinary townspeople. As game animals, however, they retained high value as elite food. While Queen Juana of Castile resided in the castle of Tordesillas in the early 1500s, in addition to her regular supplies of hens, eggs, salmon, and honey, one Francisco Simón was contracted to provide her with a daily supply of partridges and rabbits.[116] The court in Madrid made special arrangements for the provision of certain exclusive foods to the households of visiting ambassadors; these regularly included partridges and rabbits.[117] As the urban middle classes grew and tried to adopt the customs and habits of elites, hunting may have been beyond their reach, but the consumption of game animals was not. The banquet menus of the townspeople of Burgos, for example, always featured partridges and doves for their symbolic value; the consumption of game birds occasionally rose so high that the city council had to temporarily prohibit their sale.[118] The records of a seventeenth-century bourgeois household in

Catalonia support this pattern, demonstrating that even this completely urban family consumed some game birds as part of its regular diet.[119]

Hunting larger game animals, meanwhile, became the exclusive province of aristocratic men, serving to symbolically emphasize their power and masculinity.[120] Game animals were pursued with crossbows (as long as one did not use the unsportsmanlike tactic of poisoned bolts), with falcons, on horseback, or with hounds, all of which required a degree of training and expense available only to elites.[121] Francisco de Monzón's 1544 *Libro primero del espejo del príncipe christiano*, a treatise on the proper education of princes, emphasized the value and appropriateness of hunting as a royal activity. By the seventeeth century, one of the palace officials was the *cazador mayor*, the master of the hunt, supported by five hunters and seven *mozos de caza*, or assistants, who were charged with the maintenance and training of the horses and falcons under their care as well as with supplying the palace with the best hunting birds that could be found across Europe.[122] Such birds were often fed and trained with mutton and beef hearts, items that were otherwise reserved for hospitals and the poor, leading one to question whether the poor, in terms of food provision, carried roughly the same or less symbolic value as did hunting animals.[123] Philip III (1598–1621) and Philip IV (1621–1665) also enjoyed hunting on horseback, spearing boars with lances, "jousting with a worthy opponent, and displaying their bravery and military prowess before their followers."[124] Such descriptions emphasize the interaction between hunter and hunted and thus underline the distinction between game animals and domestic animals—the latter were essentially possessions, while hunted animals were perceived as "fellow beings engaged in a mutual dialogue of life and death."[125] With this emphasis, hunting eventually came to be perceived as more of a sport than a practical source of food, solidifying its association with aristocratic and royal status.

In a culture that strongly associated one's appearance with one's true internal nature, food customs were useful mechanisms with which to perform status. The early modern Spanish aristocracy, rather than being a rigidly demarcated category, was more like a spectrum, ranging from the grandees through the titled ranks down through hidalgos. Even the line between hidalgos and the non-noble population was not always clear or consistent, as many claimed to be hidalgos who were probably not formally recognized as such. Entry to the ranks of nobility was increasingly possible in the sixteenth and seventeenth centuries via wealth and accomplishment, and even those without title could dress, eat, and socialize in the same manner as traditional elites. Offering large banquets, hosting privileged guests, and purchasing sweets and exotic spices were forms of social performance that allowed rising urban elites to claim a degree of recognition, and even in some cases to outdo titled nobles. As this competition increased over the early modern period, local and national governments attempted to place limits on extravagant spending on food and clothing through sumptuary laws. Such laws did not have a profound impact, but the effort, combined with a certain amount of resistance from nobles who may not have had as much readily available wealth as new urban elites, led to a shift in emphasis to sophistication in behavior at the table rather than the quantity and expense of food. Aristocrats were able to maintain control over certain exclusive customs such as despensas and hunting, but on the whole, commerce and education made elements such as sugar, forks, and table manners more available to ever-larger segments of the population.

4

Vice and Virtue, Body and Soul

SO FAR WE HAVE EXAMINED FOOD AND DRINK IN TERMS
of their accessibility, cultural associations, and usefulness in performing
social identity in early modern Spanish society. But what about their
relationship to the soul? What and how one ate could reflect—or affect—
one's moral and spiritual state. We saw in chapter 1 how the Galenic model
of humors was based on the understanding that one could balance one's
natural physical inclinations by choosing the appropriate foods. The same
was true of one's spiritual health, as poor dietary choices could encourage
sin, and wise ones could be used to correct moral shortcomings. Early
modern dietary treatises warned against eating in excess, which was beastly
and gluttonous. They also suggested that the purpose of fasting was to
bring physical desires under the control of the soul, but that it should not
be done in excess or merely to put on a display of holiness. Any imperfections of the body were thought to reflect imperfections of the soul;
food could allow each to act on the other for better or for worse.[1] Food
could also express virtue and vice in the larger context of a community. A
society could support its needy through charitable gifts of food, though in
early modern Spain this commitment slowly shifted toward an emphasis
on individuals needing to work and provide for themselves. Greed and

gluttony were principal concerns of seventeenth-century theorists, who feared that excess consumption and the pursuit of one's appetite was dangerous to the individual and to Spanish society as a whole.

FOOD AND VIRTUE

One of the principal themes connecting food and virtue is that of fasting. The most significant elements of Spanish fasts of course have deep roots in Judeo-Christian culture. The practice of fasting followed the model of Jesus in the desert resisting Satan as well as those of several Old Testament figures who resisted sin by denying themselves food. Regular Catholic fasting practices were well established by the early modern period and were supported by Renaissance medical traditions, derived from the classical Greeks. The liturgical calendar asked Catholics to abstain from meat and other animal products on all Fridays and many Saturdays throughout the year, the forty days of Lent, Pentecost (the Wednesday, Friday, and Saturday following the seventh Sunday after Easter), the Wednesday, Friday, and Saturday following the feast of the Exaltation of the Holy Cross in September, Advent, and the evenings before the principal festivals of the year (Candlemas, St. John, St. Peter, St. James, Assumption Day, the Nativity of Mary, All Saints' Day, and Christmas). In total, days of abstinence accounted for nearly a third of each year.

In a world where many people did not always have enough to eat, and peasants' visions of paradise nearly always centered on an exaggerated abundance of food, what purpose did this abstinence serve? Many saw the exercise of control over one's appetite as a gateway to intellectual clarity and wisdom. This was the case for Eiximenis, the fourteenth-century Franciscan scholar, who wrote that fasting "ensures that man's understanding is uplifted, elevated and prepared for wisdom and knowledge as well as for the profound consideration and contemplation of lofty, heavenly matters. . . . Through fasting, the saintly hermits and monks of old arrived at such a lofty knowledge of divine matters that never has a philosopher or great scholar been able to rival it. . . . It is clear that fasting is the mother of intelligence, wisdom and knowledge."[2] Three centuries later, a dialogue presenting a portrait of student life emphasized that the ideal scholarly diet consisted of simple and frugal fare: garbanzos, lentils, turnips, perhaps a bit of meat in stews or soups. When an aspiring student hopefully asked his fellows about the quantity of food he might expect if he joined their group, the reply was "not enough to stuff you, but enough to sustain you; if you're looking for lots of food, look elsewhere, as school is only about virtue."[3]

Abstinence was also a sign of humility and spiritual purity, especially for nobles, for whom it was a more significant sacrifice. Chrétien de Troyes' medieval romance *Perceval* (written in twelfth-century France but frequently translated and retold in Spain in the following centuries) includes the experience of the knight Bohor. On his search for the Holy Grail, Bohor is offered an extraordinary banquet of all the most sumptuous meats, fish, pastries, sauces, and wines one could imagine. He rejects them all in favor of bread and water, arguing that only these are the proper and virtuous foods of a "celestial knight."[4] The Spanish literary tradition continued this theme, as fasting was an important theme in several comedias and *autos sacramentales*, the most popular forms of drama in the sixteenth and seventeenth centuries. According to Hilaire Kallendorf, these sources suggest that fasting was a preferred method for early modern Spaniards to display their religiosity, even more than keeping the Sabbath was. Moreto's play *El mejor amigo, el rey* notes that "to fast in holy loyalty, that is a very fine devotion," and Cervantes's hagiographical drama about Cristóbal de la Cruz captures its subject's devoted religious practice with the phrase "his prayer is continuous and fervent, his fasting inimitable."[5] Such connections between fasting and spirituality were echoed in Juan de Soto's seventeenth-century conduct book, which explained fasting as "a chastisement that the body piously accepts, either for the flesh to be subjected to the spirit, or to practice obedience, or for men to come as close as they can to divine grace."[6] As we saw previously in the discussion of the culinary restrictions of religious communities, monks and nuns ate a simple diet in pursuit of simplicity and to avoid the temptations of the flesh. The biographer of the seventeenth-century Valencian beata María de Jesús wrote that her daily meals consisted of "cabbage leaves or melon rinds from the kitchen refuse, which she boiled in water, and added a bit of pepper and garlic with a drop of oil. . . . If it tasted too good, she would mix in a quantity of ashes, so that it would lose its flavor." The beata made a point of never tasting meat and ate only hard and moldy bread.[7] The implication was that this physical self-denial brought her into a state of greater spiritual purity.

The spiritual benefits of fasting came from restrictions on eating meat in particular, leading to an implicit contradiction with both the Galenic and informal hierarchies of food, which prioritized meat as the most socially and physically valuable foodstuff. The post-Roman Germanic elements of Spanish heritage embraced meat, especially that of game animals, for its powerful associations with health, strength, nobility, and masculinity. At the same time, Spain's roots in the Greco-Roman tradition favored bread, oil, wine, and vegetables, and the Christian elements layered on top of that were suspicious of meat because of its association with desire and appetite. (Montanari has argued that meat became a more significant element in the European diet after the fifth century and would have become the center of that diet had it not been for the explicit opposition of the church.[8]) Meat was considered so superior to vegetables that the use of olive oil, now considered to be the mainstay of the "Mediterranean diet," in the early modern period was regarded as a sign of deprivation, to be used only when one did not have access to lard.[9] Therefore abstinence from meat for religious reasons was maintained as an important principle by church officials but was never embraced enthusiastically by the populace.

To replace meat, Catholic fasting practices encouraged the consumption of fish during days of abstinence, even though it ranked low in the hierarchy of food preferences.[10] In Gaspar Castaño de Sosa's 1590 expedition to New Mexico, the group found an abundance of river fish but complained of hunger until they encountered herds of deer, which provided them with what they considered to be "real" food. In Abel Alves' description, Castaño and his people saw themselves as adventurers, not ascetics; "they desired the flesh of land animals as they desired land and mineral wealth."[11] This preference held true in other parts of Europe as well; a Dutch recipe book from the fifteenth century includes a Lenten recipe for dough and salmon molded in the shape of small partridges, a playful preparation that suggested that fish was better if one could pretend it was fowl.[12] In England, as traditional Catholic practices were challenged by the Reformation, fish was one of the first casualties. The English crown tried to maintain meatless days in a kind of "political Lent" designed to maintain the fishing industry, but it was unsuccessful; English fish consumption dropped dramatically once the religious imposition was removed.[13] Similar attitudes appear in Spanish recipe books. Domingo Hernández de Maceras includes recipes for fish but in a section dedicated to foods for fasting days, implying that one would not consume such foods otherwise.[14] Salsete's monastic recipe book includes a section on fish but introduces it by saying, "See how you can make Lent easier on your community with this variety of preparations," suggesting that one had to invest some effort in making it palatable.[15] Even the Pia Almoina of Barcelona, a charitable institution that provided food for the poor, provided servings of meat whenever possible, in spite of the fact that Barcelona as a coastal city would have had greater access to fresh fish.[16] Indeed, choosing to eat fish on non-fasting days was considered a sign of Judaism, especially if it coincided with traditional Jewish fasting days and not Christian ones. The assumption seems to have been that one would only eat fish under some sort of religious obligation.[17]

In spite of the religious virtue associated with abstinence from meat, elites did not take such restrictions very seriously, as eating well was an important part of their performance of status. Alfonso de Aragón, the early fifteenth-century Duke of Gandía, regularly ate meat on Fridays but paid his confessor the sum of one real every time he did, in a neat bid to satisfy personal appetite, the requirements of status, and his religious guilt all at once.[18] Antonio Pérez, the royal secretary who was accused of murder in the 1580s, defiantly continued to eat the fine foods appropriate to his elite status during his imprisonment, even when this coincided with the fasting season of Lent.[19] Doctors and apothecaries were warned not to bend easily to the pleas of those who sought a medical dispensation to avoid the fasts prescribed by the church: "this is of great scandal to the republic, seeing that there is hardly a household without one or two people who claim to need to eat meat when they could get by with eggs."[20]

Even bishops and archbishops, in spite of their positions as exemplars and high-ranking authorities of the church, probably had consumption habits that echoed those of the nobility rather than the principles of the church. It seems that the farther down in the church hierarchy they were, the more its members adhered to the ideals of abstinence as virtuous. The same was true of the gender hierarchy, as feminine orders followed the ideal dietary regimen more strictly than did the masculine ones.[21] Secular clergy practiced more days of abstinence than did their superiors but still consumed substantial amounts of meat. Members of the regular orders relied more on vegetables and legumes (in addition to the ubiquitous bread and wine), even though, as we have seen, they increasingly gave in to the temptation to add meat to their diet over the early modern period. Nor were kings ideal models in this matter. Charles III of Navarre generally ignored Saturday fasts and those on the evenings before principal holidays; instead he made offerings to the church and to the poor as a more visible symbol of his religiosity and power. Practical matters could also intervene. In Charles's court, those who participated in the fast of the vigil of All Saints' Day in 1406 agreed to do so a day early, to be able to participate in the feast welcoming the Viscount of Castellbó to the court.[22] Within the royal household itself, rations listed for the servants in 1562 include a daily half-pound of lard even for "fish days," when meat products were not to be eaten, suggesting that the court was not striving to model the full practice of abstinence.[23] Wholeheartedly keeping the proper religious fasts, while symbolically important, seems to have been reserved for those with a particular degree of commitment and willingness to go against the general cultural preferences for meat and lard, or those who had no choice in the matter. By the eighteenth century, the perceived spiritual value of fasting had begun to die out, and the church gradually reduced the official number of abstinence days.

While refraining from food was seen as an exercise in religious virtue, food itself could represent purity and goodness in certain circumstances. As royal courts grew in size and sophistication in the sixteenth and seventeenth centuries, a popular literary technique was to contrast the artifice, greed, and manipulation of the court with the wholesome and idyllic countryside. These arguments were nearly always illustrated with examples of food, which reflected the corruption of the court and the simple virtue of rural life. Enea Silvio Piccolomini's sixteenth-century satire of court life warned those who came to the court in pursuit of good food and drink that they were likely to be disappointed: "Do not think that they will bring you any other meat but that of old oxen, goats, pigs and bears. . . . The meat you will eat is likely to be cold, though twice-cooked, dirty and flavorless, smelling of smoke and full of ash and charcoal, or cooked without grease, salt or spices." He compared this to the rich variety of fine foods that were consumed by lords and kings, such as apples and pippins "like those of gold said to be guarded by the Hesperides," but concluded that the only thing better than this was the food of ordinary citizens, "who eat in an honest and ordered fashion with their wives and children in their homes," or that of peasants and shepherds, "who, among their sheep, eat fresh chestnuts and flavorful apples with the milk of their own flock, drinking from the clear fresh water of the rivers."[24] Antonio de Guevara's treatise *Menosprecio de Corte y alabanza de aldea* (Disdain of the court and praise of the village), as its title suggests, also celebrated the innocence, tranquility, and virtue of rural life in contrast to the contrary qualities of the court. In Guevara's description, the contrast centered on bread, the central element of the Spanish diet. He argued that the bread one was obliged to purchase in Madrid was likely to be too hard, black, sour, damp, or either burned or undercooked, while in a village one could eat "bread of white flour, well milled, prepared slowly, thrice sifted, baked in a large oven, made with good water, white as snow and soft as a sponge."[25] Country life and peasant food could even symbolize *limpieza de sangre*, purity of blood, the Spanish near-obsession with demonstrating an absence of Jewish or Muslim heritage. Golden Age theater made frequent connections between peasants and pork, with images related to raising and butchering pigs, to suggest that wholesome country folk were more likely to be free of the perceived taint of these (non-pork-eating) groups than their courtly counterparts.[26]

ISSUES SUCH AS FASTING AND THE CONTRAST BETWEEN urban and rural values show us the perceived moral qualities of food in relation to the individual consumer. Spaniards also used food for the benefit of others, as an important element of charity. In medieval and early modern Europe, the poor were more than simply people without resources. They played an important role in the moral structure of society, in that all good Christians had an obligation to provide charity to the needy. In order for the wealthy and elite to be good Christians, therefore, the needy had to exist to provide objects for their beneficence. This was especially true as elites increasingly pursued wealth, possessions, and admiration and thus faced the challenge of reconciling their worldly ambition with the Christian values of poverty and humility. The religious injunction of carrying out good works to achieve salvation in its origins carried an emphasis on charity in the form of food, as suggested by the Book of Matthew's account of Judgment Day, in which Jesus asks the multitude whether they have fed the hungry and clothed the naked. Much of the need for charity for the poor, therefore, was met by church institutions and private individuals, at least in the late medieval period. This support could take the form of coins or, even more directly, offerings of food. Before the development of individualized place settings in the seventeenth century, the most common form of eating meat, even in noble houses, was to carve pieces onto a slab of bread, which served as a sort of plate. After the meal, this bread was often left aside on the household's alms plate, to be given to the poor.[27] The picaresque author Francisco de Santos in his panoramic *Día y noche de Madrid* describes the crowds of beggars who flocked to the houses of nobles who were known to give out charitable donations of food. An onlooker remarks "How much is achieved by him who gives charity to the needy! Oh, the greatness of such charity given with love!" and goes on to narrate several examples of good people assisting the poor in this way.[28]

When institutions such as charitable brotherhoods and hospitals, or the court itself, took on such donations, they did so with an eye to the performative aspect as much as the practical, to maximize the display of themselves as good Christians.[29] For example, such groups often provided meals for symbolic numbers of poor people such as twelve or twenty-four, with a ritual dinner and footwashing.[30] María de Luna, Queen of Aragon in the late fourteenth century, provided food each day for seven poor women. She often invited monks and beguines to her table as a symbol of generosity and frequently dedicated offerings of food to the needy. Such actions earned her a reputation of being a serious and capable ruler, one who acted in the interests of her people.[31] The seventeenth-century archbishop of Seville, Jaime de Palafox y Cardona, personally provided a meal for twelve beggars and a child on each Thursday of the year in his own palace.[32] A particularly elaborate display of charity (in Spain, as well as in many of the other royal courts of Europe) was that of Maundy Thursday, the Thursday before Easter, which commemorates Jesus washing the feet of his disciples and the Last Supper. The Spanish monarch on this day would welcome thirteen beggars into the palace, wash their feet, and serve each of them a meal. Twelve would be seated at the same table, representing Jesus and the apostles, and the thirteenth was given a small table apart, representing Judas. The beggars were given glass chalices of wine and water, poured by the king himself, and after the meal he gave them new clothing and coins.[33] As we have seen, Spanish kings increasingly took their meals in isolation into the seventeenth century, distancing themselves from court elites, but this custom remained. As a form of transgressive commensality (eating with people with whom one would not normally share a table) it carried even more symbolic value of religious generosity. In all of these cases, the purpose of such charity was often more performative than practical. While such gifts of food were surely appreciated by those who received them, they responded more to the interests of those who provided food than to the needs of the poor themselves.

Through the late medieval period, poverty was considered to be a fairly minor issue, one that could best be managed by individuals and parishes providing gifts of food as part of a routine of Christian charity. Gradual increases in the levels of poverty in the fourteenth and fifteenth centuries, however, began to put a strain on this system, resulting in the establishment of local institutions (principally confraternities and hospitals) dedicated to charity, particularly in the form of providing food. The church stepped up its direct involvement as well. In eastern Spain in the early fourteenth century, cathedral chapters in Catalonia, Valencia, and Mallorca established foundations whose principal goal was to provide one daily meal of bread, meat, and wine for the indigent. Over the course of their first hundred years, the number of those they served nearly doubled. Facing the strain of rising prices and increasing numbers of poor, the cathedral officials of Lleida around 1400 changed their tactics from providing a daily meal to handing out cash.[34] This measure would prove to be a foreshadowing of later events, as local authorities, charitable institutions, and royal advisors began to change their approach to charity and poverty. In the late medieval period, charity had most often meant a direct connection between donor and recipient through tangible gifts like food. This exchange was meant to be spiritually and socially rewarding to the donor; it was not meant to remedy the actual problem of poverty. Through the sixteenth and seventeenth centuries, as poverty continued to rise and the state took on increasing responsibilities related to the well-being of its subjects, the indigent came to be seen as a political and social problem to be solved rather than a natural element in a Christian society. Consequently, donations of food lost their role as a public sign of Christian virtue.

The most important factors leading to this change were substantial population growth and increased movement from rural to urban areas, coupled with rising prices and stagnant wages caused by inflation. The new nature and scale of urban poverty across western Europe required an approach much broader and more substantial than symbolic individual donations. For a time, community-funded institutions could fill the gap; confraternities organized hospitals and increased their efforts to feed and care for the most desperate cases.[35] The influence of hospitals in urban areas increased dramatically in the fifteenth and sixteenth centuries— Córdoba had eight in the fourteenth century but added seventeen more in the following one. There were over thirty hospitals in the city of Burgos at a time when the city's population barely reached ten thousand, and Salamanca had twenty-eight by the early sixteenth century when its population was around twenty-four thousand.[36] This shift to hospitals also signified a change in the principal source of charity. Previously, the individual donors who supported the poor had mostly been traditional elites, who provided gifts of food as part of their noblesse oblige. Charitable organizations such as confraternity-run hospitals, though, were more likely to depend on the contributions of the bourgeoisie. Like dining customs themselves, this seems to have been an area in which socially ambitious merchants were able to appropriate the very virtues that used to distinguish the nobility.[37]

These local charitable institutions could not keep up with the demands of poverty for long. While numerous, these institutions were fairly small in scale. On average across Europe they were likely to have twenty-five to thirty beds each, and the typical hospital in Spain had even fewer.[38] Their methods were essentially an attempt to extend to a greater number of people the practice of providing meals and occasionally a temporary bed, a practice whose ultimate goal was not to solve poverty but to exercise virtue. On a larger scale, this was impractical, and Spaniards began to view poverty and charity as issues that should be managed by the state rather than by individuals. As early as 1526, the humanist Juan Luis Vives in his *De subventione pauperum* argued that responsibility of caring for the poor should fall on the shoulders of civil authorities rather than on those of the church.[39] The first step in this shift was to establish more municipal hospitals (run and funded by city authorities rather than by charitable brotherhoods) and to encourage the consolidation of smaller local organizations. For example, in Seville, the new Hospital del Espíritu Santo and the renovated Hospital del Amor de Dios took over the charitable duties of several smaller religious brotherhoods (including the goods and rents that funded them), so that the latter disappeared as sources of charity.[40] Cofradías, as we saw in chapter 2, offered frequent meals to the poor in the sixteenth and seventeenth centuries. While such groups were still prominent and active in the eighteenth, instructions about food, and especially meals provided to the poor, disappear from their charter books, probably as a result of decisions at the episcopal level. The bishopric of Oviedo in 1769, for example, decreed that cofradías were not allowed to offer meals or refreshments for others as part of their activities, under the penalty of a fifty-ducat fine.[41]

City governments had already taken on the expectation that they would guarantee a safe and accessible food supply to all of their residents; it was not difficult to extend this expectation to cover the impoverished. Such a duty came partly out of the desire of city officials to avoid unrest and partly out of the growing role of the early modern state. If, as Marie Kelleher argues, early ideas of public health followed Galenic principles, city authorities were then responsible for plentiful and uncontaminated food as a way of preserving the health of the body politic.[42] City ordinances increasingly addressed the issues of feeding the poor. Seventeenth-century municipal guidelines about food supplies in Madrid emphasized that pork products (including lard, offal, and various kinds of sausage) needed to be in ready supply, considering that these were essential in meeting the needs of the poor.[43] They also required that giblets be reserved for provision to the poor and the hospitals, rather than being sold in the public markets.[44] Rations of bread and beef were established for prisoners held in the court's jail, and in 1662 the city's public defender (*procurador de los pobres*) asked city authorities to require those who held the yearly contracts for providing meat to include each day the offal and entrails from two ram carcasses to feed the neediest in jail. He argued that even if this were not enough to provide each prisoner with a ration of meat every day, "he who did not receive any one day would be consoled the next."[45]

Along with this practical change in the source of food-based charity came a shift in how poverty was understood. Late medieval poverty was often considered to be a transitional state, where families might be temporarily in need of support but could ultimately recover. The population growth and inflation of the sixteenth century, however, resulted in much larger numbers of able-bodied poor, people who had the physical and mental capacity to support themselves but who simply could not find work. Such individuals did not fit as easily in the late medieval mindset about those deserving of Christian charity. It was easier to conflate them with beggars and vagabonds, those who represented a threat to the community, rather than see them as an opportunity to practice virtue.

By the early seventeenth century, poverty had come to be perceived as a civic issue more than as a moral one, and the state faced the question of how to distinguish the truly needy, those who were deserving of help, from those who were (or were perceived to be) simply avoiding work. Municipal officials and local religious organizations alike began to place limitations on the spectrum of people they were willing to help and struggled to clearly define those limits. The hospital of Santa María la Real in Burgos was established to provide meals to poor pilgrims and local residents who could not support themselves but rejected "rogues and vagabonds."[46] The Hospice for Poor Beggars, founded in Madrid in 1673 to gather the homeless off the city streets and give them beds and meals, welcomed all the needy except those who acted in any way that was "offensive to God or harmful to the Republic." Its regulations also excepted the mentally ill, who were sent to another hospital as well as those who presumably were able (and thus obliged) to find some sort of occupation.[47] The seventeenth-century instructions for Madrid's alcaldes de casa y corte, the city officials responsible for public order, viewed the growing number of urban poor with a decidedly jaundiced eye:

> Most of these people are vagabonds, or thieves and pimps. . . . All of them are living in sin with lost women, and only care about eating and drinking and gambling. . . . They send their children out to beg for their dinner, even injuring them, breaking an arm or a leg to provoke more pity and compassion. . . . Many of the poor in this court are healthy and strong and could be sent to the presidios or to the galleys.[48]

The older tradition of elites providing charitable handouts of food to the needy, when the needy now seemed more threatening than helpless, no longer appeared to be a virtuous practice; instead, it could almost be perceived as perpetuating lawlessness and disorder.

The city of Seville tried in 1675 to address the problem of determining who was genuinely deserving of assistance by designing an "examination of the poor," presided over by a member of the city council, to screen potential beggars and provide the acceptable ones with a license to receive charitable handouts.[49] Madrid attempted a similar project, designing small bronze tablets with descriptions that were the early modern equivalent of ID cards to identify the worthy poor. Burdened by impracticality—it was too costly and cumbersome to supply all the needy with such tablets and too easy for beggars to share them—this experiment failed. Another option for hospitals and poorhouses was to have the residents themselves take part in the management and maintenance of the institutions. In Madrid's Royal Hospice for Poor Beggars, the poor who were given food and beds were expected to contribute to the hospice by serving as doormen, cooks, or laundresses, or even by going to the market to beg for donations of vegetables for their communal meals.[50] One now had to clearly deserve charity and contribute something in return.

Even the blind, who historically had been recognized as a group worthy of charity, found themselves under increasing suspicion. In urban areas, where they were often organized into brotherhoods, the blind supported themselves by performing music on the streets, offering prayers, or reciting news reports. In the late seventeenth century, Madrid's Hospice for Poor Beggars refused to take in the able blind, arguing that they had their own support network and ways to earn money.[51] But even these methods came into question by Madrid city officials, who around the same time noted that the blind used to be productive, getting up early to visit private residences and offer prayers, but that more recently they simply begged on the street and made nuisances of themselves. Even their musical performances and presentation of news items had become questionable: "They go about singing satires and romances, and frivolous and indecent verses. . . . Others invent false accounts and miracles that never happened. . . . They are not content only with announcing these things in public places, but they also sing and play their guitars, gathering an audience and distracting people from the business they should be doing."[52] At a time when concerns about idleness and low economic productivity were at their height, such "distractions" were unacceptable from the authorities' point of view, even from those who were simply trying to support themselves.[53]

As the poor increasingly became perceived as a social problem rather than as people deserving of help, the rhetoric of charity changed as well.

Waiting at the door of a noble household for a handout of bread may not have been an ideal social safety net, but it relied on the assumption that the wealthy had a responsibility to the rest of society and could demonstrate their status and generosity through the virtuous gift of charity. By the seventeenth century, these individual relationships had vanished, and the poor had to demonstrate that they were worthy of charity. The language of petitions from individuals who sought charitable assistance from the government, such as those from Seville in the late sixteenth century, suggests the proper formula for this relationship. Fernando de Meneses studied medicine at Salamanca and came to Seville to find work, but he spent all his savings on the trip and requested help from the city council. So did Francisco Vélez, an executioner, pleading that his salary was not enough to take care of his children, and doña Francisca de Quesada, widow of a city official, who was sick and asked for help to buy clothes. In these and hundreds of other such petitions, two elements were always present: an expression of legitimate need and appropriate humility of the petitioner and the superiority of those who were in a position to assist. In Fernando's words, "I cannot in any way get by without your favor and support," or in doña Francisca's, "I hope that out of your greatness and charity you will view me with mercy."[54] This rhetoric was similar to that implied by the earlier generosity of nobles, but in this case the donor in a position of superiority was a representative of the government. Charity had been, for elites, a way to publically confirm their social position and their Christian virtue. With these changing attitudes toward the poor, however, established elites did not seem to mind losing this opportunity. Luis Haranburu Altuna has argued that nobles and the church both supported sumptuary laws that limited the size of banquets, in part because they increasingly resented the secondary purpose of these meals in providing leftovers to the poor.[55] Now the emphasis was that individuals had to be responsible for themselves, not for each other, and when they were not able to be, they appealed to the state. Although, as we shall see later, charitable donations of food continued to be an important element in funerals, in normal circumstances they ceased to be part of the relationship between the wealthy and the needy in Spanish society. Food became a merely practical element of efforts to address poverty and avoid social unrest rather than a symbol of virtue.

WHILE FOOD MAY HAVE DISAPPEARED FROM QUOTIDIAN charitable donations to the poor, it retained its power as a symbolic gift in the context of funerals. In the early seventeenth century, the Asturian writer Luis de Valdés declared that "the act of passing from this life to the next should be celebrated with food." Funerals were public occasions, in which representatives of an entire community were meant to participate, from neighbors to religious orders to cofradías to the poor, and the positive relationships between these groups could be visibly established through gifts of food. Valdés' statement reflected a common attitude toward funerals in early modern Spain, where families of the deceased were expected to offer ceremonial meals at funerals, burials, and annual memorial masses. The provision of food was woven into funeral ceremonies in several ways. One of these was the funeral meal itself, offered by the relatives of the deceased for family members and friends. Valdés went on to comment that such funeral meals had come to be so abundant and excessive that some communities, particularly in his home region of Asturias, had acquired special cauldrons in which to prepare them, big enough for two cows or more.[56] Such meals always included substantial amounts of bread and wine. In the funerary banquets documented in Barcelona, on meat days, the principal dish was often mutton in a spiced parsley sauce, and on abstinence days, fish and vegetables, usually spinach or cabbage.[57]

The social rank of both hosts and guests was expressed in the quality and quantity of the food provided. People of average means tended to serve one course to a small group of immediate family and friends, while wealthier families served at least two courses to an average of twenty to twenty-five guests.[58] An anonymous traveler to Asturias described how all those who attended a requiem mass were offered "magnificent amounts of food and drink, in accordance with the abilities of the family of the deceased. To the poor they provide bread and cider, and perhaps broth and meat, and alms; to the elite, a full meal as sumptuous and well presented as possible."⁵⁹ In late fourteenth-century Barcelona, Alamanda, the wife of Gabriel Jacoví, stated in her will that she wished for her slave to be sold to pay for a sufficiently impressive funeral meal.⁶⁰ In some areas, this practice lasted into the mid-twentieth century, though in most of Spain it began to die out in the eighteenth century. As late as the nineteenth century, Catalan records still made the distinction between "fat funerals," which included arrangements for a substantial family meal, and "thin funerals," which did not.⁶¹ If the home of the deceased was not large enough to accommodate the number of guests, table settings and cooking utensils could be rented, and tables and benches would be set up in the streets, adding to the element of public display.

Gifts of food also served as reciprocation for support and services related to a burial. In many regions, it was common for the family of the deceased to give food to those who carried the body to the cemetery. This exchange was so ingrained in Galicia that families without sufficient resources could find themselves without pallbearers. One church official from Postmarcos de Abaixo (Santiago) complained of priests left waiting for an indigent family to struggle to bring a coffin to the graveside, as "where no meal is offered, no one will help."⁶² Meanwhile, when families were able to offer plentiful food, then bread, wine, and meat were often brought along with the cadaver to the church, and feasting would take place there, sometimes to the consternation of church officials. In 1511, there were complaints in the bishopric of Mondoñedo about the long-standing custom of "eating and drinking and setting up tables inside the churches, and what is worse, putting jugs and platters on the altars, using them like sideboards," on the days of burials as well as two distinct holidays celebrating the dead.⁶³ Similar offerings of food were made to the churchmen who presided over a funeral, the numbers of whom also served as a sign of the wealth and status of a family. Even farmers and laborers usually managed to invite between six and eight clergymen, and moderately well-off townspeople could invite and provide food for up to twenty.⁶⁴ When a funeral was held in a monastery, to garner the regular prayers of the monks, the family would offer in payment a meal for the monks (either directly in food, or an equivalent monetary donation) on the day of the funeral and on its yearly anniversary. In his will of 1328, Pedro de Huértolo, who lived near the Benedictine monastery of San Juan de la Peña in Aragon, donated a vineyard and a field to the monastery under the condition that they would use those resources to provide two rams for a dinner for the monks once a year.[65] In the monastery of Santa Anna in Barcelona, the monks were able to feed themselves throughout most of the year on such donations.[66]

Another important and visible role played by food at funerals was in the form of charitable offerings made by the family of the deceased to the poor. In some cases these offerings were made at the family meal described previously, to the poor who came to beg. Other donations were made in the form of bread and wine at the burial site itself, offered in return for prayers. Such gifts were usually planned in advance, their quantity stipulated in the deceased's will; they were often repeated for some years afterward on the anniversary of the donor's death and on All Saints' Day.[67] The Galician hidalgo Roi Díaz de Cadórniga stated in his will in 1572 that he would provide for the poor during each week of Lent "a pot of cooked chestnuts with oil and rye bread and an *azumbre* of wine, and a pair of sardines for each person."[68] The most common offering to the poor took the form of simple bread, humble but sustaining, and carrying the religious echoes of Jesus' offering of bread to his disciples. Guillem d'Orta in 1393 established a fund so that after his death, each year on November 2, an offering of bread would be left on his tomb.[69] The challenge of leaving edible offerings of bread upon the graves of the deceased may have led to the curious recipes for "tomb buns" found in a handwritten sixteenth-century recipe collection, presumably a simple, inexpensive and durable form of preparing bread, rather like ship's biscuit.[70] Offerings of grain were perhaps a more practical substitute, and easier for small-scale landowners who grew their own. Joan Armentera from the Catalan village of Santa María de Corcó in 1441 designated in his will a gift of over a hundred pounds of wheat (slightly less than two bushels) to the poor who attended his funeral.[71] Most donations of grain or bread were dedicated to the poor or to charitable organizations, though some were also to convents and monasteries to facilitate their assistance of the indigent. While such donations were similar in many ways to the meals that religious brotherhoods provided to the poor (discussed earlier in this chapter and in chapter 2), the cofradías used their meals in part to establish and display their collective identity as an organization. Funeral meals, in contrast, were more about confirming the identity of the individual and his or her position in the community. They were also made (or arranged for in their wills) by individuals seeking to do good works in the memory of their loved ones more than as a solution to poverty. For example, Nicolás Bernard of Calatayud established in his will of 1494 that his wine cellar and vineyards in the parish of San Torcuato de Calatayud were to be left to the dean and chapter of his local collegiate church under the condition that they provide a meal once each year for five poor people in memory of the five wounds of Christ and for the soul of his wife María.[72]

Here there was an interesting tension between the desire for display and the desire for modesty as befitted a Christian burial. While any public occasion was an important stage for the presentation of one's rank and status, funerals were also meant to invoke the humility and simplicity that would speak to the quality of the soul of the deceased. Elite families who would have spent substantial amounts of money on carriages, clothing, and banquets during their lives, hesitated to carry this ostentation over to their funerals. Indeed, the wealthiest often opted for the simplest rituals. This does not mean that they neglected the opportunity for display and self-promotion: providing funerary meals for the poor functioned as the perfect solution, as it was a public exercise of Christian charity that could benefit the soul of the departed and simultaneously serve to demonstrate the wealth and influence of the family. Presumably the goal was to lessen the burden on one's own soul or that of one's kin through an act of charity, an act similar to the purchase of a number of masses to be said on the anniversary of one's death. However, legends persisted in the rural communities of Cantabria in northern Spain about nightly processions of the dead. Indeed, in 1662 a group of people were accused and put on trial for dressing up as the penitent dead and wandering around the village at night, capitalizing on those very fears.[73] Perhaps the funeral offerings of bread to the poor, especially those that took place in cemeteries, were made with the intent of quieting the dead as much as nurturing the living.

While bread was the simplest and most common gift of food to the poor, some took advantage of the opportunity to engage in a greater show of generosity. A funeral could be perceived as a kind of last-ditch bid for self-improvement, in which one could make a final effort to improve one's image through a dramatic act of charity. Indeed, just as competition grew in the sixteenth century over public displays of wealth and sophistication through carriages, clothing, and banquets, so was there also an increase in the amount spent on funeral offerings to the poor, perhaps as a way to counterbalance in death the material excesses that had been embraced in life. In the northern city of Gijón in the late sixteenth century, one resident provided funds for complete meals for all of the local poor who attended his funeral and prayed for his soul. Another, not to be outdone, invited all the poor of the town to share a formal meal "with table and tablecloth" not only on the day of her burial but also for two days afterwards and decreed that they should all be served wine twice at each meal.[74] One sixteenth-century Madrid city councilman requested in his will a very simple burial for himself, insisting that "all the pomp and fuss of the world is of no use to the soul." But he also left four thousand maravedís for bread to distribute among the poor (when a two-pound loaf of bread was worth about ten maravedís, so the equivalent of roughly eight hundred pounds of bread). Several of the members of the Council of Castile—and often the most wealthy—identified in their wills that at their death they wanted their bodies to be quietly buried "with a minimum of noise and applause" but left money for regular offerings of bread, wine, and meat to their parish or local convent and for anniversary masses with donations of bread for the poor.[75]

Just as confraternities gradually abandoned their provision of meals for the poor, hospitals shifted their burden to the state, and as elites grew less and less interested in addressing poverty through personal donations, so did the practice of providing these funerary offerings to the poor gradually die out. The meals themselves remained important; Ilana

Krausman Ben-Amos has suggested that funeral dining over time became more centered on maintaining connections between kin and neighbors and less concerned about charitable support for needy strangers.[76] The church itself came to criticize the dangerous levels of expenditures that could be reached in providing food at funerals. As early as 1541, the synod of Mondoñedo in Galicia tried to place a simple limit of twelve guests on funeral meals, including heirs, relatives, and clergymen, though it acknowledged that it might be necessary sometimes to invite more.[77] The synod of Oviedo in 1553 expressed its concern over the degree to which the families of the dead were obliged to feed their guests, often spending most of the value of the estate on funeral meals without being able to leave enough even to fulfill the terms of the will. As a result, the bishop decreed that heirs were prohibited, under the threat of excommunication and a fine of a thousand maravedís, from providing meals to anyone who was not a blood relative within the fourth degree (and also prohibiting nonrelatives from demanding such meals). Exempt from this prohibition were "gentlemen and the rich," who presumably left enough funds to cover such meals as well as their other obligations. The ban on meals also did not include the dinners that were traditionally served to the churchmen who officiated over all religious ceremonies relating to the funeral.[78] (These prohibitions were repeated in the synod of 1769, which makes one wonder how effective they had been.) As late as the early nineteenth century, church officials in Cantabria were still trying to restrict the practice of funerary meals, which as they saw it were "capable of ruining a house with expenses that are beyond its means . . . adding to the weight of mourning for a parent that of working to prepare the meal that must be provided, when they should be dedicating themselves instead to hearing mass, confessing and taking communion to lessen the burden on the souls of the dead."[79] Another blow to this practice came from a more practical issue, as the sharing of space and food between the living and the dead came to an end in the late eighteenth century with reforms that moved cemeteries outside of city limits.[80] The principal motivations for this change, which happened across Europe, were practical and hygienic, as urban populations grew and it was no longer feasible to bury the dead in churchyards and urban cemeteries. However, this shift also affected perceptions of the dead and their relationship with the living, as it was no longer possible to share quotidian space with the dead, and the tradition of offering meals at their tombs faded away.

CHARITABLE GIFTS OF FOOD TO THE POOR OR AT FUNER-als were perhaps the most important expression of food as virtue, but gifts in other circumstances also worked to establish positive connections between individuals and groups and to solidify relationships. The symbolic importance of gifts draws in part on Germanic influence from the Middle Ages, where the possession of wealth was not as important as an end in itself as it was as a means to redistribute resources and to acquire power and status in feudal society.[81] Gifts in this sense could even be dangerous, since they could be used to coerce the receiver into an unwanted obligation. Most often, though, gifts functioned as an important form of informal and mutual support. When the recipient was socially superior or more powerful than the giver, gifts of food represented service and loyalty. The fifteenth-century kingdom of Navarre was chronically short of wheat and often had to import it from Aragón and Castile, but local elites who hosted the king still managed to provide baskets of wheat bread as a symbolic gift.[82] The peasants of southeastern Spain each year symbolically enacted their fidelity and obedience to their lord by inviting him to a feast of bread, wine, and meat; in some cases, the yearly taxes included a representative pot of cabbage or legumes.[83] Sometimes such gifts could be imposed as a kind of punishment: as the result of a conflict over water rights in 1482 between the monastery of Santa María de Veruela and the city council of Magallón (Zaragoza), the monastery was obliged to provide once a year a meal of bread, meat and wine to a group of thirty city officials, along with six cántaras of wine (some seventy liters) for the festivals of Saint Stephen.[84]

When gifts went in the other direction, from the more powerful to the less, the giver's generosity could represent his greater authority but also his generosity and patronage. The guidelines for Spanish ambassadors to Rome in the late sixteenth century instructed them to use every opportunity to display the power of the Spanish monarchy, particularly through gifts of food: "When you entertain guests, provide the pages and servants of cardinals and ambassadors with refreshments of cold cuts, cheeses, hams, and pies, fruit, bread, and wine; and for the prelates and gentlemen different wines, and ice water if it is summer."[85] Marino Cavalli, a Venetian diplomat renowned for his influence and experience, noted that one of the most essential tools at an ambassador's disposal was a good chef.[86] Payment for service in noble households and the palace often included "rations," either servings of prepared food or set amounts of foodstuffs such as grain and wine. The dozens of servants who attended Queen Isabel de Borbón in the 1620s, for example, received such daily rations, and in fact one of the reasons for the constant shortage of palace funds under Charles II was the growing number of people who ate from the palace kitchen.[87] Many around the palace took these provisions for granted as part of their salary, but their symbolic value as a gift was underscored when in 1677 a servant of the Marchioness de los Vélez was arrested for attempting to sell his mistress's rations to a tavern. Although the servant protested that this was common practice, he was formally accused of acting "rashly and audaciously against royal decorum" for violating the protocol of the gift.[88]

Gifts and exchanges of food also helped to define and solidify working and political relationships. A typical late medieval custom in Aragón was to celebrate the completion of a substantial purchase with a meal to which the buyer treated the seller and the witnesses.[89] City officials regularly offered meals to the people they hired for certain projects: in Zaragoza in the early 1400s, for example, councilmen offered a meal of bread, wine, and fruit to those who were supervising the construction of its principal bridge, as well as to musicians and other performers who came to provide entertainment for the yearly Corpus Christi celebrations.[90] The monks of San Martín in Madrid, following the successful resolution of a legal difficulty over tithes levied on a particular vineyard, thanked the judge in the case with a gift of twelve pounds of fine chocolate; their records also indicate expenses for twice-yearly special dinners for the brothers who kept their accounts.[91] In Murcia, certain positions such as town crier and guards of the public jail were paid in food rather than wages.[92] While sugar was still rare enough to be prized in the mid-sixteenth century, it was often given as a Christmas gift or tip; the aldermen of Madrid received forty pounds of sugar each as a bonus at Christmas and Easter.[93] Meals were nearly always incorporated into important diplomatic occasions, to cement alliances and promote peaceful relations. In fifteenth-century Jaén, near what was then the border between Christian- and Muslim-controlled territories, the condestable don Miguel Lucas de Iranzo occasionally entertained the Moors from nearby Cambil with banquets that were "very sumptuous, with many hens and capons, goslings and kid goats and very delicate wines."[94] When a city or court received a visit from another ruler's ambassadors, tradition held that they were to be welcomed not only with a banquet but also with gifts of food left in their lodgings. In July 1472, a group of ambassadors from the court of Charles the Bold of Burgundy spent over a week in Zaragoza, and city officials stocked their pantries with an impressive array of meat, poultry, fish, fine wine, fruit, and sweets.[95]

Gifts of food or meals were often provided as symbolic accompaniments to more substantial offerings. In cases where landowners in their wills bequeathed donations of land to their local monastery or religious confraternity, such bequests regularly included stipulations that some of the income from the land should be set aside to provide a yearly meal for the monks or brothers. The value of the gift clearly lay in the land itself more than in the meal, but the meal served as an annual reminder to the recipients of the donor's generosity. Similarly, when lands were held in long-term rental arrangements or when income from certain offices was pledged to charitable organizations, such agreements were celebrated with an annual meal between the owner and the person or group who received the benefits of the arrangement.[96] Doña Mencía de Torres, the wife of a Segovian official, dedicated a substantial amount of money to having her own tomb placed in the city's Parral monastery, accompanied by the gift of three hens and two capons.[97] Hens were a traditional and symbolic gift of this kind, to the extent that they frequently accompanied a payment or even came to replace it, and many early modern rents and tributes were calculated and paid in pairs of hens. The cathedral of Toledo regularly received such payments; the birds were redistributed in turn among its chapter members and recorded in a set of account books that were simply labeled "Hens."[98]

Exchanges of food on a more local and personal level reflected quotidian connections of friendship and romance. In Barcelona in the late fourteenth century, a young man pursued the hand of a young woman, Margarida, and their courtship was carried out via gifts of food. Margarida's response to his petition was to give him a lobster, telling him he should eat it for love and then visit her. In return, he brought her pears, peaches, and Mallorcan cheese.[99] Late on a summer night in Madrid in 1676, a group of musicians wandered about the city visiting different houses and playing requests. One woman, hearing them pass by, came out to ask them to sing for her and offered them chocolate in return. Shortly thereafter, they visited another household, performed, and requested refreshments; they were rewarded with fried pork rinds and wine.[100] The seventeenth-century *Reglas de educación*, a series of vignettes and dialogues about student life, included one exchange in which a student comments that his mother has asked him to pass by the plaza after school to pick up some cherries. His companion asks why he would go so far out of his way, and he replies that there is an old woman greengrocer there who often gives them an extra handful of cherries or head of lettuce "because her daughter worked for a time for my mother and sister." Such a gift may seem like an insignificant detail. Nevertheless, it holds a prominent place in this brief treatise on manners, intended to provide lessons about ideal behavior and the importance of such social exchanges.[101] Over time, such interactions could solidify into more significant relationships. Gonzalo de Rueda, a student at the University of Valladolid, rented a room in a boarding-house (*posada*) during his stay in that city, as was typical of many students. When he took on a part-time job working in a monastery, the monks gave him access to their leftover food as part of his payment. Gonzalo in turn passed on this generosity to his hosts, bringing home every day a loaf of bread, an azumbre of wine, and occasionally servings of fish, beans, or eggs. His hosts became so accustomed to this relationship that after three years, when Gonzalo decided to leave for another posada, they begged him not to go, promising that they would not charge him anything for room and board if he would agree to stay with them, teach their children to read, and continue to bring them food from the monastery.[102] Breaking the conventions of gifts by refusing to offer or accept food could be indicative of serious breaches of confidence. In the case of Juan de Lara, accused of killing his wife María Hipólita, he feared that she was having an affair with a certain Balthasar de Rosales. Their maid Stefanía explained to investigators that Balthasar was a frequent visitor to the Lara household. The investigators asked whether Balthasar ever ate with them, and she replied that though he was often there at mealtimes and they invited him to eat with them, he refused to eat with Juan.[103] In a husband's eyes, such a refusal could only fan his suspicion that some sort of violation of his trust had taken place, and ultimately he took revenge through murder.

VICE AND GLUTTONY

Just as we have seen powerful associations between food and virtue, so could food be a source of sin. In the Middle Ages, food was "perceived to be a physical necessity that represented a moral and spiritual danger[,] . . . a potential source of perdition" for the soul.[104] Even the iconography of the Last Supper, which represents Jesus and the apostles sharing a meal, traditionally features a table laden with food but rarely represents anyone actually eating. As Bruno Andreolli notes, the table is represented more as an altar, while the only ones who seem genuinely interested in the food it bears are the hopeful dogs and cats around the legs of the table. In visual representations of other food-centered Biblical stories such as the wedding at Cana, humans are detached from or wary of the act of eating.[105] As much as food served as a mechanism to carry out acts of virtue, its uncontrolled consumption was a powerful symbol of vice and gluttony. This association goes back to the traditions of early Christianity, which emphasized the value of simple, plain foods and the importance of restraining the appetites of the belly and the sexual organs. The second-century bishop Clement of Alexandria warned Christians against becoming "captives of pleasure" with the temptations of sweets and wine, and the early church fathers gradually extended the practice of fasting as an element of spiritual discipline.[106] Overindulgence, then, was associated with lust, impurity, wastefulness, dullness of thought, and lack of self-control, and in the fourth century gluttony earned its place as one of the capital sins. It was also potentially the most dangerous, since it was the most common, and even the first in the Biblical history of humanity as suggested by the story of Adam and Eve in the garden. Gluttony was thus perceived to be a "gateway sin" for the others—succumbing to gluttony made one more susceptible to the sin of lust, and so on through the chain of greed, wrath, sloth, envy, and pride.[107]

Gluttony (which included excessive eating and drinking, and any consumption dedicated only to pleasure) was a particular concern of late medieval and early modern Spanish writers. It appeared frequently as a theme in St. Vincent Ferrer's Sermons, and it occupied the whole fifth section of Eiximenis's "Terç del Crestiá." Just as fasting was a virtue because it led to wisdom, intellectual clarity, and spiritual purity, so an excessive interest in food was perceived to be parallel to an obsession with "carnal delights," which in turn could endanger the soul. As Francisco de Monzón advised in his sixteenth-century book of advice to princes, "If this world finds you eating and drinking delicacies and giving yourself to carnal delights, be assured that you will not enjoy [spiritual] glory.... Heaven is reached by good works, not by gluttony." He supported this with a string of Biblical examples of fasting and spirituality and a warning that Adam and Eve were expelled from paradise as a result of their greed.[108] He then complained that early modern Spaniards surpassed even the ancient Romans in their pursuit of excess, developing "new arts of gluttony," which he thought led them far from Christian practice and appropriate noble behavior.[109] Monzón clearly saw the table as a potentially dangerous context that could lead people toward vice and licentiousness, and he recommended that hosts at meals should be very careful to guard against any inappropriate words or deeds, since "the pleasure of eating and the joy of wine often lead to doing things that are offensive to God and against all good custom."[110] As late as the eighteenth century, the consumption of delicacies such as chocolate was associated with wastefulness and appetite. Gabriel Quijano in 1783 wrote a fictional dialogue between a churchman (don Gil) and a lady (doña Proba) with the intent of criticizing tertulias, social gatherings similar to the French salons. Doña Proba offers her guest conversation, coffee, and chocolate, which he rejects: "These things are not good for my stomach, which is accustomed to rougher fare." She replies that "this is the style and custom among nobles and people of fashion; such conversation is necessary to distinguish between nobles and plebeians." Don Gil counters that when people who waste their time and wealth on such things face their day of judgment, they will be only able to say that rather than helping the poor, they fed each other refreshments and chocolate.[111]

In sharp contrast to our modern concerns about obesity, early modern authors very rarely warned of the physical dangers of gluttony. Monzón mentioned in passing that overeating was harmful to the body, leading to ill health and early death, and St. Vincent Ferrer noted that it could lead to apoplexy and gout.[112] The primary concerns of those who wrote about gluttony were its dangers to one's soul and one's community, more than those to one's body. Eiximenis argued that gluttons were in danger of losing their common sense and shame and therefore were easily in danger of losing the respect of their subordinates; St. Vincent warned that excessive eating was also a potential sign of ostentation that could disrupt social harmony. He dedicated a chapter of his work on spiritual life to suppressing the body's desires related to food and drink, noting that one had to overcome greed before one could acquire any other virtue. If the table offers a variety of breads (soft, hard, white, or black), he suggested, one should reach for that which happens to be closest, not the one that is most appealing to the senses. In every case, even when one is offered a particular delicacy, one should try to leave something on one's plate as an offering to the poor: "Eat the crusts, and leave the good bread for Christ." Diners should also avoid sauces, "which have no purpose other than to excite greed."[113] These concerns were heightened in the sixteenth century, as both the Protestant and Catholic Reformations shared a concern for bodily self-discipline and conduct books began to address the importance of controlling one's appetite at the table and not eating greedily or taking more than one's share.[114] Even dietary treatises of the seventeenth century became more ascetic and included more condemnations of gluttony.[115]

Concerns about gluttony became a way for people to criticize any form of excess as a danger to all. If an uncontrolled appetite was a moral danger to the individual, it was an even greater potential danger to society. Early modern Spanish drama frequently took on such concerns, linking them to abuses of power. On stage, gluttony was often associated with the wealthy, and particularly courtiers and monarchs; there were strong associations between tyranny and kings who abandoned themselves to sensual pleasures. Both the *comedia* and the picaresque genre took abundant opportunities to satirize the clergy as well, who (quite literally) fattened themselves on their benefices.[116] With a worsening economy and occasional grain shortages in the seventeenth century, Spanish plays increasingly took a view of gluttony as corrupt and grotesque. Elites who struggled to maintain a lavish lifestyle caused damage not only to themselves but to their servants and ultimately to the rest of society when they spent beyond their means.[117] Temperance was therefore appropriate to all individuals but particularly advantageous to those in power. Many treatises on food, manners, and spirituality turned to the particular importance of moderation and avoiding greed as key characteristics of good political and social leadership.

GREED AND GLUTTONY PRESENTED SEVERAL POTENTIAL threats to good rulership in the eyes of early modern Spaniards. As we have seen earlier, in both the classical and Christian traditions, fasting was associated with mental acuity, and so overindulging was perceived to lead to poor judgment. Monzón's educational guide for princes included a full chapter on "the temperance that princes should maintain in regard to their food." He framed this issue as one of maintaining balance between body and mind, or, as he put it, "exterior man" (*hombre de fuera*) and "interior man" (*hombre de dentro*).[118] Pointing out that heavy meals dull the mind, and drawing on the example of Socrates who was said to have subsisted only on bread and milk, he insisted that the greatest wise men and philosophers through history are known to have eaten infrequently and in small amounts. Monzón argued that the same virtues should hold for governors and princes: "the more power and freedom they have to eat in excess, the more praiseworthy it is when they refrain." Abstaining from excess meant that princes would always be hardworking, would be prepared to take on important business, and would serve as good examples to their subjects. He even suggested that a good prince not only would eat moderately as an example but would also create laws that prohibited his subjects from overindulging, as (he believed) the ancient Romans and the Egyptian pharaoh Ahmose II had done.[119] The early fifteenth-century Portuguese king João I and his sons were respected for their moderation in food and drink, and there seemed to be a general culture among the Portuguese nobility at this time that discouraged drinking to excess.[120] Monzón pointed to them as good models to follow, noting that in Portugal "all the nobles are very measured in their eating, because the king and his brothers are." He acknowledged that "the greatness of princes is enhanced by having tables filled with a greater quality and quantity of delicacies than those of other men," but at the same time he argued that it would be praiseworthy of them to refrain from partaking too freely and spending too excessively on these. If a prince's table was appointed according to his royal status, so must he "be ruled by virtue, and abstain as a Christian, and he should eat what is appropriate rather than as much as he can, and should not strive to imitate those vain and immoral princes that we have identified as being such gluttons."[121] The theme of moderation and self-control also plays a key role in *Reglas de urbanidad* (Rules of etiquette), in which a group of fictional students and their guest discuss food and table manners in the context of student life. One of the first things the visitor asks is how much food the students receive. The students respond that they always have enough but that they never eat in excess, because "it is in the manner of beasts, not of men, to stuff themselves," and one notes that "a certain wise King never sat down at his table without an appetite, and he never left it overfull"; they prided themselves in following his example.[122]

Commensality also provided opportunities for danger and deception.

As we have seen in chapter 3, sharing meals was an important element in developing social networks, especially in the court. A particular subset of conduct books appeared in the sixteenth century, oriented to instructing those who were newly arrived at court. These included extensive commentaries on how to get invited to banquets and how to make the most of the connections that could be acquired there.[123] In the seventeenth century, their attention turned more to morality and the pitfalls of focusing on the meals more than on the connections. For elites who were expected to have some role in governing others, it was particularly important for them to be able to govern themselves, in conversation and loyalty as well as in appetite. Both Monzón and Guevara chided those who were willing to eat with their families' enemies only for the sake of partaking in an excellent feast.[124] Writers also warned of the ways in which food could be used as a mechanism for manipulation. Núñez de Castro's famous description of the seventeenth-century court, *Sólo Madrid es Corte*, emphasized that appetite and gluttony were the sworn enemies of the ideal characteristics of the courtier, which are reason, willpower, and understanding. Núñez de Castro wrote that banquets, which were usually perceived as events centered around generosity and networking, were actually veritable minefields of danger: if political friendships were fundamentally about loyalty and keeping secrets, banquets worked against that. He went so far as to suggest that there were spies who engineered banquets precisely to draw sensitive information out of people, because wine and the excess of food are the perfect ways to get people to speak unguardedly.[125] "There are fewer glosses on the Bible than there are commentaries on some phrase overheard of the royal minister at the table," noted Guevara.[126] Along the same lines, the sixteenth-century Polish diplomat Christopher Varsevicius warned that "many voluntarily profess at table more than they would confess under torture."[127] Other writings in the advice-to-princes genre emphasized that princes and ministers should be very careful about whom they invite to their tables. Guevara suggested that ministers close to the king should never accept invitations to eat with others, precisely because of the conversations that might take place. If the conversation turned to politics, there could easily be points raised that the minister would not be able to respond to for security's sake. By not responding, however, other guests may take his silence for approval, and thus any number of political conflicts or misunderstandings could result from the simple requirements of dinner conversation.[128]

THE LAST OF THE PERCEIVED DANGERS OF GLUTTONY WAS its capacity to drain the economic productivity of the country. This was a principal concern during the seventeenth century, as Spain faced growing economic and political challenges. The decades from 1620–50 included military losses to the Dutch and the French, rebellions on the part of Catalonia and Portugal, serious food shortages, and the failure of a reform plan instituted by Philip IV and his minister Olivares to improve the country's fiscal problems. Politicians and scholars struggled to address and explain this crisis, to the extent that a new political-literary genre appeared of treatises written by the *arbitristas*, essayists who proposed a wide range of reforms addressing Spain's ills. While their principal concerns were inflation, unemployment, and the depopulation of rural areas, arbitristas often framed their discussion of these problems in the language of religious and physical malady. As noted earlier, Philip IV summoned a council (the Junta de Reformación) that met over several years in the 1620s to address the economic problems facing the empire. While this council debated possible solutions such as sumptuary decrees, the reduction of taxes, and broader fiscal reform, it clearly perceived all of these issues to be closely interwoven with morality and virtue (or the absence thereof). Recommendations for sumptuary laws, for example, argued that Spaniards' taste for luxury in food, dress, and household goods "has destroyed virtue in all the Provinces and impoverished them, increasing vice." Another list of economic problems facing the Council identifies them as "having been introduced by our sins." Such phrases connecting economic and political decline to vice, immorality, and excess (particularly in food and clothing) echoed frequently throughout the Junta's recommendations.[129] Such wasteful opulence was perceived as working in opposition to charity, as elites spent money on themselves rather than doing their Christian duty in supporting the less fortunate.[130]

While the sixteenth century saw competition among elites to host elaborate banquets and acquire ever more expensive food items, Spaniards in the seventeenth century became more critical of such excess. Francisco de Santos's narrative portrait of a typical seventeenth-century Madrid man of means conveys a clear disdain for a life measured almost entirely in terms of food:

> He requests something light for breakfast, to not ruin his appetite at midday, since he is only thinking of how much he will eat later. They bring him some preserves; he takes two bites and realizes that he is hungry, so he asks for something more substantial. They bring a capon; he eats the breast and the rump, picks out the choicest bits, and gradually leaves only the skeleton. . . . [He reads until dinnertime.] They call him to the table, where various delicacies await: he eats them all, from entrees to desserts. He rises from the table using a pick to clean his teeth, without paying attention to what picks at his conscience. . . . Out with friends, he asks for drinks to go with his cinnamon biscuits, while he and his companions complain of how bored they are.

Such a description was a far cry from the delighted recountings of endless delicacies that had characterized descriptions of elite meals in the fourteenth and fifteenth centuries. The narrator concludes with the curt observation that death awaits us all, and the rich should not lose sight of the poor: "It isn't enough for these sluggards to make themselves blind and deaf to the sad and necessary complaints of the poor, but they must try to take away what little they have left."[131] In addition to denouncing the simple selfishness of such greed while others were going hungry, writers such as Francisco de Ledesma warned courtiers of the economic dangers to their own households. In spite of the emphasis that we have seen on developing political connections through dining, Ledesma argued that it was best to eat at home, because the social pressure to pursue expensive delicacies could lead to economic ruin.[132] Juan de Soto's conduct book *Obligaciones de todos los estados* included several admonishments to elites to reduce their excesses, especially in the form of meals, banquets, and hunting, precisely the things they had formerly pursued to distinguish themselves. He included excesses in eating and drinking along with envy, fornication, and idol worship as the "works of the flesh" that drew men away from God and wasted their fortunes.[133] Antonio de Torquemada, in a satirical dialogue, included an extensive criticism of the poor example set by nobles who "used to save money for their needs, and now are always overextended, because they spend everything on food and drink.... In this, we see reason ravaged and good order lost."[134] Torquemada's worry that people of ordinary means would follow the bad example of noble excess tied into the arbitristas' general concern about economic decline. Philip III's Junta de Reformación expressed concern that "many men without means get together to eat and snack at the *figón*, and drink wine from canteens that they get from the taverns[,] ... and they spend twenty or thirty reales on what is hardly worth half that, and leave their wives and children without sustenance."[135] The Council of Castile in 1712 argued to the king that Spaniards had traditionally been modest in their dress and sparing in their consumption of food but that the growth in commerce with other nations, along with "the grandeur and opulence that this Monarchy achieved under the reign of Charles V," led them into greater vice and undue pride. This was the same problem, they argued, that had befallen Rome, and "all the other nations that reigned over the world, but then were no longer able to rule over others when they could no longer rule their own appetites."[136]

Civil authorities thus perceived excess food consumption to be related to moral weakness. Overindulging in any food, especially in a public setting, became a metaphor for indolence, immorality, and economic decline. Certain foods came under particular scrutiny. Wine and the production and sale of luxury foods such as chocolate were frequent targets of criticism, as they were thought to be connected to unseemly idleness. In the early seventeenth century, Madrid authorities fretted that the production of chocolate had grown so dramatically that too many men were occupied in grinding and selling chocolate on the streets, "especially strong boys who could otherwise serve in the armies or be in some other way useful to the republic," implying that chocolate sales were not the most productive use of their labor.[137] Similarly, they criticized the increasing popularity of flavored waters, iced drinks, and candied nuts, suggesting that these had no practical purpose other than luring people to spend their money and socialize in the street all day, "without being the least bit useful to the republic and in fact causing it great harm."[138] Even the Council of Castile addressed the king in 1678 in regard to the economic damage caused by Spaniards spending their money on "extraordinary and exquisite drinks," warning that those who did so were leaving their children and families without bread and arguing (unsuccessfully, in this case) that such stands should be banned altogether. The Council perceived the combination of public socializing and the sale of food and alcoholic drink to be a serious threat, leading to scandal, sin, idleness, vice, and corruption.[139] City authorities attempted to limit such dangers by placing restrictions on taverns, whose principal purpose was to sell wine. Their licenses did not allow them to sell food, or even to have benches or tables, to discourage people from bringing their own food from nearby street vendors. Owners were also prohibited from allowing gambling or card games to take place in their taverns.[140] Authorities hoped to keep these sites from encouraging "the presence of idle men and unsavory women pursuing at all hours the vices of greed, lust, and gaming," but given the frequency of complaints about such immorality, their efforts must have been largely unsuccessful.[141]

While the arbitristas associated gluttony and excess with poor leadership, economic decline, and general immorality, they also worried about the relationship between food, political corruption, and favoritism. As we saw in chapter 3, Madrid elites in the seventeenth century maintained access to private food stores called despensas, where they kept personal supplies of fine foods and delicacies, and to figones, which functioned as gourmet taverns that were allowed to sell luxury foods such as partridge, venison, and trout. The Junta de Reformación of the 1620s identified the problematic nature of the latter, "where they sell hens and capons, hares and kid goats and royal tarts and other indolent things at excessive prices. . . . They take the best mutton legs from the butchers, leaving only bones for the poor."[142] Similar exchanges happened further down the social scale. In 1509 the city council of Antequera heard a complaint that butchers were receiving gifts of bread and wine in return for providing better cuts of meat to tavernkeepers and other "low people," which in the council's view was most harmful to the republic.[143] The greatest challenge officials faced in correcting this issue was the complicity of local authorities, who were more than willing to turn a blind eye in return for receiving hens and other delicacies from the *figoneros* at a substantial discount. Madrid city officials complained of this as well, saying that their authority was completely disregarded when they tried to impose any limits on the despensas.[144] This connection between gifts of food and the manipulation of authority was an ongoing theme in the Junta's discussions. They expressed particular concern about Madrid, where it seemed that gifts of food held particular sway with the 104 constables who represented the judicial system at the local level. The Junta feared that men wanted to hold this office so that in the marketplace "they would be given their meat without bones, and the best choice of fruit and all their other food supplies." If these products were only for the officials themselves, the Junta concluded, this would be more acceptable, but the constables used their influence to procure food to give to their friends and to merchants in return for discounts. The Junta perceived this as a danger not only to justice and commerce but also to the poor, whose money did not go as far when "the powerful people can buy their meat without bones."[145] Madrid's magistrates noted with some sarcasm that "the aficionados of gluttony" would be in favor of maintaining the despensas because their provision of all kinds of luxury foodstuffs added glory and fame to the court. In their view, however, the despensas were nothing but troublesome sources of vice, and their exclusivity simply raised the prices of products that otherwise would have been accessible to everyone via the public marketplace.[146]

DISCUSSIONS OF THE VICES RELATED TO EXCESS CONsumption, especially when they focused on the threat of economic ruin or political corruption, generally targeted men as the problem. Women, however, were certainly not neglected as subjects when it came to discussions of proper behavior regarding food. Early modern conduct literature emphasized firm self-control for women, noting that they should keep their movements restrained, their gaze lowered, and their appetites firmly restricted. Even the ideal woman's laugh should be discreet, keeping the mouth closed. All of these elements suggested that women were not to draw attention to their own bodies, behaviors, or attitudes.[147] Eiximenis, in his advice on the proper education of the daughters of sovereigns, supported these views, especially in the context of eating: "They should be taught to eat properly, for they must eat little in quantity and that little should be eaten elegantly, without raising their eyes and by guiding their hands very skillfully, while always keeping their mouths closed apart from when they are taking in a mouthful."[148] The Portuguese Pinheiro da Veiga, who visited Spain in the early seventeenth century, described as an example of perfect feminine manners the encounter between doña María de Meneses and the princess Ana Mauricia, older sister to the future Philip IV. Pinheiro wrote that doña María brought the princess a jar of preserved cherries, and the little girl offered her one. Doña María politely refused, saying, "Does Your Highness not see that it would be discourteous for me to eat in front of her?" to which the princess replied charmingly, "Please, take it, and I will look away."[149] Such negotiation demonstrates the connection between restraint of the appetite, respect for the royal family, and proper feminine grace.

More commonly, it was assumed that women (especially those who were not royal) lacked such firm self-control and that their appetites were likely to lead to excessive greed, immorality, and spending. Martín Pérez's 1316 confessor's guide warned that delicacies were particularly dangerous to women: "There are some women who live for dainty treats, who eat to satisfy their tastebuds more than their stomachs[,] . . . which leads many of them to break Lent and other fasts in pursuit of these treats, and their wines and other concoctions made with herbs and spices clearly lead them towards sin."[150] The sumptuary laws that attempted to limit spending on clothing often were predicated on the assumption that women were more naturally inclined to such expenses than men, and the same held true for food. One of the vignettes in Santos's *Día y noche de Madrid* features a man who meets a charming group of women, who in turn persuade him to invite them to dine with him. The women not only request a variety of delicacies (partridge, squab, wine, and fruit) but also surreptitiously slip as much food as they can into their pockets. By the end of the day they have manipulated the man into spending all of his money on fine meals for them, and he has none left to feed his own family.[151] Several of the Santos stories combine these themes of the dangers of the city, the dangers of manipulative women, and the dangers of food, all of which conspired to tempt men to spend their money unwisely. Camilo Borghese, a papal nuncio who visited the Spanish court in 1562, expressed the same concerns rather more bluntly: "The man who wishes to flatter a woman sends her something to eat, which as soon as it lands in her possession is devoured voraciously in one's presence, and one sees them eating in the street as if they were goats."[152] Even the Junta de Reformación became concerned about the specter of female gluttony, using it to argue for increased restrictions on the figones (taverns that served fine delicacies). They argued that the availability of such foods "is the cause of many mortal sins, because there are many gluttonous women who would commit a mortal sin in exchange for a meat pie."[153]

Another instance of women's disordered relationship with food (and potential danger to men) was the fear of women using food as poison. If women's role in the domestic sphere was associated with the provision of food and comfort, poison was the symbolic reversal of these elements: woman as aggressor rather than caretaker and food as deadly rather than life-giving, and all the more threatening for being invisible and coming from a presumably trusted source. Women's use of poison also reversed traditional relationships of power, as it was one of the few ways women could influence, threaten, or even kill those much more powerful than themselves. Jerónimo de Pasamonte, a sixteenth-century Aragonese military adventurer, wrote in his autobiography that he spent some time in Gaeta, Italy, in the service of a Captain Aguirra. He lamented not having the ability to cook, which led to an uncomfortable dependence on a series of hosts. In his three years in Gaeta he stayed in seven different houses and apparently believed that he experienced some degree of food-related persecution in nearly all of them. In his first lodging, he was pursued by his host's Tunisian wife (whom he described as a morisca, a Muslim who has only superficially converted to Christianity), who wished him to marry one of the young women from the neighborhood. He refused and eventually moved to a different house but feared that the morisca continued to plot with the other neighborhood women against him and accused her of bringing him eggs and bread poisoned "with cat brains and a thousand fiendish tricks."[154] Even when he found a fellow Spaniard to share lodgings with, he eventually suspected that man's wife of also trying to poison his food and to lead him toward sin. Pasamonte saw a clear connection between women, food, and witchcraft in each of these cases; he claimed to have overheard the morisca boast to the neighbors about how fortunate women were to be the cooks, "to put in the food what we want, and to do as we wish at the expense of men!"[155] One may read in his reaction his concern (expressed with perhaps a degree of paranoia) about being in unfamiliar territory and depending on others for food and shelter, but it is interesting that this fear took the shape of women and poisoned food (perhaps the only way a morisca woman could conceivably have power over a military man.)[156]

In addition to the dangers of women's gluttony, immorality, and the threat of poison, authorities were also wary of the role of women who worked as providers of food in public areas. As we have seen in chapter 2, Madrid city authorities repeatedly expressed concerns about women selling food on the street, which they associated with impropriety and dissolution rather than with economic entrepreneurship. They took issue with women who sold rosquillas (small doughnut-like cakes) and fruit on festival days along the Prado, the tree-lined boulevard on what was then the eastern edge of the city, suspecting that such women used these treats merely as cover for passing messages to the men in the carriages along the promenade.[157] The introduction of a new kind of milk cake, influenced by those made by the peasant women of Valladolid, threw Madrid city officials into fresh fits of concern about the rise of gluttony and the difficulty of controlling women. As we have seen, urban authorities were strongly inclined to perceive connections among sweets, women's role as street vendors, and the problem of shortages of labor in more respected occupations: "We have seen the introduction of things called milk cakes [*tortillas de leche*]. . . . These are [sold by] women workers who come from outside [Madrid] with their haversacks, all in the interest of increasing this gluttony and earning money so that they all may leave off working as servants or learning other professions and work on becoming vagabonds and thieves." The officials' complaint goes on to describe "the immense number of women" who have set up street stands to sell nuts, fruits, and vegetables (curiously, at this point, abandoning its previous emphasis on sweet cakes):

> Even though some might argue that it is helpful to have people selling these things in the streets, since there are many who cannot go out on their own or do not have servants to send out to shop for them, we say there is no one who does not manage to buy meat and bread, and in the same way they can get everything else they need . . . so that it would be better to not have so many people involved in these things who can and should be working in service or other things of greater value to the republic.[158]

The denunciation that began by targeting the vice and gluttony related to the sale of milk cakes and other "unjustifiable treats" quickly devolved into a diatribe against women who did not choose to maintain traditional domestic occupations and the presumed socioeconomic and moral damage that could result.[159]

In a wide range of moral, religious, political, and economic contexts, food had powerful connotations with vice and virtue, with the soul as well as the body. The provision of food to others could serve as a beneficent act of charity, as a gift (with or without the proverbial strings attached), or as a lure to provoke the sharing of information. One could succumb to the sin of gluttony and be ruined by appetite. Or one could resist the temptations of food in the pursuit of self-control; such an act was perceived to be morally beneficial for individuals, a political imperative for rulers, and collectively necessary to preserve the economic stability of the empire.

Conclusion

IN EARLY MODERN SPAIN, PEOPLE PERCEIVED THEMSELVES
and others as belonging to clearly defined categories of gender, status,
age, occupation, and religion. Each of these categories carried certain
assumptions about proper behavior and appropriate relationships with
others. Such behavior and relationships could be expressed in a number
of visible ways, such as clothing, terms of address, or relative position in
a procession. In a culture that valued appearances and relied on these
visible cues for the proper maintenance of social order, food was a particularly useful mechanism for the performance of social identity. Dining
habits could publicly convey people's social position, religious loyalties,
expectations of others, even the authority of their officials and rulers at
the local and national levels. A person's various categories of identity
were associated with certain food choices by medical tradition, informal
custom, and law. Dining customs such as gifts of food and the seating
order of guests were meant to reinforce the proper social hierarchies in
people's relationships with each other. One's appearance was meant to
closely correspond to one's actual nature in regard to these categories — a
monarch's stomach was not suited to turnips, peasants were not meant to
eat lamb, monks and nuns expressed their faith through an ascetic diet

of fish and vegetables, and the proper social order depended on everyone acting their part.

Reflecting early modern Europeans' understandings of themselves as a society of orders, the majority of food customs were practiced to emphasize and reinforce difference in degree and kind. Anyone attending or observing a banquet could see that the guests at the first table were superior to those at the second table. Kings projected their authority by hosting large banquets, or by dining alone in front of an audience, in either case with carefully ritualized protocols of table service. Family members ate separately from their servants. Ambassadors and other political elites enjoyed a level of access to special foods such as rabbit, partridge, and lamb that others lacked. Christians enthusiastically embraced the consumption of pork and kept close watch on their neighbors to see whether a stew prepared on a Friday night or a distaste for blood sausage might suggest the hidden practice of heresy. Confraternities prepared meals of cabbage and beans as charitable offerings to the poor and consolidated their own communities with feasts of mutton, fruit, sweets, and good wine. Women were responsible for preparing food for their families, though authorities tried to limit their food-related activities outside the home and feared that women were too susceptible to their desires for sweets and idleness. Men were the only ones who were able to elevate food preparation to a respected profession and proudly publicized their accomplishments through cookbooks and service in aristocratic households. Peasants were prohibited from hunting large game animals, while nobles enjoyed such activity as entertainment. Even the nature of charity shifted away from direct, individual donations of food at festivals and funerals toward the greater marginalization of poor people, framing them no longer as objects of Christian charity but as vagabonds and ne'er-do-wells who needed to be controlled by civic authorities.

While these assumptions and behaviors served to highlight the differences between social categories, there was also a degree of flexibility in how one displayed oneself, especially regarding social status. A common stereotype of the early modern social structure holds that the noble estate was clearly defined and distinct from the rest of society, but the definition and practice of nobility was far more nuanced and uncertain. Some traditional landed elites found themselves economically challenged while some urban merchants found themselves newly wealthy; sales of noble titles blurred the distinction of heritage. Maintaining a certain appearance was the best way to claim a particular social position, and creating such appearances was within the reach of an increasingly large sector of the population. Those with little wealth could spend extravagantly on fine dinners, masking their poverty elsewhere. Those with wealth but no title could invest in luxury spices and tableware in imitation of their presumptive superiors; anyone with access to a degree of education could develop their rhetorical skills and table manners to present themselves as a worthy dining companion. Foodstuffs and customs that in the fourteenth century were the exclusive province of aristocrats became increasingly available to a wider population by the seventeenth.[1] Sugar, cinnamon, manjar blanco, and fruit all began as markers of elite status and trickled their way down to be appropriated by broader urban markets. The same was true of table manners; where a fourteenth-century nobleman could distinguish himself by picking up his food with three fingers instead of five and not wiping his mouth on the tablecloth, some generations later even poor university students were learning to make proper use of silverware. Even monks and nuns came to be less rigidly distinct from the lay population in their eating habits. Though they traditionally pursued regular fasts and a limited diet as a way of demonstrating their spiritual dedication and rejection of worldly temptations, their meals gradually came to resemble those of the rest of society as they increased their consumption of meat, wine, and sweets. The only exception to this gradual softening of the social hierarchy was the royal family, which in Spain succeeded in setting itself ever more apart from its subjects. The king's retinue experienced a shift from being peripatetic and relying on principal subjects for the provision of food to settling in a fixed court and providing food and lodging to courtiers and guests. This shift echoed a change in the idea of kingship itself, from an emphasis on collegiality among the powerful to the supremacy of the monarch; with less commensality came greater symbolic distance between ruler and subjects.

The emphasis on appearance and the social developments of education and table manners all reflect a greater appreciation of the value of self-control, or "self-fashioning" in Stephen Greenblatt's famous term.[2] Lineage and title were still significant, but people came to be identified by their occupations, abilities, and earned wealth as well, all elements that reflected their individual achievement rather than their inherited value. This development paralleled the growing criticism of excess that characterized discussions of the empire's economic situation in the seventeenth century. Just as elites turned their attention away from loading their tables with dizzying quantities of food toward sophistication and the tasteful selection of ingredients, so moralists criticized the gluttony and wastefulness of the court, and those outside the circles of power could vaunt their moral superiority and freedom from corruption as represented by their simple, honest cuisine. Treatises on food, education, and the economy all agreed that good government and social order relied on everyone from citizens to monarchs to curb their appetites and govern their desires. While Europe continued to be characterized by a stepped social hierarchy and the perception of distinct social categories until well into the modern period, food habits in the sixteenth and seventeenth centuries show the beginning of a gradual smoothing out of the extremes. Hosts no longer competed with each other to impress their guests at banquets featuring hundreds of different dishes; practicing Catholics could gradually reduce the number of days they were expected to fast. Food remained (and remains) one of the most important mechanisms of social interaction, but with the transition to modernity, it would no longer be vital to seek the distinction of being seated "at the first table."

NOTES

INTRODUCTION

1. Moreno de la Torre, *Diario*, 103, 117. See chapter 3 for a discussion of the significance of being seated "at the first table." Unless otherwise noted, all translations are my own.

2. Moreno de la Torre, *Diario*, 104.

3. Moreno de la Torre, *Diario*, 90, 96.

4. The king had appointed him *merino mayor*, a kind of regional ombudsman, and he became *mayordomo*, or financial manager, of the recently established Convent of the Conception. See Moreno de la Torre, *Diario*, 25.

5. Contreras, *Alimentación y cultura*, 207.

6. Piccinni, "Family and Domesticity," 125.

7. Douglas, "Deciphering a Meal," 249–75.

8. Devroey, "Food and Politics," 88.

9. Montanari, "Introduction," 7.

10. Profeti, "Comer en las tablas," 83–85.

11. Riera i Melis, prologue to García Marsilla, *La jerarquía de la mesa*, 13.

12. The best examples of this sort of work are Braudel's three-volume *Civilization and Capitalism* and the essays collected in Forster and Ranum, eds., *Food and Drink in History*.

13. See for example Mintz, *Sweetness and Power*; Visser, *Much Depends on Dinner*; and Mennell, *All Manners of Food*.

14. See the work of Montanari, Revel, Flandrin, and Camporesi. The best recent work on early modern Europe is summarized in volumes 3 and 4 of Bloomsbury's

Cultural History of Food, edited by Parasecoli and Scholliers, and parts 5 and 6 of *Food: A Culinary History*, under the direction of Flandrin and Montanari.

15. Simón Palmer, *La alimentación y sus circunstancias*; Castro Martínez, *La alimentación en las crónicas castellanas bajomedievales*; Martínez López, ed., *Historia de la alimentación rural y tradicional*.

16. See for example the excellent collection of essays in Barceló Crespí and Riera i Melis, eds., *XIV Jornades d'estudis historics locals*.

17. Valles Rojo, *Cocina y alimentación en los siglos XVI y XVII*; Eiras Roel, *Historia de la alimentación en la España moderna*.

18. The majority of available sources by their nature are weighted toward the preferences and experiences of elites. While I have tried to extend my analysis to include as broad a range of the Spanish population as possible, this work reveals more about townspeople and the wealthy than about peasants and the rural population.

19. Another important element of Spain's historical identity was, of course, its American empire following the explorations and conquests of the late fifteenth and early sixteenth centuries. As I note in chapter 3, the impact of peninsular food habits on the Americas was much greater than the reciprocal effect on Spain, especially in the first century or so after the conquest. Much excellent work has been done on the food history of the colonies, so I have chosen here to retain a focus only on Spain. For the colonies, see among others Earle, *The Body of the Conquistador*; Garrido Aranda, *Cultura alimentaria de España y América*; and Dunmire, *Gardens of New Spain*.

20. Albala, *Eating Right in the Renaissance*, 185.

1. BASIC FOOD PRACTICES AND BELIEFS

1. Riera i Melis, "Jerarquía social y desigualdad alimentaria," 201.

2. García Gómez, *Carlos V a la mesa*, 34.

3. The social ramifications of hunting different animals will be discussed in chapter 3.

4. Piccinni, "Family and Domesticity," 141.

5. d'Aulnoy, *The Ingenious and Diverting Letters*, 133.

6. Covarrubias, *Tesoro de la lengua castellana o española*, 568v.

7. *Olla podrida* was its Castilian name; its other manifestations include the Galician *pote*, the Catalan *escudella*, and the Andalusian *cocido*.

8. Covarrubias, *Tesoro de la lengua castellana o española*, 1175.

9. Pozzo, *El diario del viaje a España del Cardenal Francesco Barberini*, 154 (page numbers for Pozzo are from the Spanish translation that accompanies the Italian original); Martínez Montiño, *Arte de cozina* (1611), 9v. While the latter's second last name is presented as Motiño in the first edition of *Arte*, later editions list

him as Montiño, and his name is most frequently spelled that way by modern authors.

10. *Libro de mayordomía de gastos de cocina*, Biblioteca Nacional de España (hereafter BNE) MS 1654, February 14, 1674.

11. Martínez Montiño, *Arte de cozina*, 21.

12. The list was for those who were applying to manage figones, taverns that provided relatively expensive and high-quality foods. For their list of proposed foods, see Archivo Histórico Nacional (hereafter AHN), Consejos, SACC, libro 1203, f. 614–23v.

13. The cinnamon-sugar combination appears far more frequently in the 1490 *Llibre del Coch* than it does in the early fourteenth-century *Sent Sovi*. Cinnamon bark was grown in China and Sri Lanka; cloves came from the Moluccas, and nutmeg came from Indonesia; all of these became more accessible with the rise of Spanish and Portuguese trade networks. Sugar, imported from the Middle East and Egypt until it began to be produced in Brazil in the mid-sixteenth century, gradually replaced honey as the predominant sweetener. For the Benedictine monks, see *Libro de mayordomía de gastos*, for example December 24, 1678, and February 19, 1679; for Pinheiro's comments, see Santamaría Arnaiz, *La alimentación de los españoles bajo el reino de los Austrias*, 691.

14. d'Aulnoy, *The Ingenious and Diverting Letters*, 46.

15. Riera i Melis, "Jerarquía social y desigualdad alimentaria," 102.

16. Augustine, *Sermons*, part 3, vol. 7, 301.

17. Paul Freedman, "Eating Out," 104.

18. Prats and Rey, "Las bases modernas de la alimentación tradicional," 57–58; García Sánchez, "La alimentación popular urbana en Al-andalus," 224.

19. Pujol y Bertran, "Alimentació i nutrició a Mallorca, segle XVII," 374. Montanari's estimates for early modern Europe are lower, at 500–600 grams per person per day, but he also notes that bread consumption was higher than average in Spain and Italy. See Montanari, *El hambre y la abundancia*, 107, 113.

20. Sreenivasan, "Food Production," 13.

21. In the city of Jaén in the late fifteenth century, for example, there was one oven for every sixty houses. See Rodríguez Molina, "La alimentación en el antiguo Reino de Jaén," 50.

22. Castro Martínez, *El abastecimiento alimentario en el reino de Granada*, 156–76.

23. García Marsilla, *La jerarquía de la mesa*, 110.

24. Rodríguez Molina, "La alimentación en el antiguo Reino de Jaén," 52.

25. Castro Martínez, *El abastecimiento alimentario en el reino de Granada*, 156.

26. AHN, Sala de Alcaldes de Casa y Corte (hereafter SACC), libro 1173, ch. 35, "faltas de pan."

27. A standard *pan* weighed two Spanish pounds (*libras*), or around 920 grams. See Eiras Roel, *Historia de la alimentación en la España moderna*, 36n2.

28. "Regarding the bread for the lord's table, one must obtain the best wheat, prepared by good bakers, and it should be baked every day, and there should be another bread for those who eat in the household [i.e., servants] and for the sick." See Yelgo de Vazquez, *Estilo de servir a príncipes*, 10v.

29. For more on proper table manners, chapter 3.

30. Serrano Larráyoz, *La mesa del rey*, 177.

31. Díaz, *Diez siglos de cocina en Madrid*, 38.

32. Eiras Roel, *Historia de la alimentación en la España moderna*, 42n11.

33. Saavedra, *La vida cotidiana en la Galicia del Antiguo Régimen*, 136, 144.

34. Haranburu Altuna, *Historia de la alimentación y de la cocina en el País Vasco*, 155, 170–75.

35. García Marsilla, *La jerarquía de la mesa*, 259.

36. Serra i Clota, "Comportaments alimentaris i factors socioeconòmics," 538.

37. García Gómez, *Carlos V a la mesa*, 62.

38. Prats and Rey, "Las bases modernas de la alimentación tradicional," 58; Burgo López, "El consumo alimentario del clero regular femenino," 233.

39. Serrano Larráyoz, "Aproximación a la alimentación del ejército navarro," 570n13.

40. Lobera de Avila, *Vergel de sanidad*, 43.

41. *Constituciones, y instrucciones de la hermandad del Real Hospicio de Pobres Mendigos*, 102.

42. García Marsilla, *La jerarquía de la mesa*, 90. For more on the hot, cold, wet, and dry characteristics of food in the Galenic system, see later in this chapter.

43. See chapter 4 in this book.

44. Castro Martínez, "Comer en la Alhambra de Granada," 144.

45. Izquierdo Benito, *Abastecimiento y alimentación de Toledo*, 96.

46. Martínez Martínez, "Hacia la configuración del modelo alimentario feudal," 359n21.

47. Burgo López, "El consumo alimentario del clero regular femenino," 233.

48. Díaz, *Madrid: Bodegones, mesones, fondas y restaurantes*, 181. A recipe for home-made hippocras may be found in *Recetas y memorias para guisados*, BNE MS 6058, 63.

49. González Palencia, *Consejo de Castilla: Sala de Alcaldes de Casa y Corte*, 11–12. For general references to documentation that exists in the SACC, I am citing González's catalog; in cases where I am quoting from specific documents that I have consulted in the AHN, I refer to them by their archival signature.

50. Pujol y Bertran, "Alimentació i nutrició a Mallorca, segle XVII," 375.

51. García Gómez, *Carlos V a la mesa*, 69.

52. Lobera de Avila, *Vergel de sanidad*, 46.
53. Sendra i Beltran, "Variacions en l'evolució de la dieta alimentària dels monjos benedictins," 418.
54. "Recepta para engordar pollos en muy breve tiempo," *Receptas experimentadas para diversas cosas*, BNE MS 2019, 124v.
55. AHN, Consejos, SACC, libro 1210, f. 686.
56. Garrido Aranda, "La bebida en cuatro tratadistas españoles," 190.
57. For a contemporary description of such ice wells, see Micón, *Alivio de los sedientos*, especially 97–99.
58. Santamaría Arnaiz, *La alimentación de los españoles bajo el reino de los Austrias*, 753; Simón Palmer, *La alimentación y sus circunstancias en el Real Alcázar de Madrid*, 23.
59. Cavallo and Storey, *Healthy Living in Late Renaissance Italy*, 227–28.
60. Micón, *Alivio de los sedientos*, 237.
61. For an excellent examination of the cultural transmission and significance of chocolate, see Norton, "Tasting Empire: Chocolate and the European Internalization of Mesoamerican Aesthetics," 660–91, and *Sacred Gifts, Profane Pleasures*.
62. Pérez Samper, "Chocolate, té y café," 205.
63. González Palencia, *Consejo de Castilla: Sala de Alcaldes de Casa y Corte*.
64. Garrido Aranda, "La bebida en cuatro tratadistas españoles," 191–92.
65. Montanari, "El papel del Mediterráneo en la definición de los modelos alimentarios de la Edad Media," 77. See also García Marsilla, *La jerarquía de la mesa*, 163; and Laudan, *Cuisine & Empire*, 174–75.
66. Vinyoles i Vidal, "Alimentació i ritme del temps a Catalunya," 151.
67. Castro Martínez, *El abastecimiento alimentario en el reino de Granada*, 40–43.
68. Haranburu Altuna, *Historia de la alimentación*, 151–53, 197.
69. See, for example, Fàbrega, *La cultura del gust als països catalans*; and Pérez Samper, "Cataluña y Europa a la mesa," 251–72.
70. García Marsilla, *La jerarquía de la mesa*, 165.
71. Martínez López, ed., *Historia de la alimentación rural y tradicional*, 61; Pérez Samper, "Cataluña y Europa a la mesa," 253–58.
72. This system was first described by the classical Greek physician Hippocrates and more fully developed by the second-century scholar Galen, whose works were considered authoritative well into the eighteenth century. For a more thorough discussion of food and the Galenic humors, see Powell's introduction to Galen, *On the Properties of Foodstuffs* (*De alimentorum facultatibus*), particularly 12–18.
73. Examples of the many early modern treatises on the medicinal qualities of food include Vilanova, *De regimine sanitatis* (1307); Lobera de Avila, *Vergel de*

sanidad (1542); Núñez de Oria, *Aviso de sanidad* (1572); and Álvarez Miravall, *La conservación de la salud del cuerpo y alma* (1601). Of these, Vilanova was the most influential; a Spanish translation was published in 1519 and several editions were produced through the seventeenth century. The best modern edition of Vilanova is Cruz Cruz, *Dietética medieval.* For an excellent general discussion of these ideas, see Albala, *Eating Right in the Renaissance*, particularly chapter 1.

74. Fitzpatrick, "Body and Soul," 153.

75. Piquer, "Discurso sobre la enfermedad del Rey nuestro señor," *Colección de documentos inéditos para la historia de España* (hereafter C O D O I N), vol. 18, 156–87, quotation on p. 183.

76. Gentilcore, "Body and Soul, or Living Physically in the Kitchen," 147.

77. Grieco, "Food and Social Classes in Late Medieval and Renaissance Italy," 308; see also Montanari, *El hambre y la abundancia*, 93.

78. Gutiérrez Nieto, "El campesinado," 64.

79. "Carne de pluma," Real Academia Española, *Diccionario de Autoridades*, tomo 2 (Madrid, 1729), accessed April 29, 2016, http://web.frl.es/DA.html.

80. Grieco, "Body and Soul," 147; see also chapter 4 in this book.

81. Grieco, "Food and Social Classes in Late Medieval and Renaissance Italy," 305.

82. For a discussion of fish and its relative social value, see chapter 4.

83. Riera i Melis, "Jerarquía social y desigualdad alimentaria," 91.

84. Montanari, *El hambre y la abundancia*, 106; Carmona García, *Crónica urbana del malvivir*, 186–89. For Spain, see Vassberg, *Land and Society in Golden Age Castile*, 79–83.

85. This hierarchy was carried over to the colonies in the Americas, where Spaniards received substantial land grants to raise sheep, which soon numbered in the millions. See Butzer and Butzer, "Transfer of the Mediterranean Livestock Economy to New Spain," 161–62.

86. Piccinni, "Family and Domesticity," 129–30; Benito, "Food Systems," 48; Cruselles and Narbona, "Los modelos alimentarios de una sociedad jerarquizada," 78.

87. Krondl, "Food Systems: Pepper, Herring, and Beer," 60. One exception was the region between Toledo and Salamanca in West-Central Spain, one of the only parts of the country that was (and still is today) known for raising high-quality beef; there beef and veal were consumed more than mutton. The seventeenth-century cook Domingo Hernández de Maceras, who wrote one of the most influential early modern recipe collections, relied much more heavily on beef than did his culinary counterparts, reflecting his forty years of residence in Salamanca.

88. Izquierdo Benito, *Abastecimiento y alimentación de Toledo*, 80.

89. García Marsilla, *La jerarquía de la mesa*, 260, for Gandía; González Palencia, *Consejo de Castilla: Sala de Alcaldes de Casa y Corte* for Madrid.
90. García Marsilla, *La jerarquía de la mesa*, 78.
91. Cruz Cruz, *Alimentación y cultura*, 273.
92. Levi-Strauss, "The Culinary Triangle," 40–47.
93. Martín, *La mujer y el caballero*, 53.
94. Serra i Clota, "Comportaments alimentaris i factors socioeconòmics," 533.
95. Serrano Larráyoz, "Aproximación a la alimentación del ejército navarro," 567, 575–76.
96. Soto, *Obligaciones de todos los estados*, 90v.
97. Montanari, "Introduction," 18.
98. Andreolli, "Food Representations," 157.
99. Garrido Aranda's estimates for the average daily food consumption of poor, middling, and wealthy families in the early seventeenth century include regular amounts of meat and animal fat even at the lowest levels of income, and Pujol y Bertran's estimates for an average family's daily meals in seventeenth-century Mallorca include at least small portions of cheese, fish, or pork. See Garrido Aranda, "Acerca de la dieta familiar española del Barroco," 194–96; and Pujol y Bertran, "Alimentació i nutrició a Mallorca," 371–78.
100. Manuppella, ed., *O "Livro de Cozinha" da Infanta D. Maria de Portugal*, xxxii.
101. Pérez de Herrera, *A la catolica real magestad del Rey don Felipe III*, 16.
102. AHN, Consejos, SACC: libro 1217, f. 24, quotation f. 30; libro 1247, f. 116.
103. Alves, *Animals of Spain*, 151.
104. Contreras, *Alimentación y cultura*, 225.
105. Santamaría Arnaiz, *La alimentación de los españoles bajo el reino de los Austrias*, 1479.
106. Despojos: "se llaman también las sobras o relieves de alguna cosa, como los despojos de la mesa o comida." Menudo: "vale también despreciable, y de poco o ninguna consecuencia," también "plebeyo o vulgar." See Real Academia Española, *Diccionario de Autoridades*, tomo 3 (1732) and tomo 4 (1734), accessed April 29, 2016, http://web.frl.es/DA.html.
107. Castro Martínez, *El abastecimiento alimentario en el reino de Granada*, 255.
108. AHN, Consejos, SACC: libro 1203, f. 639; libro 1247, f. 147; libro 1276, f. 111; libro 1278, f. 127.
109. *Constituciones, y instrucciones de la hermandad del Real Hospicio*, 103.
110. Zamora, *Diario de los viajes hechos en Cataluña*, cited in Pérez Samper, "Privacidad doméstica: La mesa y la servidumbre," 115.
111. Serra i Clota, "Comportaments alimentaris i factors socioeconòmics," 538.

112. AHN, Consejos, SACC: libro 1234, f. 48; libro 1246, f. 141, and elsewhere; Santamaría Arnaiz, *La alimentación de los españoles bajo el reino de los Austrias,* 255–59.

113. Santamaría Arnaiz, *La alimentación de los españoles bajo el reino de los Austrias,* 234.

114. Fitzpatrick, "Body and Soul," 158.

115. Eiximenis, "Terç del Crestià," 159.

116. León Pinelo, *Anales de Madrid,* BNE MS 18117, 94v.

117. Cruz Cruz, *Dietética medieval,* 119, 121.

118. "Son muchos y buenos los lugares que ellos poseyan y no los cultivaban casi para cosa de sustancia, ni plantavan sino de higueras, cerezos, ciruelos, duraznos, y parras para pasas." See *Expulsión justificada de los moriscos españoles* (1612), 64v.

119. Albala, "Introduction," 25.

120. Granado Maldonado, *Libro del arte de cozina;* Hernández Maceras, *Libro del arte de cozina.*

121. García Marsilla, *La jerarquía de la mesa,* 205.

122. *Cartas del Baile General de Valencia,* cited in García Marsilla, *La jerarquía de la mesa,* 143.

123. Vinyoles i Vidal, "Alimentació i ritme del temps a Catalunya," 130. See Montanari, *Cheese, Pears, and History in a Proverb,* for a discussion of the particular significance of the pear to early modern Europeans.

124. Conde y Delgado de Molina, "Fonts per a l'estudi del consum alimentari," 30; Pérez Samper, "Privacidad doméstica," 90; Serrano Larráyoz, *La mesa del rey,* 211–14.

125. Riera i Melis, "Estructura social y sistemas alimentarios en la Cataluña bajomedieval," 211.

126. "Que en ninguna mesa de qualquier calidad que fuesse, no pudiesse aver mas de dos frutas de principio, y dos en fin, y quatro platos cada vno de su manjar y que de allí no se excediesse." See *Actas de las Cortes de Castilla,* vol. 1, 371.

127. Cruselles and Narbona, "Los modelos alimentarios de una sociedad jerarquizada," 77. Riera i Melis argues that, at least in the late Middle Ages, fruit was a luxury available only to the wealthy; see "Jerarquía social," 92. By the seventeenth century there was growing commerce throughout the peninsula in fruit from Murcia, Valencia, and Aragón, which made possible the greater consumption of a greater variety of products; see Santamaría Arnaiz, *La alimentación de los españoles bajo el reino de los Austrias,* 1432.

128. Grieco, "Food Production," 40–41.

129. Santamaría Arnaiz, *La alimentación de los españoles bajo el reino de los Austrias,* 1444.

130. Heal, "Food Gifts, the Household and the Politics of Exchange in Early Modern England," 56.

131. Santamaría Arnaiz, *La alimentación de los españoles bajo el reino de los Austrias*, 1132, 1141.

132. Pujol y Bertrán, "Alimentació i nutrició a Mallorca, segle XVII," 375; Pérez López, "Las cuentas de la casa Sala," 459.

133. "De vianda lo que basta no para hartar sino para sustentar; mucha comida buscala en otra parte no en la escuela a donde se trata solo de virtud." See *Reglas de urbanidad expuestas en forma dialogada*, BNE, MSS 12955/68, fol. 6.

134. Freedman, "Eating Out," 102.

135. Lope de Vega, *La moza de cántaro*, act 2, scene 16.

136. Quevedo, *Las Batuecas del Duque de Alba*, quoted in Díaz, *La cocina del Barroco*, 71–72.

137. García Marsilla, *La jerarquía de la mesa*, 249.

138. Ball, "Water, Wine, and Aloja," 61–62.

139. Luján, *La vida cotidiana en la España del Siglo de Oro*, 25.

140. "El sótano o soportal en que se hace y guisa de comer a la gente pobre y ordinaria." See Real Academia Española, *Diccionario de Autoridades*, tomo 1 (1726), accessed April 29, 2016, http://web.frl.es/DA.html.

141. García Marsilla, *La jerarquía de la mesa*, 159.

142. Núñez de Castro, *Sólo Madrid es corte*, 22.

143. Núñez de Castro, *Sólo Madrid es corte*, 12.

144. Santamaría Arnaiz, *La alimentación de los españoles bajo el reino de los Austrias*, 1479.

145. Dursteler, "Food and Politics," 86.

146. Benito, "Food Systems," 42.

147. Castro Martínez, *El abastecimiento alimentario en el reino de Granada*, 105, 110.

148. Victor Magagna describes this as "a market economy regulated formally and informally through moral principles emphasizing justice and the subsistence needs of households, graded according to a hierarchy of status, property, and power." See Magagna, "Food and Politics: The Power of Bread in European Culture," 74. See also Kelleher, "Eating from a Corrupted Table," 51.

149. Izquierdo Benito, *Abastecimiento y alimentación de Toledo*, 41–42.

150. See Greer, "Constituting Community," 52–53.

151. AHN, Consejos, SACC, libro 1173, ch. 36.

152. AHN, Consejos, SACC, libro 1173, ch. 35.

153. AHN, Consejos, SACC, libro 1173, f. 114.

154. Kelleher, "Eating from a Corrupted Table," 58.

155. Riera i Melis, "Jerarquía social y desigualdad alimentaria," 185.

156. Soto, *Obligaciones de todos los estados*, 78v.
157. Soto, *Obligaciones de todos los estados*, 93.
158. A H N, Consejos, S A C C, libros 1197–1409, for the alcaldes' records from 1573 –1817. For a list of the alcaldes' essential responsibilities, see libro 1173.
159. Rodríguez Molina, "La alimentación en el antiguo Reino de Jaén," 77.
160. A H N, Consejos, S A C C: libro 1198, f. 85; libro 1173, f. 120v.
161. Castro Martínez, *El abastecimiento alimentario en el reino de Granada*, 94–95.
162. Izquierdo Benito, *Abastecimiento y alimentación de Toledo*, 69.
163. A H N, Consejos, S A C C: libro 1256, f. 11; libro 1203, f. 639, f. 642. For additional examples of the supplies guaranteed to ambassadors, see libro 1239, f. 505–10.

2. SOCIAL GROUPS AND COLLECTIVE IDENTITY

1. Vinyoles i Vidal, "Alimentació i ritme del temps a Catalunya," 134.
2. Though today we consider gender to be performative and flexible, in the early modern period, with a few very rare exceptions, it was perceived to be fixed and permanent.
3. Capel, *La gula en el siglo de oro*, 24.
4. Castro Martínez, *La alimentación en las crónicas castellanas bajomedievales*, 81, 83.
5. Dursteler, "Food and Politics," 95.
6. From the Crónica de D. Pedro, quoted in Manuppella, *O "Livro de Cozinha" da Infanta D. Maria de Portugal*, xxvi.
7. *Cortes de los antiguos reinos de León y Castilla*, tomo 1, vol. 3, 55–58.
8. Castro Martínez, *La alimentación en las crónicas castellanas bajomedievales*, 79.
9. Riera i Melis, "Jerarquía social y desigualdad alimentaria," 195.
10. Monzón, *Libro primero del espejo del príncipe christiano*, 110v.
11. García Marsilla, *La jerarquía de la mesa*, 174.
12. This translates loosely as "rations" and probably had its origin in simply allowing servants to take their meals from the kitchen of the royal household. By the sixteenth and seventeenth centuries *raciones* were fixed as particular quantities of bread, wine, and meat that generally corresponded to the recipient's position rather than his or her actual alimentary needs.
13. D. García de Toledo to Francisco de Eraso, February 24, 1562, C O D O I N, vol. 26, p. 431–37.
14. Simón Palmer, "Las bebidas en el Palacio Real de Madrid en tiempo de los Austrias," 169.
15. *Etiquetas de palacio*, B N E M S 12816; see also a condensed version published in Rodríguez Villa, *Etiquetas de la Casa de Austria*.
16. Martínez Montiño, *Arte de cozina*, 6v.

17. Monzón, *Libro primero*, 110v–111.
18. This included a corresponding emphasis on table manners, about which there is a more extended discussion in chapter 3s.
19. See Elias, *The Court Society*, 78–104.
20. Ampudia de Haro, *Las bridas de la conducta*, 62.
21. Celada, *La cocina de la Casa de Alba*, 125, 128.
22. Díaz, *Diez siglos de cocina en Madrid*, 46.
23. Valles Rojo, *Cocina y alimentación en los siglos XVI y XVII*, 20.
24. Rodríguez Villa, *Etiquetas de palacio*, 15.
25. González de Salcedo, *Nudrición real o preceptos de cómo se ha de educar a los reyes mozos*, 123.
26. Pinheiro da Veiga, *Fastiginia*, 112–13.
27. Pinheiro da Veiga, *Fastiginia*, 102.
28. *Libros de acuerdos municipales de Santander*, vol. 1, 97–98.
29. *Libros de acuerdos municipales de Santander*, vol. 1, 100–101.
30. For more on the theatricality and political elements of dining at elite tables, see Albala, *The Banquet*.
31. Castro Martínez's study of municipal regulations and court records related to food in sixteenth-century Granada suggests that household food purchases were normally made by men. Most denunciations were for things like milk that had been watered down; women described how they would discover this in their kitchen after the men had brought it home. See Castro Martínez, "Comer en la Alhambra de Granada," 151.
32. Mas i Forners, "L'alimentació de la mà d'obra assalariada," 523–24.
33. Vigil, *La vida de las mujeres en los siglos XVI y XVII*, 124.
34. Torremocha Hernández, *La vida estudiantil en el Antiguo Régimen*, 53. See Piccinni, "Family and Domesticity," emphasizes the historical role of women in the kitchen, 131–34.
35. Guevara, *Epístolas familiares*, 278.
36. Vigil, *La vida de las mujeres en los siglos XVI y XVII*, 46, 79.
37. See chapter 1 of this book.
38. Francisco de Santos, *Día y noche de Madrid*, 131.
39. Vigil, *La vida de las mujeres en los siglos XVI y XVII*, 114; Pennell, "Professional Cooking, Kitchens and Service Work," 121, and "Family and Domesticity: Cooking, Eating, and Making Homes," 124.
40. Gil Ambrona, "Entre la oración y el trabajo," 62.
41. Such associations have deep historical roots: while Greek and Roman women of the classical period were responsible for maintaining ordinary households, they were not allowed to participate in banquets or symposia, and both societies

thought of formal cooking as a masculine profession. See Haranburu Altuna, *Historia de la alimentación*, 108.

42. The only exception over the course of two centuries of Habsburg rule was the woman who accompanied Mariana of Neuburg to the Spanish court after her marriage to Charles II. She is mentioned in palace records as "the female German cook who has come in the service of Her Majesty" but not identified by name. See Archivo del Palacio, Sec. Adm. Leg 880, Oficios de Boca de la Real Casa, 1690.

43. Guevara, *Aviso de privados*, 141.

44. Manuppella, *O "Livro de Cozinha" da Infanta D. Maria de Portugal*, lxiii–lxvi.

45. Albala, "Professional Cooking, Kitchens, and Service Work," 126.

46. Guerrero Mayllo, *Familia y vida cotidiana de una élite de poder*, 344, 347.

47. Especially since it paid a miserably low salary of three ducados a month. See Santamaría Arnaiz, *La alimentación de los españoles bajo el reino de los Austrias*, 277.

48. Spivakovsky, "La Princesa de Eboli," 17.

49. Pennell, "Professional Cooking," 109.

50. Pérez Samper, "Cocineras, escritoras y lectoras," 94–96; see also Vinyoles i Vidal, "Alimentació i ritme del temps a Catalunya," 145.

51. Martínez Montiño, *Arte de cozina*, prologue.

52. Albala, "Introduction," 6.

53. Pérez Samper, "Cocineras, escritoras y lectoras," contains an excellent discussion of women's recipe collections across western Europe from the Renaissance through the twentieth century.

54. Pérez Samper, "Cocineras, escritoras y lectoras," 102.

55. Valles Rojo, *Cocina y alimentación en los siglos XVI y XVII*, 35–39; *Manual de mugeres*.

56. Manuppella, *O "Livro de Cozinha" da Infanta D. Maria de Portugal*, xiii.

57. *Receptas de pivetes, pastilhas e vvas perfumadas y conserbas*, BNE MS 1462.

58. *Receptas experimentadas para diversas cosas*.

59. Pérez Samper, "Cocineras, escritoras y lectoras," 89.

60. Perry, "Las mujeres y su trabajo curativo en Sevilla, siglos XVI y XVII," 42.

61. *Receptas de pivetes*, f. 65.

62. Perry, "Las mujeres y su trabajo curativo en Sevilla," 40–47.

63. Garrido Aranda, Hidalgo Nuchera, and Muñoz Hidalgo, "Los manipuladores de alimentos en España y América," 196.

64. *Libros de acuerdos municipales de Santander*, 377, 383; Izquierdo Benito, *Abastecimiento y alimentación de Toledo*, 47–48. Ida Altman's work on Cáceres and Trujillo also suggests that bakers were female; see *Emigrants and Society*, 109.

65. Ortega López, "La participación laboral de la mujer en un señorío aragonés," 73.
66. Today's traditional Spanish markets still reflect this distinction, as rabbits are sold in the chicken and egg stalls, instead of in the meat stalls alongside lamb, beef, and pork.
67. Bravo Lozano, "Fuentes para el estudio del trabajo femenino en la edad moderna," 23, 25.
68. Serrano Larráyoz, *La mesa del rey*, 177.
69. Castro Martínez, *El abastecimiento alimentario en el reino de Granada*, 311; Izquierdo Benito, *Abastecimiento y alimentación de Toledo*, 82.
70. Bravo Lozano, "Fuentes para el estudio del trabajo femenino en la edad moderna," 22.
71. See for example the testimony of Ana de Bendicho, María Pérez, and Luisa Grandela in the case of Juan de la Cruz, A H N, Consejos, Indultos de Viernes Santo, leg. 5589.
72. López Iglesias, "Oficios y actividades de las mujeres ovetenses en el antiguo régimen," 51–52. There is no reason to think that Oviedo would have been unusual in this regard.
73. Prieto Palomo, "El abastecimiento alimentario en el Madrid del siglo XVII," 420–26.
74. A H N, Consejos, S A C C, libro 1173, ch. 55.
75. Santamaría Arnaiz, *La alimentación de los españoles bajo el reino de los Austrias*, 351. The prohibition on women serving wine and its exceptions were repeated in the early 1600s, with the licenses including the age and physical description of the women in question, presumably to prevent the licenses being shared with others. See A H N, Consejos, S A C C, libro 1173, título de las tabernas de corte, f. 120v.
76. A H N, Consejos, S A C C, libro 1201, f. 174–76; Prieto Palomo, "El abastecimiento alimentario en el Madrid del siglo XVII," 417–18.
77. A H N, Consejos, S A C C, libro 1200, f. 376, f. 495.
78. Laudan, *Cuisine & Empire*, 168–70.
79. For more on fasting, see chapter 4 in this book.
80. Montanari, *El hambre y la abundancia*, 115.
81. The term "old Christians" in Spanish (*cristianos viejos*) refers to families who had been Christian for several generations, as opposed to "new Christians" who were relatively recent converts from Judaism or Islam.
82. A H N, Inquisición, leg. 234, exp. 7 (Pedro Calvo) and 6 (Francisco de Andino, Felipe Lazaro, and Juan de la Peña).
83. Piccinni, "Family and Domesticity," 131.

84. Fàbrega, *La cultura del gust als països catalans*, 29.
85. Prats and Rey, "Las bases modernas de la alimentación tradicional," 53.
86. Nalle, "Self-correction and Social Change in the Spanish Counter-Reformation," 304.
87. Describing the fifteenth-century banquets offered by the condestable don Miguel Lucas de Iranzo of Jaén (who had a substantial number of Muslim clients), a chronicler noted that although the host offered "very delicate wines," his Muslim guests partook of them only in small amounts. See Rodríguez Molina, "La alimentación en el antiguo Reino de Jaén," 96.
88. Motis Dolader, "Alimentación y comensalidad," 44.
89. Serrano Larráyoz, *La mesa del rey*, 241.
90. Rodríguez Molina, "La alimentación en el antiguo Reino de Jaén," 98.
91. Motis Dolader, "Alimentación y comensalidad," 127.
92. Quoted in Hernando, "Els moralistes i l'alimentació a la baixa edat mitjana," 292.
93. Izquierdo Benito, *Abastecimiento y alimentación de Toledo*, 67.
94. The best study of this phenomenon is Gitlitz and Davidson, *A Drizzle of Honey*.
95. My examples and conclusions for this section are drawn from representative samples from seventeenth-century trials of suspected Judaizers and *moriscos* in the court of the Inquisition of Toledo, one of the principal courts in Castile. See AHN Inquisición, leg. 130–34, 193, 196.
96. Sánchez Moya, "El ayuno del Yom Kippur entre los judaizantes turolenses del siglo XV," 302.
97. AHN, Inquisición, leg. 133, exp. 10.
98. AHN, Inquisición, leg. 134, exp. 21.
99. Castro, *Cervantes y los casticismos españoles*, 25.
100. Fàbrega, "La cultura del cerdo en el Mediterráneo, entre el rechazo y la aceptación," 223, 229.
101. AHN, Inquisición, leg. 133, exp. 10.
102. AHN, Inquisición, leg. 134, exp. 21.
103. Sixteenth- and seventeenth-century cookbooks generally specified the use of pork fat (*tocino*) in the preparation of meat dishes. See AHN, Consejos, SACC, libro 1203, f. 614–23v.
104. Sendra i Beltran, "Variacions en l'evolució de la dieta alimentària dels monjos benedictins," 421.
105. AHN, Inquisición, leg. 133, exp. 9.
106. Rule of St Benedict, chapters 39, 40, and 36.
107. Ferrer, *Tratados espirituales de San Vicente Ferrer*, 70–71.

108. Gadea, "El monasterio de San Benito el Real de Valladolid," accessed April 29, 2016, http://viajarconelarte.blogspot.com.es/2014/01/el-monaste rio-de-san-benito-el-real-de.html. See also Egido, "La grandeza benedictina: San Benito el Real de Valladolid," 4–10.

109. Sendra i Beltran, "Variacions en l'evolució de la dieta alimentària dels monjos benedictins," 419.

110. Barceló Crespí, "La dieta alimentària a la Cartoixa de Valldemossa (segle XV)," 393, 403.

111. Canabal Rodríguez, "El sistema alimenticio de los conventos femeninos tole-danos en la baja Edad Media," 409.

112. Vinyoles i Vidal, "Alimentació i ritme del temps a Catalunya," 136.

113. Because of this tension between nobility and poverty, Montanari has argued that monastic communities functioned as a kind of mediator between high and low dietary practices, even "ennobling" such humble foods as cheese and fruit. See *Cheese, Pears, and History in a Proverb*, 17–18.

114. Burgo López, "El consumo alimentario del clero regular femenino," 229–35.

115. AHN, Consejos, SACC, libro 1224, f. 115.

116. *Constituciones de la congregación de San Benito de la Observancia* (Madrid 1612), ch. 43, 136v–137.

117. *Constituciones de la congregación de San Benito de la Observancia*, ch. 43, 137.

118. *Libro de mayordomía de gastos*.

119. Salsete, *El cocinero religioso*.

120. García Marsilla, *La jerarquía de la mesa*, 223.

121. Vizuete Mendoza, "La dieta alimenticia en la religiosidad femenina de San Clemente de Toledo," 253–56.

122. *Libro de mayordomía de gastos*, July 11, 1675.

123. Indeed, following a decline in wine production in Europe after the fall of the Roman Empire, medieval monasteries were crucial in redeveloping the culti-vation of wine grapes. See Torres, "Producción y comercialización del vino en el Mediterráneo," 198.

124. Vinyoles i Vidal, "El rebost, la taula i la cuina dels frares barcelonins al 1400," 143.

125. *Constituciones de la congregación de San Benito de la Observancia*, ch. 43, 137v.

126. *Libro de mayordomía de gastos*, March 11, 1679.

127. Monks and priests in Spain have always had the reputation of eating well, as can be seen in any number of popular sayings and proverbs; see examples in Gómez Díaz, "'Buen alimento, mejor pensamiento': El consumo en un convento almeriense a finales del s. XVII," 377–78.

128. Salsete, *El cocinero religioso*, iv.

129. Pérez Samper, *La alimentación en la España del Siglo de Oro*, 68.

130. Domínguez Ortiz, "Aspectos del vivir madrileño durante el reinado de Carlos II," 237n4; see also Gómez Díaz, "'Buen alimento, mejor pensamiento': El consumo en un convento almeriense a finales del s. XVII," 392–93.

131. Salsete, *El cocinero religioso*. This collection also includes references to chocolate, though these recipes were added in a different hand; see p. xxxii.

132. Saavedra, *La vida cotidiana en la Galicia del Antiguo Régimen*, 145.

133. Haranburu Altuna, *Historia de la alimentación*, 129.

134. Laudan, *Cuisine & Empire*, 180.

135. Pérez Samper, "Privacidad doméstica," 129.

136. *Constituciones de la congregación de San Benito de la Observancia*, 132.

137. Vinyoles i Vidal, "Alimentació i ritme del temps a Catalunya," 125, 142.

138. *Constituciones de la congregación de San Benito de la Observancia*, 139.

139. Canabal Rodríguez, "El sistema alimenticio de los conventos femeninos toledanos en la baja Edad Media," 411.

140. Laudan, *Cuisine & Empire*, 180.

141. *Libro de mayordomía de gastos*, April 26, 1674 (visiting abbots); July 7 and 28 and August 4 and 11, 1674 (ice).

142. Burgo López, "El consumo alimentario del clero regular femenino," 233–34.

143. *Constituciones de la congregación de San Benito de la Observancia*, 193.

144. *Constituciones de la congregación de San Benito de la Observancia*, 115v.

145. *Constituciones de la congregación de San Benito de la Observancia*, 169, 175v.

146. Quoted in Sendra i Beltran, "Variacions en l'evolució de la dieta alimentària dels monjos benedictins," 231.

147. For an overview of early modern European institutional culture, see Goldgar and Frost, "Introduction," i–xviii.

148. Gautier, "Eating Out in the Early and High Middle Ages," 103.

149. Rodríguez-San Pedro Bezares, *La universidad salmantina del Barroco*, 25.

150. Rodríguez-San Pedro Bezares, *La universidad salmantina del Barroco*, 19–27; Santamaría Arnaiz, *La alimentación de los españoles bajo el reino de los Austrias*, 949.

151. "Por más duro y rústico que sea un ingenio humano, si le labran con doctrinarle bien, le harán ser sabio y discreto." See Monzón, *Libro primero del espejo del príncipe christiano*, f.23.

152. Monzón, *Libro primero del espejo del príncipe christiano*, f. 61v.

153. Pérez Samper, "Privacidad doméstica," 111; Sala Balust, *Constituciones, estatutos y ceremonias de los antiguos colegios seculares de la Universidad de Salamanca*, vol. 4, 99.

154. Rodríguez-San Pedro Bezares, *La universidad salmantina del Barroco*, 402; Santamaría Arnaiz, *La alimentación de los españoles bajo el reino de los Austrias*, 953.

155. Eiximenis, "Dotzè del Crestià," 113.

156. *Reglas de urbanidad*, 3.

157. Rodríguez-San Pedro Bezares, *La universidad salmantina del Barroco*, 22, 27.

158. See for example the comments of Pedro Fernández de Navarrete in 1626, quoted in Rodríguez-San Pedro Bezares, *La universidad salmantina del Barroco*, 24.

159. Torremocha Hernández, *La vida estudiantil en el Antiguo Régimen*, 27.

160. Torremocha Hernández, *La vida estudiantil en el Antiguo Régimen*, 17.

161. Díaz, *La cocina del Barroco*, 28.

162. AHN, Universidades, leg. 371, for the *colegio mayor* of San Ildefonso of the University of Alcalá de Henares. See also Santamaría Arnaiz, *La alimentación de los españoles bajo el reino de los Austrias*, 954–1141. For similar information from other *colegios mayores*, see María Angeles Pérez Samper, *La alimentación en la España del Siglo de Oro*, 131.

163. *Constituciones del Colegio del Arzobispo de Toledo*, from Sala Balust, *Constituciones, estatutos y ceremonias de los antiguos colegios seculares de la Universidad de Salamanca*, tomo 4, 101.

164. Rodríguez-San Pedro Bezares, *La universidad salmantina del Barroco*, 377.

165. Rodríguez-San Pedro Bezares, *La universidad salmantina del Barroco*, 382–87.

166. Torremocha Hernández, *La vida estudiantil en el Antiguo Régimen*, 33.

167. Rodríguez-San Pedro Bezares, *La universidad salmantina del Barroco*, 375.

168. Pérez Samper, *La alimentación en la España del Siglo de Oro*, 150.

169. Pérez Samper, *La alimentación en la España del Siglo de Oro*, 164.

170. Pérez Samper, "Privacidad doméstica," 106.

171. Santamaría Arnaiz, *La alimentación de los españoles bajo el reino de los Austrias*, 954.

172. *Constituciones del Imperial y Real Seminario de Nobles de Barcelona de Cordelles*, quoted in Pérez Samper, "La alimentación como indicativo de un estilo de vida," 57.

173. López López, *Comportamientos religiosos en Asturias durante el Antiguo Régimen*, 188.

174. For the confraternities, see Flynn, *Sacred Charity*; for a study of the connection between confraternities, theater, and public health and welfare, see Ball, *Treating the Public*.

175. Pezzi Cristóbal, "Fiesta religiosa y ostentación social," 271–78.

176. In the ordinances of the Cofradía de San Antonio Abad in Benavente, for example, fourteen of the forty chapters refer to meals. See Ansón Calvo, Manzano

Ledesma, and González Alonso, "Un ejemplo de sociabilidad gastronómica," 782, 788.

177. Ansón Calvo, Manzano Ledesma, and González Alonso, "Un ejemplo de sociabilidad gastronómica," 788.

178. García Marsilla, *La jerarquía de la mesa*, 170.

179. Mantecón Movellán, *Contrarreforma y religiosidad popular en Cantabria*, 161–65; Ansón Calvo, Manzano Ledesma, and González Alonso, "Un ejemplo de sociabilidad gastronómica," 788.

180. Riera i Melis, "Jerarquía social y desigualdad alimentaria," 103.

181. Carmona García, *Crónica urbana del malvivir*, 144.

182. Falcón Pérez, "Banquetes en Aragón en la Baja Edad Media," 512.

183. Ansón Calvo, Manzano Ledesma, and González Alonso, "Un ejemplo de sociabilidad gastronómica," 787.

184. Izquierdo Benito, *Abastecimiento y alimentación de Toledo*, 152.

185. Eiras Roel, *Historia de la alimentación en la España moderna*, 37, 51.

186. Martínez García, *La asistencia a los pobres en Burgos*, 158.

187. Martínez García, *La asistencia a los pobres en Burgos*, 121–22.

188. Flynn, *Sacred Charity*, 63.

189. Ansón Calvo, Manzano Ledesma, and González Alonso, "Un ejemplo de sociabilidad gastronómica," 787.

190. Lera de Isla, "Cuando Madrid se hizo Corte: La famosa Ronda de Pan y Huevo," 3–6. The Hermandad still exists in Madrid and continues to maintain a soup kitchen for the poor. Riera i Melis notes that for poor rural families of northeastern Spain, at least during the first wave of expansion of the hospitals, an average day's food may well have been less than what was typically provided by charitable institutions. See "Jerarquía social y desigualdad alimentaria," 94.

191. Ansón Calvo, Manzano Ledesma, and González Alonso, "Un ejemplo de sociabilidad gastronómica," 788.

192. Izquierdo Benito, *Abastecimiento y alimentación de Toledo*, 147.

193. Martínez García, *La asistencia a los pobres en Burgos*, 122.

3. STATUS AND CHANGE

1. *Novísima recopilación de las leyes de España*, libro 6, título 2, ley 9.

2. Atienza Hernández, *Aristocracia, poder y riqueza*, 39.

3. Hernando, "Els moralistes i l'alimentació a la baixa edat mitjana," 285; see also Martín Pérez, *Libro de las confesiones*.

4. The Spanish word she uses is "honra," which translates as "honor" in the sense of fame, good name, and reputation. See Saint Teresa, *Camino de perfección*, 454.

5. Ródenas Vilar, *Vida cotidiana y negocio en la Segovia del Siglo de Oro*, 133.
6. Ródenas Vilar, *Vida cotidiana y negocio en la Segovia del Siglo de Oro*, 17, 140.
7. Pezzi Cristóbal, "Fiesta religiosa y ostentación social," 271–78.
8. Guerrero Mayllo, *Familia y vida cotidiana de una élite de poder*, 305; see also Alvarez-Assorio Alvariño, "Rango y apariencia," 267.
9. Ródenas Vilar, *Vida cotidiana y negocio*, 141, 148.
10. Albala, *Eating Right in the Renaissance*, 185.
11. Guerrero Navarrete, "Aproximación cualitativa y cuantitativa a la dieta urbana en el siglo XV," 247.
12. Riera i Melis, "Jerarquía social y desigualdad alimentaria," 88, 105, 204.
13. Quoted in Albala, "Introduction," 2.
14. Riera i Melis, "Jerarquía social y desigualdad alimentaria," 202; García Marsilla, *La jerarquía de la mesa*, 237.
15. See for example *Recetas y memorias para guisados*; Ferrer i Mallol, "Figues, panses, fruita seca i torrons," 191–208; and Martínez Martínez, "Hacia la configuración del modelo alimentario feudal," 359.
16. "Non es dulce el sabor quanto el precio es pequeño," quoted in Valles Rojo, *Cocina y alimentación en los siglos XVI y XVII*, 131.
17. García Marsilla, *La jerarquía de la mesa*, 248.
18. Pérez Samper, *La alimentación en la España del Siglo de Oro*, 114–15.
19. Monzón, *Libro primero del espejo del príncipe christiano*, 108.
20. This difference carried over to physical health as well, as elites became more likely to suffer from problems related to the consumption of excess fat and protein. See Serrano Larráyoz, *La mesa del rey*, 251.
21. The Toledan confectioner Miguel de Baeza drew substantially on Arab and Andalusian texts for his *Quatro libros del arte de la confitería* (Alcalá, 1592).
22. *Arte de cozina*, 9v, 15, 17.
23. Pozzo, *El diario del viaje a España del Cardenal Francesco Barberini*, 156, 336.
24. Simón Palmer, *La alimentación y sus circunstancias en el Real Alcázar de Madrid*, 35.
25. Bernardino de Mendoza to Philip II, January 24, 1582, CODOIN v. 92, p. 253.
26. The French term *blancmange*, which now describes a molded dessert based on cream, sugar, and almonds, originally referred to the chicken-based *manjar blanco*, which appeared in late medieval recipe books across Europe but seems to have had particular popularity in Spain.
27. Yelgo de Vazquez, *Estilo de servir a príncipes*, chapter 19, "in which the cook is instructed on the different dishes he should know how to prepare," 147–56. The variations included *manjar blanco* baked in empanadas, made with cheese curd, or served as a torte.

28. Santamaría Arnaiz, *La alimentación de los españoles bajo el reino de los Austrias*, 962; Rodríguez-San Pedro Bezares, *La universidad salmantina del Barroco*, vol. 3, 386–87.

29. *Libro de mayordomía de gastos*, see for example January 1 and 4 and February 14, 1679.

30. Bartolomé Sánchez, Luis Hernández and Diego Lainez all had licenses in 1596 to sell manjar blanco "to whomever they wished," and in 1615 Diego de la Peña had two stands in the Plaza Mayor for the same purpose. See AHN, Consejos, SACC: libro 1198, f. 79, and libro 1203, f. 134. See also Santamaría Arnaiz, *La alimentación de los españoles bajo el reino de los Austrias*, 20, 23.

31. Laudan, *Cuisine & Empire*, 190–92.

32. Saavedra, *La vida cotidiana en la Galicia del Antiguo Régimen*, 149.

33. The first Europeans to adopt corn as "people food" were northern Italians, who used it to create polenta. See Haranburu Altuna, *Historia de la alimentación*, 170–73.

34. Haranburu Altuna, *Historia de la alimentación*, 179.

35. Laudan, *Cuisine & Empire*, 202. Nicolás Monardes, a sixteenth-century physician and botanist, wrote an extensive catalog of what he considered to be the most important properties of dozens of New World foods, including tobacco, corn, pineapple, and peanuts. See Monardes, *La historia medicinal de las cosas que se traen de nuestras islas occidentales*.

36. The best discussion of this process is Norton, "Tasting Empire: Chocolate and the European Internalization of Mesoamerican Aesthetics." See also Coe and Coe, *The True History of Chocolate*.

37. Colmenero de Ledesma, *Curioso tratado de la naturaleza y calidad del chocolate*, 6–7.

38. Doctors' report from April 17, 1693. See *Documentos inéditos referentes a las postrimerías de la Casa de Austria en España*, 95.

39. Colmenero de Ledesma, *Curioso tratado de la naturaleza y calidad del chocolate*, 4v.

40. *The Ingenious and Diverting Letters*, 147. D'Aulnoy's accounts are not entirely credible, but her descriptions of chocolate match other contemporary accounts.

41. "Yo no he de ir a vuestros Palacios, ni entro en ellos, ni bebo vuestro chocolate, ni quiero confesaros, porque hasta que os quitara con la ayuda de Dios esta profanidad, no os avía de absolver." See Antonio de Ezcaray, *Voces de dolor nacidas de la multitud de pecados*, 63.

42. Santamaría Arnaiz, *La alimentación de los españoles bajo el reino de los Austrias*, 717.

43. Moreno de la Torre, *Diario*, 133.
44. For chocolate as part of eighteenth-century tertulias, see Pérez Samper, "Chocolate, té y café," 177. For the Cervera family, see Sarasúa, "Upholding Status: The Diet of a Noble Family in Early Nineteenth-Century La Mancha," 47.
45. Santamaría Arnaiz, *La alimentación de los españoles bajo el reino de los Austrias*, 713, 1451; AHN, Consejos, SACC, libro 1219, fol. 342. Though the sale of chocolate from street stands was briefly prohibited in 1644, several additional licenses were granted beginning in 1646. Francisco de Santos's *Día y noche de Madrid*, first published in 1663, frequently mentions chocolate as part of common eating habits (34, 38, 57, 142). However, it remained difficult to find in rural areas through the late eighteenth century. See Saavedra, *La vida cotidiana en la Galicia del Antiguo Régimen*, 148.
46. AHN, Consejos, SACC, libro 1173, fol. 98v.
47. Domínguez Ortiz, "Aspectos del vivir madrileño durante el reinado de Carlos II," 237n4.
48. Sarasúa, *Criados, nodrizas y amos: El servicio doméstico en la formación del mercado de trabajo madrileño*, 217. The chocolate grinders' guild was formed in 1772; see AHN, Consejos, SACC, 1772, fols. 608–703.
49. AHN, Inquisición, leg. 133, exp. 9, fol. 25.
50. They calculated that according to the proper ingredients (cocoa, sugar, achiote, cinnamon, pepper, and almonds), a pound of good chocolate should cost eleven reales, when it was being sold at five and a half. See AHN, Consejos, SACC, libro 1173, fols. 99–99v.
51. AHN, Consejos, SACC, libro 1173, ch. 50, "Modo de visitar al señor presidente y otras personas."
52. Guevara, *Menosprecio de corte y alabanza de aldea*, 44.
53. Devroey, "Food and Politics," 85.
54. This theme of gaining influence through generosity was reflected in various ways in sixteenth-century advice as well. Francisco de Ledesma's advice on raising elite children consistently recommended the importance of humility and demonstrating one's position by yielding to others: "If you walk with one who is your equal, do not jockey for position, but give way. . . . If you are rich, be generous to the poor, and God will see that you will not lack. . . . If you are in the town hall, take the lowest seat." See Ledesma, *Documentos de la buena crianza*, 6, 16, 24.
55. Monzón, *Libro primero del espejo del príncipe christiano*, 111v.
56. Guevara, *Aviso de privados*, 143.
57. *Colección de avisos de la nobleza a sus hijos*, BNE, MSS 10857, 114.

58. Guevara, *Aviso de privados*, 138–39.

59. Bravo Lozano, "Fuentes para el estudio del trabajo femenino en la edad moderna," 24.

60. Vigil, *La vida de las mujeres en los siglos XVI y XVII*, 125.

61. Castillo Solórzano, *Niña de los embustes, Teresa de Manzanares* (1634), quoted in Fernández Pérez, "La mujer trabajadora del barroco a través de la picaresca," 4.

62. Lacour, "Faces of Violence Revisited: A Typology of Violence in Early Modern Rural Germany," 657.

63. Moreno de la Torre, *Diario*, 103.

64. Pozzo, *El diario del viaje a España del Cardenal Francesco Barberini*, 16–17.

65. Pérez Samper, "Privacidad doméstica," 129.

66. Yelgo de Vazquez, *Estilo de servir a príncipes*, 38v.

67. Guevara, *Avisos, y advertmiento de la diligencia, que un señor deve usar en criar los hijos*, 53.

68. *Constituciones, y instrucciones de la hermandad del Real Hospicio*, 104.

69. The most influential ideas on this topic are those of Elias, *The Civilizing Process* and *The Court Society*.

70. See Elias, and for Spain, Ampudia de Haro, *Las bridas de la conducta*, xv–xvi.

71. Devroey, "Food and Politics," 89.

72. Riera i Melis, "Jerarquía social y desigualdad alimentaria," 199.

73. Capitán Díaz, "Educación, urbanidad y buenos modales en el siglo XVI español," 279–87.

74. The principal early modern Spanish conduct books, especially those that include an emphasis on table manners, are Francesc Eiximenis, *Lo Crestià* (c. 1380); Juan Luis Vives, *Diálogos sobre la educación* (1538); Antonio de Torquemada, *Coloquios satíricos* (1553); Lucas Gracián Dantisco, *Galateo español* (1593); and Francisco de Ledesma, *Documentos de la buena crianza* (1599).

75. From a sonnet by Galvez de Montalvo, included in the front matter of Dantisco, *Galateo español*.

76. Gracián, *Galateo español*, 7v. See also *Reglas de urbanidad*, 8.

77. Gracián, *Galateo español*, 12v, 107v.

78. Ledesma's *Documentos de la buena crianza* (1599), for example, is principally oriented toward children and includes the same kind of advice directed previously to adults about keeping elbows off the table and not slurping the soup. See *Documentos de la buena crianza*, 11–13.

79. Pérez Samper, "La alimentación como indicativo de un estilo de vida," 58.

80. Celada, *La cocina de la Casa de Alba*, 117.

81. Cruz Cruz, *Alimentación y cultura*, 373.

82. Cruz Cruz, *Alimentación y cultura*, 372; Ledesma, *Documentos de la buena crianza*, 12.

83. The Cordelles constitution emphasizes repeatedly that students should not eat with both hands nor use their hands to dip into the salt or serve themselves food. Such warnings suggest that these behaviors must still have been common. See Pérez Samper, "La alimentación como indicativo de un estilo de vida," 57.

84. Pozzo, *El diario del viaje a España del Cardenal Francesco Barberini*, 72.

85. García Marsilla, *La jerarquía de la mesa*, 174.

86. Ródenas Vilar, *Vida cotidiana y negocio*, 167–68.

87. Guerrero Mayllo, *Familia y vida cotidiana de una élite de poder*, 306, 316.

88. Ródenas Vilar, *Vida cotidiana y negocio*, 137; Mercado, *Dialogos de Philosophia natural y moral* (Granada, 1558), quoted in Alvarez-Assorio Alvariño, "Rango y apariencia," 264.

89. Mercado, *Dialogos*, quoted in Alvarez-Assorio Alvariño, "Rango y apariencia," 264.

90. García Marsilla, *La jerarquía de la mesa*, 78.

91. Soto, *Obligaciones de todos los estados*, 39v.

92. Piccolomini, *Tractado de la miseria de los cortesanos*, 7v–8.

93. In this discussion I am focusing principally on food, but early modern Spaniards embraced similar extravagance in their clothing and other possessions. See López Álvarez, *Poder, lujo, y conflicto en la corte de los Austrias*; and Wunder, "Women's Fashions and Politics in Seventeenth-Century Spain."

94. González Arce, *Apariencia y poder*, 197.

95. *Actas de las Cortes de Castilla*, vol. 1, 95, 370.

96. *Actas de las Cortes de Castilla*, vol. 1, 371.

97. Vinyoles i Vidal, "Alimentació i ritme del temps a Catalunya," 143.

98. The Council to Philip III, January 9, 1620, in González Palencia, *La Junta de Reformación*, 35.

99. Muzzarelli, "Reconciling the Privilege of a Few with the Common Good," 599. See also Riera i Melis, "Jerarquía social y desigualdad alimentaria."

100. "Memoria de los maravedies que yo Bartolome Perez gasto en comida y otras cosas nezesarias para el servizio de mi señor Antonio Perez," April 1585, AHN, Consejos, leg. 50232, exp. 119.

101. Guerrero Mayllo, *Familia y vida cotidiana de una élite de poder*, 306.

102. Carmen Sarasúa, "Upholding Status," 42.

103. AHN, Consejos, SACC, libro 1247, f. 1–6.

104. Castro Martínez, *El abastecimiento alimentario en el reino de Granada*, 230.

105. "Ya no se tiene por señor el que no la tiene, ni aun por caballero de importancia." See AHN, Consejos, SACC, libro 1173, f. 94.

106. González Palencia, *Consejo de Castilla: Sala de Alcaldes de Casa y Corte.*
107. AHN, Consejos, SACC, libro 1247, f. 1–6.
108. AHN, Consejos, SACC, libro 1173, ch. 61.
109. González Palencia, *La Junta de Reformación*, 212. See also chapter 4 in this book.
110. Riera i Melis, "Jerarquía social y desigualdad alimentaria," 100–101.
111. Ladero Quesada, "La caza en la legislación municipal castellana," 206–7.
112. Ladero Quesada, "La caza en la legislación municipal castellana," 204.
113. Izquierdo Benito, *Abastecimiento y alimentación de Toledo*, 80.
114. AHN, Consejos, SACC, libro 1173, f. 106v.
115. Hilton 1973, quoted in Montanari, "Introduction," 11.
116. Valles Rojo, *Cocina y alimentación en los siglos XVI y XVII*, 136.
117. See chapter 1 in this book.
118. Guerrero Navarrete, "Aproximación cualitativa y cuantitativa a la dieta urbana," 262.
119. Pérez López, "Las cuentas de la casa Sala," 457.
120. Haranburu Altuna, *Historia de la alimentación*, 128.
121. Ladero Quesada, "La caza en la legislación municipal castellana," 206.
122. Rodríguez Villa, *Etiquetas de la Casa de Austria*, 165.
123. González Palencia, *Consejo de Castilla: Sala de Alcaldes de Casa y Corte*, 136; Castro Martínez, *El abastecimiento alimentario en el reino de Granada*, 238–39.
124. Alves, *Animals of Spain*, 192.
125. Alves, *Animals of Spain*, 4.

4. VICE AND VIRTUE, BODY AND SOUL

1. The model for understanding ties between food and holiness remains Bynum, *Holy Feast and Holy Fast.*
2. Eiximenis, "Terç del Crestià," 162.
3. "De vianda lo que basta no para hartar sino para sustentar; mucha comida buscala en otra parte no en la escuela a donde se trata solo de virtud." See *Reglas de urbanidad*, 6.
4. Andreolli, "Food Representations," 162.
5. Kallendorf, *Sins of the Fathers*, 123–29; Moreto quotation p. 124, Cervantes quotation p. 129.
6. Soto, *Obligaciones de todos los estados*, 12.
7. Pons Fuster, "Mujeres y espiritualidad: Las beatas valencianas del siglo XVII," 79.
8. Montanari, *El hambre y la abundancia*, 25.
9. Pérez Samper, *La alimentación en la España del Siglo de Oro*, 81.

10. Riera i Melis implies that ordinary Spaniards consumed fish only because of this ecclesiastical imposition. See "Jerarquía social y desigualdad alimentaria," 94.

11. Alves, *Animals of Spain*, 152–53.

12. Albala, "Introduction," 12.

13. Krondl, "Food Systems," 51.

14. Hernández de Maceras, "Pescados, huevos, y potajes en días de vigilias," in *Libro de arte de cozina*, 72.

15. "Mira cuán suave puedes hacer la cuaresma a tu comunidad con la variación de los guisos." See Salsete, *El cocinero religioso*, 112.

16. Echániz Sans, "La alimentación de los pobres asistidos por la Pia Almoina de la catedral de Barcelona," 181.

17. See for example AHN, Inquisición, leg. 132, exp. 4, trial of Antonio Alferez de Ricamonte, 1652.

18. García Marsilla, *La jerarquía de la mesa*, 207.

19. "Memoria de los maravedies que yo Bartolome Perez gasto en comida y otras cosas nezesarias para el servizio de mi señor Antonio Perez," April 1585, AHN, Consejos, leg. 50232, exp. 119.

20. Soto, *Obligaciones de todos los estados*, 97.

21. García Marsilla, *La jerarquía de la mesa*, 211–17; Serrano Larráyoz, *La mesa del rey*, 238.

22. Serrano Larráyoz, *La mesa del rey*, 239.

23. D. García de Toledo to Francisco de Eraso, February 24, 1562, CODOIN, vol. 26, p. 436.

24. Piccolomini, *Tractado de la miseria de los cortesanos*, 7–8v.

25. Guevara, *Menosprecio de corte y alabanza de aldea*, 32.

26. Gutiérrez Nieto, "El campesinado," 61. See chapter 2 of this book for more discussion of religion and food choices.

27. Celada, *La cocina de la Casa de Alba*, 114.

28. Santos, *Día y noche de Madrid*, 32.

29. See also chapter 2 for the example of confraternities.

30. Riera i Melis, "Pobreza y alimentación," 41.

31. García Marsilla, *La jerarquía de la mesa*, 208.

32. Carmona García, *El extenso mundo de la pobreza*, 213.

33. Rodríguez Villa, *Etiquetas de la Casa de Austria*, 46.

34. Riera i Melis, "Pobreza y alimentación en el Mediterráneo Noroccidental en la Baja Edad Media," 53–61; "Estructura social y sistemas alimentarios en la Cataluña bajomedieval," 215.

35. Carmona García has argued that the role of these hospitals has been exaggerated, since small brotherhoods often called their gathering places "hospitales" even if they did not regularly provide meals or other charitable support (*Crónica urbana del malvivir*, 142). Even if they did not do enough to meet all the needs of all the urban poor, their role was significant enough to merit discussion here.

36. Martínez García, *La asistencia a los pobres en Burgos*, 10–27.

37. García Marsilla, *La jerarquía de la mesa*, 250; Riera i Melis, "Estructura social y sistemas alimentarios en la Cataluña bajomedieval," 210.

38. Martínez García, *La asistencia a los pobres en Burgos*, 27.

39. Dursteler, "Food and Politics," 91.

40. Carmona García, *Crónica urbana del malvivir*, 131–32, 137.

41. Ansón Calvo, Manzano Ledesma, and González Alonso, "Un ejemplo de sociabilidad gastronómica," 786.

42. Kelleher, "Eating from a Corrupted Table," 60.

43. AHN, Consejos, SACC, libro 1173, ch. 38, "puerco fresco y sus despojos."

44. AHN, Consejos, SACC, libro 1203, f. 639.

45. AHN, Consejos, SACC, libro 1247, f. 147.

46. Martínez García, *La asistencia a los pobres en Burgos*, 45.

47. *Constituciones, y instrucciones de la hermandad del Real Hospicio*, 2, 63.

48. AHN, Consejos, SACC, libro 1173, ch. 52.

49. Carmona García, *El extenso mundo de la pobreza*, 53.

50. *Constituciones, y instrucciones de la hermandad del Real Hospicio*, 67, 85, 110.

51. *Constituciones, y instrucciones de la hermandad del Real Hospicio*, 59.

52. AHN, Consejos, SACC, libro 1173, ch. 53, "Ciegos y los daños de consentirlos," 82v–83.

53. Note the similarity between this and concerns about women working in the marketplace, noted in chapter 2 of this book.

54. Carmona García, *El extenso mundo de la pobreza*, 27–30.

55. Haranburu Altuna, *Historia de la alimentación*, 127.

56. Valdés, *Memorias de Asturias*, quoted in López López, *Comportamientos religiosos en Asturias*, 77.

57. Equip Broida, "Els àpats funeraris segons els testaments vers el 1400," 267.

58. Equip Broida, "Els àpats funeraris segons els testaments vers el 1400," 265–67.

59. López López, *Comportamientos religiosos en Asturias*, 78.

60. Equip Broida, "Els àpats funeraris segons els testaments vers el 1400," 267.

61. Equip Broida, "Els àpats funeraris segons els testaments vers el 1400," 265.

62. Castro, *A lume manso*, 161–62.

63. López López, *Comportamientos religiosos en Asturias*, 76.

64. Castro, *A lume manso*, 166–67.

65. Lapeña Paul, "Notas en torno al sistema alimentario en un monasterio altoaragonés en la Edad Media," 386.

66. Equip Broida, "Els àpats funeraris segons els testaments vers el 1400," 264–65.

67. Equip Broida, "Actitudes religiosas de las mujeres medievales ante la muerte," 215–16.

68. Saavedra, *La vida cotidiana en la Galicia del Antiguo Régimen*, 141.

69. Riera i Melis, "Estructura social y sistemas alimentarios en la Cataluña bajomedieval," 214.

70. "Bizcochos del sepulcro," in *Recetas y memorias para guisados*.

71. Riera i Melis, "Jerarquía social y desigualdad alimentaria," 96.

72. Will of Nicolás Bernard, April 1494, AHN, Clero, car. 3638n10. Consulted via the Portal de Archivos Españoles (hereafter PARES), April 29, 2016, http://pares.mcu.es.

73. Mantecón Movellán, *Contrarreforma y religiosidad popular en Cantabria*, 96.

74. López López, *Comportamientos religiosos en Asturias*, 72–73.

75. Guerrero Mayllo, *Familia y vida cotidiana de una élite de poder*, 372–79.

76. Krausman Ben-Amos, "Gifts and Favors: Informal Support in Early Modern England," 319–20. Her analysis is of England, but I suspect that similar patterns hold true for Spain.

77. Castro, *A lume manso*, 171.

78. López López, *Comportamientos religiosos en Asturias*, 76.

79. Mantecón Movellán, *Contrarreforma y religiosidad popular en Cantabria*, 94.

80. López López, *Comportamientos religiosos en Asturias*, 83.

81. González Arce, *Apariencia y poder*, 182.

82. Serrano Larráyoz, *La mesa del rey*, 161–63.

83. Riera i Melis, "Jerarquía social y desigualdad alimentaria," 103; Serra i Clota, "Comportaments alimentaris i factors socioeconòmics," 539.

84. "Trasunto del proceso sobre el ador de agua en Magallón" (Zaragoza, October 1482), AHN, Clero, Car. 3788n7; consulted via PARES, April 29, 2016, http://pares.mcu.es.

85. Bort Tomo, "La vida en la embajada de Roma en la época de Don Juan de Zúñiga Requesens (1568–1580)," 456.

86. Dursteler, "Food and Politics," 97.

87. Simón Palmer, *La alimentación y sus circunstancias en el Real Alcázar de Madrid*, 29.

88. Simón Palmer, "Las bebidas en el Palacio Real," 170.

89. Lapeña Paul, "Notas en torno al sistema alimentario en un monasterio altoaragonés en la Edad Media," 379.

90. Falcón Pérez, "Banquetes en Aragón en la Baja Edad Media," 509–10.
91. *Libro de mayordomía de gastos*, June 30, 1674 (chocolate); January 7 and July 3, 1679 (accountants).
92. Martínez Martínez, "Hacia la configuración del modelo alimentario feudal," 353.
93. Santamaría Arnaiz, *La alimentación de los españoles bajo el reino de los Austrias*, 668.
94. Rodríguez Molina, "La alimentación en el antiguo Reino de Jaén," 96.
95. Falcón Pérez, "Banquetes en Aragón en la Baja Edad Media," 510.
96. Such arrangements are noted in cases of litigation over the ownership or proper use of such lands and offices. See, among many other examples, the case brought by Juan García Múñoz Mozo, Archivo de la Real Audiencia y Chancillería de Valladolid, Registro de Ejecutorias, caja 1470, 58, 1589, or that brought by Lope Rodríguez, Registro de Ejecutorias, caja 898, 9, 1557. These and similar cases may be viewed in PARES.
97. Ródenas Vilar, *Vida cotidiana y negocio*, 43.
98. Izquierdo Benito, *Abastecimiento y alimentación de Toledo*, 74.
99. Vinyoles i Vidal, "Alimentació i ritme del temps a Catalunya," 150.
100. AHN, Consejos, Indultos de Viernes Santo, leg. 5590, Francisco de Peredo.
101. *Reglas de educación y urbanidad expuestas en forma dialogada*, 4v.
102. Torremocha Hernández, "Las noches y los días de los estudiantes universitarios," 59. The student accepted the offer and stayed on at the original *posada*.
103. AHN, Consejos, Indultos de Viernes Santo, leg. 5590, Juan de Lara (1675).
104. Grieco, "Body and Soul," 143.
105. Andreolli, "Food Representations," 152.
106. Laudan, *Cuisine & Empire*, 169.
107. Grieco, "Body and Soul," 145. Grieco phrases this in terms of the eight capital sins as they were categorized in the early church; I have reduced it to the seven that were commonly understood after the influence of the sixth-century Pope Gregory the Great. For another excellent discussion of the perception of the deadly sins in early modern Spanish culture, see Kallendorf, *Sins of the Fathers*.
108. Monzón, *Libro primero del espejo del príncipe christiano*, 101.
109. Monzón, *Libro primero del espejo del príncipe christiano*, 108.
110. Monzón, *Libro primero del espejo del príncipe christiano*, 111v.
111. Gabriel Quijano, *Vicios de las tertulias*, quoted in Pérez Samper, "Chocolate, té y café," 186–98.
112. Monzón, *Libro primero del espejo del príncipe christiano*, 100v; García Marsilla, *La jerarquía de la mesa*, 71.

113. Ferrer, *Tratados espirituales de San Vicente Ferrer*, 72.
114. See for example Hernando de Talavera, Archbishop of Granada, "Solazoso y provechoso tractado contra la demasia de vestir y de calçar y de comer y de bever," in *Breve y muy provechosa doctrina de lo que deve saber todo christiano*, 325–416; or Luis Lobera de Avila, *Vergel de sanidad*.
115. Gentilcore, "Body and Soul, or Living Physically in the Kitchen," 149–50.
116. Kallendorf, *Sins of the Fathers*, 113–14.
117. Kallendorf, *Sins of the Fathers*, 116.
118. Monzón, *Libro primero del espejo del príncipe christiano*, 100.
119. Monzón, *Libro primero del espejo del príncipe christiano*, 100–103.
120. Manuppella, *O "Livro de Cozinha" da Infanta D. Maria de Portugal*, lii.
121. Monzón, *Libro primero del espejo del príncipe christiano*, 110.
122. *Reglas de urbanidad*, 6.
123. See for example *Colección de avisos de la nobleza a sus hijos*; and Palmireno, *El estudioso cortesano*.
124. Guevara, *Aviso de privados*, 143.
125. Núñez de Castro, *Sólo Madrid es corte*.
126. Guevara, *Aviso de privados*, 218.
127. Dursteler, "Food and Politics," 97.
128. Guevara, *Aviso de privados*, 217–18.
129. González Palencia, *La Junta de Reformación*, 46 (1620).
130. Muzzarelli, "Reconciling the Privilege of a Few with the Common Good," 598.
131. Santos, *Día y noche de Madrid*, 40–42.
132. Ledesma, *Documentos de la buena crianza*, 20–23.
133. Soto, *Obligaciones de todos los estados*, 11v, 69.
134. Torquemada, *Coloquios satíricos*, 632–33.
135. "Puntos de gobierno, especialmente para Madrid, que conviene reformar," n.d. (1621?), in González Palencia, *La Junta de Reformación*, 212.
136. AHN, Consejos, leg. 51438.
137. AHN, Consejos, SACC, libro 1173, f. 98v.
138. AHN, Consejos, SACC, libro 1173, f. 191.
139. AHN, Consejos, leg. 7167, exp. 22.
140. AHN, Consejos, SACC: libro 1203 (licenses); libro 1173, f. 119v (gambling and card games).
141. AHN, Consejos, SACC, libro 1173, f. 94.
142. "Puntos de gobierno, especialmente para Madrid, que conviene reformar," n.d. (1621?), in González Palencia, *La Junta de Reformación*, 212.
143. Castro Martínez, *El abastecimiento alimentario en el reino de Granada*, 235–36.

144. AHN, Consejos, SACC, libro 1173, f. 95.
145. "Puntos de gobierno, especialmente para Madrid, que conviene reformar," n.d. (1621?), in González Palencia, *La Junta de Reformación*, 212.
146. AHN, Consejos, SACC, libro 1173, f. 96v.
147. Montandon, ed., *Dictionnaire raisonné de la politesse et du savoir-vivre*, 200.
148. Eiximenis, "Dotzè del Crestià," 123.
149. Pinheiro da Veiga, *Fastiginia*, 59.
150. Martín Pérez, quoted in Hernando, "Els moralistes i l'alimentació a la baixa edat mitjana," 293.
151. Santos, *Día y noche de Madrid*, 57–58.
152. Díaz, *Diez siglos de cocina en Madrid*, 44.
153. "Puntos de gobierno, especialmente para Madrid, que conviene reformar," González Palencia, *La Junta de Reformación*, 212.
154. Although the brains of meat animals were consumed and appreciated, cat brains were considered to be dangerous. Nola's recipe for roast cat (the only early modern recipe that mentions felines) indicates that the head must be discarded, as "he who eats them will lose his senses and judgment." See Nola, *Coch*, xlii.
155. Pasamonte, "Vida y trabajos de Jerónimo de Pasamonte," 41.
156. Enrique Suárez Figaredo, in the introduction to the electronic version of the BAE text, describes Pasamonte toward the end of his life as "sickly, neurotic and profoundly religious." Accessed April 29, 2016,http://users.ipfw.edu/jehle /CERVANTE/othertxts/VidaPasamonte.htm.
157. AHN, Consejos, SACC, libro 1173, f. 103.
158. AHN, Consejos, SACC, libro 1173, f. 104v–105v. They made similar arguments about women who sold chocolate instead of working as washerwomen, suggesting that such endeavors were more about "idly roaming about and enjoying their youth" than actual economic productivity. See Libro 1173, f. 98v.
159. See also the discussion of women and work in chapter 2. One danger of such arguments was that in their attempts to avoid such judgmental characterizations, some women went to the other extreme. Yelgo de Vazquez, in a chapter on the importance of properly managing a household's funds, tells the story of his friend who married an unusually stingy woman. Arguing that all treats and sweet things were associated with "bad women," she fed her family only salads for dinner, offered bread to the members of her household with a reluctant sigh, and engaged in constant arguments with her husband over food. Yelgo emphasized at the end of his tale that a housewife, while she must avoid being wasteful, still needed to maintain the quality of food

appropriate to her family's position and avoid excess parsimony. See *Estilo de servir a príncipes*, 87v–96v.

CONCLUSION

1. This agrees with Stephen Mennell's argument for the "diminishing contrasts and increasing varieties" he perceives in early modern France and England. See Mennell, *All Manners of Food*, 322.
2. Greenblatt, *Renaissance Self-Fashioning*.

GLOSSARY

adafina: A pot of legumes, vegetables, eggs, and meat, typically prepared as a Jewish Sabbath meal.

aguardiente: Clear, distilled spirits; frequently taken in small amounts for breakfast.

alcaldes de casa y corte: In the court of Madrid, city officials whose duties included maintaining order and the supervision of public markets and the sale of food and drink.

aloja: Beverage sold at street stands; a mildly fermented mixture of water, honey, and spices.

arroba: A unit of liquid measure, equal to approximately fifteen liters.

azumbre: A unit of liquid measure, equal to approximately two and a half liters.

bodegón, bodegoncillo: Small tavern or cantina that sold drinks and inexpensive simple meals.

cántara: A unit of liquid measure, equal to approximately eleven liters.

cofradías: Lay religious brotherhoods, often organized for charitable purposes.

converso: A Jew converted (often under duress) to Catholicism.

Cortes: A representative government assembly.

despensa: A pantry or storage area; in Madrid, often maintained by wealthy families to keep supplies of valuable food items.

despojos: The organs and offal of meat animals and poultry (necks, lungs, intestines, etc.), generally considered appropriate food for the poor.

ducado: A unit of money, equivalent to 375 maravedís.

figón: Especially in Madrid, a tavern catering to wealthier customers, allowed to sell exclusive foods such as partridge and venison.

letuario: Electuary; a sweet paste made from honey and orange peel, sold in street markets and often eaten for breakfast.

manjar blanco: A chicken dish prepared with rice flour and sweetened almond milk, with roughly the consistency of a pudding.

morisco: A Muslim converted (often by force) to Catholicism.

olla podrida: Literally, "rotten pot;" a stew of vegetables and legumes, with the possible addition of meat, cooked for a long time over a low fire. A common main dish.

real: A unit of money, equal to thirty-four maravedís.

maravedí: A unit of money; fewer than ten maravedís would purchase a meal on the street.

BIBLIOGRAPHY

ARCHIVES AND MANUSCRIPT MATERIALS

Archivo Histórico Nacional, Madrid (AHN)

Sala de Alcaldes de Casa y Corte (SACC), Libros 1173, 1198, 1200, 1201, 1203, 1210, 1217, 1234, 1239, 1246, 1247, 1256, 1276, 1278.

Clero, carpetas 3638, 3788. Consulted via the Portal de Archivos Españoles, http://pares.mcu.es.

Consejos, Indultos de Viernes Santo, legajos 5589, 5590.

Inquisición, legajos 130–34, 193, 196, 234.

Universidades, Colegio Mayor de San Ildefonso de la Universidad de Alcalá de Henares, legajo 371.

Archivo del Palacio, Madrid

Sec. Adm. Legajo 880, Oficios de Boca de la Real Casa.

Biblioteca Nacional de España (BNE)

Colección de avisos de la nobleza a sus hijos. MS 10857.

Etiquetas de palacio. MS 12816.

León Pinelo, Antonio. *Anales de Madrid.* MS 18117.

Libro de mayordomía de gastos de cocina del convento benedictino de San Martín de Madrid. MS 1654.

Receptas de pivetes, pastilhas e vvas perfumadas y conserbas. MS 1462.

Receptas experimentadas para diversas cosas. MS 2019.

Recetas y memorias para guisados. MS 6058.

Reglas de urbanidad expuestas en forma dialogada. MS 12955/68.

Bibliography

PUBLISHED WORKS

Actas de las Cortes de Castilla. Vol. 1. Madrid: Imprenta Nacional, 1861.

Albala, Ken. *The Banquet: Dining in the Great Courts of Late Renaissance Europe.* Urbana: University of Illinois Press, 2007.

———. *Eating Right in the Renaissance.* Berkeley: University of California Press, 2002.

———. "Introduction." In *A Cultural History of Food in the Renaissance*, ed. Ken Albala, 1–28. London: Bloomsbury, 2012.

———. "Professional Cooking, Kitchens, and Service Work." In *A Cultural History of Food in the Renaissance*, ed. Ken Albala, 117–34. London: Bloomsbury, 2012.

Altman, Ida. *Emigrants and Society: Extremadura and Spanish America in the Sixteenth Century.* Berkeley: University of California Press, 1989.

Alvarez-Assorio Alvariño, Antonio. "Rango y apariencia. El decoro y la quiebra de la distinción en Castilla (ss. XVI–XVIII)." *Revista de Historia Moderna* 17 (1998–99): 263–78.

Alves, Abel. *Animals of Spain: An Introduction to Imperial Perceptions and Human Interaction with Other Animals, 1492–1826.* Leiden: Brill, 2011.

Ampudia de Haro, Fernando. *Las bridas de la conducta: Una aproximación al proceso civilizatorio español.* Madrid: Siglo XXI, 2007.

Andreolli, Bruno. "Food Representations." In *A Cultural History of Food in the Medieval Age*, ed. Massimo Montanari, 151–64. London: Bloomsbury, 2012.

Ansón Calvo, María del Carmen, Fernando Manzano Ledesma, and Nuria González Alonso. "Un ejemplo de sociabilidad gastronómica: Las comidas de pobres y de fraternidad en las cofradías benaventanas en la Edad Moderna." In *Ocio y vida cotidiana en el mundo hispánico en la Edad Moderna*, ed. Francisco Núñez Roldán, 781–90. Sevilla: Universidad de Sevilla, 2007.

Atienza Hernández, Ignacio. *Aristocracia, poder y riqueza en la España moderna: La casa de los Osuna, ss. XV–XIX.* Madrid: Siglo XXI, 1987.

Augustine. *Sermons.* Part 3, vol. 7. Ed. John E. Rotelle, trans. Edmund Hill. Brooklyn: New City Press, 1990.

Aulnoy, Madame d' (Marie Catherine). *The Ingenious and Diverting Letters of the Lady's Travels into Spain.* 5th ed. London, 1703.

Aznar Cardona, Pedro. *Expulsión justificada de los moriscos españoles y suma de las excelencias cristianas de nuestro Rey don Felipe III.* Huesca, 1612.

Ball, Rachael. *Treating the Public: Theater, Public Health, and Public Opinion in the Atlantic World.* Baton Rouge: Louisiana State University Press, forthcoming (2017).

———. "Water, Wine, and Aloja: Consuming Interests in the Corrales de Comedias 1600–1646." *Comedia Performance* 10, no. 1 (2013): 59–92.

Bibliography

Barceló Crespí, María. "La dieta alimentària a la Cartoixa de Valldemossa (segle XV)." In *XIV Jornades d'estudis historics locals: La Mediterrania, area de convergencia de sistemes alimentaris (segles V–XVIII)*, ed. María Barceló Crespí and Antonio Riera y Melis, 393–408. Palma: Institut d'Estudis Baleàrics, 1996.

Barceló Crespí, María, and Antonio Riera y Melis, eds. *XIV Jornades d'estudis historics locals: La Mediterrania, area de convergencia de sistemes alimentaris (segles V–XVIII)*. Palma: Institut d'Estudis Baleàrics, 1996.

Benito, Pere. "Food Systems." In *A Cultural History of Food in the Medieval Age*, ed. Massimo Montanari, 37–56. London: Bloomsbury, 2012.

Bort Tomo, Esperanza. "La vida en la embajada de Roma en la época de Don Juan de Zúñiga Requesens (1568–1580)." In *Ocio y vida cotidiana en el mundo hispánico en la Edad Moderna*, ed. Francisco Núñez Roldán, 451–59. Sevilla: Universidad de Sevilla, 2007.

Braudel, Fernand. *Civilization and Capitalism*. New York: Harper and Row, 1981–1984.

Bravo Lozano, Jesús. "Fuentes para el estudio del trabajo femenino en la edad moderna: El caso de Madrid a fines del s. XVII." In *El trabajo de las mujeres, siglos XVI–XX: Actas de las VI jornadas de investigación interdisciplinaria sobre la mujer*, ed. María José Matilla and Margarita Ortega, 21–32. Madrid: Universidad Autónoma, 1987.

Burgo López, María Concepción. "El consumo alimentario del clero regular femenino en el Antiguo Régimen: El ejemplo del monasterio de San Payo de Antealtares." *Studia Historica: Historia moderna* 5 (1987): 221–40.

Butzer, Karl, and Elisabeth Butzer. "Transfer of the Mediterranean Livestock Economy to New Spain: Adaptation and Ecological Consequences." In *Global Land Use Change: A Perspective from the Columbian Encounter*, ed. Billie Lee Turner II, Antonio Gómez Sal, Fernando González Bernáldez, and Francesco de Castri, 151–93. Madrid: Consejo Superior de Investigaciones Científicas, 1995.

Bynum, Caroline Walker. *Holy Feast and Holy Fast: The Religious Significance of Food to Medieval Women*. Berkeley: University of California Press, 1988.

Canabal Rodríguez, Laura. "El sistema alimenticio de los conventos femeninos toledanos en la baja Edad Media." In *XIV Jornades d'estudis historics locals: La Mediterrania, area de convergencia de sistemes alimentaris (segles V–XVIII)*, ed. María Barceló Crespí and Antonio Riera y Melis, 409–16. Palma: Institut d'Estudis Baleàrics, 1996.

Capel, José Carlos. *La gula en el siglo de oro*. Donostia: R&B, 1996.

Capitán Díaz, Antonio. "Educación, urbanidad y buenos modales en el siglo XVI español: De *El Cortesano* al *Galateo*." In *Homenaje al Profesor Alexandre Sanvisens*, ed. Buenaventura Delgado y María Luisa Rodríguez, 279–87. Barcelona: Universidad de Barcelona, 1989.

Bibliography

Carmona García, Juan Ignacio. *Crónica urbana del malvivir (ss. XIV–XVII): Insalubridad, desamparo y hambre en Sevilla*. Seville: Universidad de Sevilla, 2000.

———. *El extenso mundo de la pobreza: La otra cara de la Sevilla imperial*. Sevilla: Ayuntamiento, 1993.

Castro, Américo. *Cervantes y los casticismos españoles*. Madrid: Alianza Editorial, 1974.

Castro, Xavier. *A lume manso: Estudios sobre historia social da alimentación en Galicia*. Vigo: Galaxia, 1998.

Castro Martínez, Teresa de. *El abastecimiento alimentario en el reino de Granada (1482–1510)*. Granada: Universidad de Granada, 2004.

———. *La alimentación en las crónicas castellanas bajomedievales*. Granada: Universidad de Granada, 1996.

———. "Comer en la Alhambra de Granada: El abastecimiento alimentario alhambreño en los primeros años de la dominación cristiana: 1492–1568." In *Comer cultura: Estudios de cultura alimentaria*, ed. Antonio Garrido Aranda, 129–53. Córdoba: Universidad de Córdoba, 2001.

Cavallo, Sandra, and Tessa Storey. *Healthy Living in Late Renaissance Italy*. New York: Oxford University Press, 2013.

Celada, Eva. *La cocina de la Casa de Alba*. Barcelona: Belacqva, 2003.

Coe, Sophie D., and Michael Coe. *The True History of Chocolate*. 3rd ed. London: Thames & Hudson, 2013.

Colección de documentos inéditos para la historia de España. Vols. 18, 26, 92. Madrid: Viuda de Calero, 1842–1883.

Colmenero de Ledesma, Antonio. *Curioso tratado de la naturaleza y calidad del chocolate*. Madrid, 1631.

Conde y Delgado de Molina, Rafael. "Fonts per a l'estudi del consum alimentari en els temps medievals: Fonts de l'arxiu de la Corona d'Arago." In *Alimentació i societat a la Catalunya medieval*, 27–50. Barcelona: Institució Milà i Fontanals, Unitat d'Investigació d'Estudis Medievals, 1988.

Constituciones de la congregación de San Benito de la Observancia. Madrid, 1612.

Constituciones, y instrucciones de la hermandad del Real Hospicio de Pobres Mendigos del Ave María, y San Fernando. Madrid, 1675.

Contreras, Jesús. *Alimentación y cultura: Perspectivas antropológicas*. Barcelona: Ariel, 1995.

Cortes de los antiguos reinos de León y Castilla. Madrid: Rivadeneyra, 1883.

Covarrubias, Sebastián de. *Tesoro de la lengua castellana o española*. Madrid, 1611.

Cruselles, José María, and Rafael Narbona. "Los modelos alimentarios de una sociedad jerarquizada: Occidente en la Edad Media." *Debats* (Institució Alfons el Magnànim) 16 (1986): 72–83.

Bibliography

Cruz Cruz, J. *Alimentación y cultura: Antropología de la conducta alimentaria.* Pamplona, 1991.

——. *Dietética medieval: El "régimen de salud" de Arnaldo de Vilanova.* Huesca: La Val de Onsera, 1997.

Devroey, Jean-Pierre. "Food and Politics." In *A Cultural History of Food in the Medieval Age*, ed. Massimo Montanari, 73–89. London: Bloomsbury, 2014.

Díaz, Lorenzo. *La cocina del barroco: La gastronomía del Siglo de Oro en Lope, Cervantes y Quevedo.* Madrid: Alianza Editorial, 2003.

——. *Diez siglos de cocina en Madrid: De los mesones de ayer a los restaurantes de hoy.* Barcelona: Folio, 1994.

——. *Madrid: Bodegones, mesones, fondas y restaurantes: Cocina y sociedad 1412–1990.* Madrid: Espasa Calpe, 1990.

Documentos inéditos referentes a las postrimerías de la Casa de Austria en España. Vol. 2. Ed. Adalbert of Bavaria and Gabriel Maura Gamazo. Madrid: Revista de Archivos, Bibliotecas y Museos, 1929.

Domínguez Ortiz, Antonio. "Aspectos del vivir madrileño durante el reinado de Carlos II." *Anales del Instituto de Estudios Madrileños* 7 (1971): 229–52.

Douglas, Mary. "Deciphering a Meal." In *Implicit Meanings: Essays in Anthropology*, 249–75. London: Routledge & Kegan Paul, 1975.

Dunmire, William. *Gardens of New Spain: How Mediterranean Plants and Foods Changed America.* Austin: University of Texas Press, 2004.

Dursteler, Eric R. "Food and Politics." In *A Cultural History of Food in the Renaissance*, ed. Ken Albala, 83–100.

Earle, Rebecca. *The Body of the Conquistador: Food, Race and the Colonial Experience in Spanish America.* Cambridge: Cambridge University Press, 2012.

Echániz Sans, María. "La alimentación de los pobres asistidos por la Pia Almoina de la catedral de Barcelona según el libro de cuentas de 1283–1284." In *Alimentació i societat a la Catalunya medieval*, 173–261. Barcelona: Institució Milà i Fontanals, Unitat d'Investigació d'Estudis Medievals, 1988.

Egido, T. "La grandeza benedictina: San Benito el Real de Valladolid." *Patrimonio: Fundación del patrimonio histórico de Castilla y León* 46 (2012): 4–10.

Eiras Roel, Antonio. *Historia de la alimentación en la España moderna: Resultados y problemas.* Santiago de Compostela, 1993.

Eiximenis, Francesc. "Terç del Crestià" and "Dotzè del Crestià." In *Francesc Eiximenis: An Anthology*, ed. Xavier Renedo and David Guixeras, trans. Robert D. Hughes. Barcelona: Tamesis/Barcino, 2008.

Elias, Norbert. *The Civilizing Process.* Oxford: Blackwell, 2000, revised ed.

——. *The Court Society.* New York: Pantheon, 1969.

Bibliography

Equip Broida (Teresa Vinyoles, Olga Bravo, Pilar Gallego, Margarida González, Montserrat Marsiñach, Núria Muñoz, Anna Rubió, and Elisa Varela). "Actitudes religiosas de las mujeres medievales ante la muerte (los testamentos de Barcelonesas de los siglos XIV y XV)." In *Las mujeres en el cristianismo medieval*, ed. Angela Muñoz Fernández, 463–75. Madrid: Asociación Cultural al-Mudayna, 1989.

———. "Els àpats funeraris segons els testaments vers el 1400." In *Alimentació i societat a la Catalunya medieval*, 263–69. Barcelona: Institució Milà i Fontanals, Unitat d'Investigació d'Estudis Medievals, 1988.

Ezcaray, Antonio de. *Voces de dolor nacidas de la multitud de pecados*. Seville, 1691.

Fàbrega, Jaume. *El convit del tirant: Cuina i comensalitat, de l'Edat Mitjana a Ferran Adrià*. Lleida: Pagès, 2007.

———. "La cultura del cerdo en el Mediterráneo, entre el rechazo y la aceptación." In *La alimentación mediterránea: Historia, cultura, nutrición*, ed. F. Xavier Medina, 217–37. Barcelona: Icaria, 1996.

———. *La cultura del gust als països catalans: Espais geogràfics, socials i històrics del patrimoni culinari català*. Tarragona: Edicions El Mèdol, 2000.

Falcón Pérez, María Isabel. "Banquetes en Aragón en la Baja Edad Media." In *XIV Jornades d'estudis historics locals: La Mediterrania, area de convergencia de sistemes alimentaris (segles V–XVIII)*, ed. María Barceló Crespí and Antonio Riera y Melis, 509–21. Palma: Institut d'Estudis Baleàrics, 1996.

Fernández Pérez, Alicia. "La mujer trabajadora del barroco a través de la picaresca." In *El trabajo de las mujeres, siglos XVI–XX: Actas de las VI jornadas de investigación interdisciplinaria sobre la mujer*, ed. María José Matilla and Margarita Ortega, 1–10. Madrid: Universidad Autónoma, 1987.

Ferrer, Vincent. *Tratados espirituales de San Vicente Ferrer*. Madrid: Edibesa, 2005.

Ferrer i Mallol, María Teresa. "Figues, panses, fruita seca i torrons." In *XIV Jornades d'estudis historics locals: La Mediterrania, area de convergencia de sistemes alimentaris (segles V–XVIII)*, ed. María Barceló Crespí and Antonio Riera y Melis, 191–208. Palma: Institut d'Estudis Baleàrics, 1996.

Fitzpatrick, Joan. "Body and Soul." In *A Cultural History of Food in the Renaissance*, ed. Ken Albala, 151–70. London: Bloomsbury, 2012.

Flynn, Maureen. *Sacred Charity: Confraternities and Social Welfare in Spain, 1400–1700*. Ithaca: Cornell University Press, 1989.

Forster, Robert, and Orest Ranum, eds. *Food and Drink in History: Selections from the Annales*. Baltimore: Johns Hopkins University Press, 1979.

Freedman, Paul. "Eating Out." In *A Cultural History of Food in the Renaissance*, ed. Ken Albala, 101–16. London: Bloomsbury, 2012.

Galen. *On the Properties of Foodstuffs (De alimentorum facultatibus)*, ed. and trans. Owen Powell. Cambridge: Cambridge University Press, 2003.

Bibliography

García Gómez, Jacinto. *Carlos V a la mesa: Cocina y alimentación en la España renacentista.* Toledo: Bremen, 2000.

García Marsilla, Juan Vicente. *La jerarquía de la mesa: Los sistemas alimentarios en la Valencia bajomedieval.* Prologue by Antoni Riera Melis. Valencia: Diputació de Valencia, 1993.

García Sánchez, Expiración. "La alimentación popular urbana en Al-andalus." *Arqueología Medieval* 4 (1995): 219–35.

Garrido Aranda, Antonio. "Acerca de la dieta familiar española del Barroco: Algunas pautas metodológicas." In *Antropología de la alimentación: Nuevos ensayos sobre dieta mediterránea,* ed. Isabel González Turmo and Pedro Romero de Solís, 171–98. Sevilla: Universidad de Sevilla, 1996.

——. "La bebida en cuatro tratadistas españoles: Lobera de Ávila, Núñez de Coria, Sorapán de Rieros, y Bails." In *Comer cultura: Estudios de cultura alimentaria,* ed. Antonio Garrido Aranda, 173–97. Córdoba: Universidad de Córdoba, 2001.

Garrido Aranda, Antonio, Patricio Hidalgo Nuchera, and Javier Muñoz Hidalgo. "Los manipuladores de alimentos en España y América entre los siglos XV y XVIII: Los gremios alimentarios y otras normativas de consumo." In *Cultura alimentaria de España y América,* ed. Antonio Garrido Aranda, 169–214. Huesca: La Val de Onsera, 1995.

Garrido Aranda, Antonio, ed. *Cultura alimentaria de España y América.* Huesca: La Val de Onsera, 1995.

Gautier, Alban. "Eating Out in the Early and High Middle Ages." In *A Cultural History of Food in the Medieval Age,* ed. Massimo Montanari, 91–106. London: Bloomsbury, 2012.

Gentilcore, David. "Body and Soul, or Living Physically in the Kitchen." In *A Cultural History of Food in the Early Modern Age,* ed. Beat Kümin, 143–64. London: Bloomsbury, 2012.

Gil Ambrona, Antonio. "Entre la oración y el trabajo: Las ocupaciones de las otras esposas, siglos XVI–XVII." In *El trabajo de las mujeres, siglos XVI–XX: Actas de las VI jornadas de investigación interdisciplinaria sobre la mujer,* ed. María José Matilla and Margarita Ortega, 57–67. Madrid: Universidad Autónoma, 1987.

Gitlitz, David M., and Linda Kay Davidson. *A Drizzle of Honey: The Lives and Recipes of Spain's Secret Jews.* New York: St. Martin's, 1999.

Goldgar, Anne, and Robert Frost. "Introduction." In *Institutional Culture in Early Modern Society,* ed. Goldgar and Frost, i–xviii. Leiden: Brill, 2004.

Gómez Díaz, Donato. "'Buen alimento, mejor pensamiento': El consumo en un convento almeriense a finales del s. XVII." *Espacio, tiempo y forma,* serie IV, *Historia moderna,* 14 (2001): 133–55.

Bibliography

González Arce, José Damián. *Apariencia y poder: La legislación suntuaria castellana en los siglos XIII–XV*. Jaén: Universidad de Jaén, 1998.

González de Salcedo, Pedro. *Nudrición real o preceptos de cómo se ha de educar a los reyes mozos*. Madrid, 1671.

González Palencia, Angel. *Consejo de Castilla: Sala de Alcaldes de Casa y Corte, catálogo por materias*. Madrid: Imp. del Seminario Conciliar, 1925.

González Palencia, Angel. *La Junta de Reformación: Documentos procedentes del Archivo Histórico Nacional y del General de Simancas*. Valladolid, 1932.

Gracián Dantisco, Lucas. *Galateo español*. Ed. Margherita Morreale. Madrid: CSIC, 1968.

Granado Maldonado, Diego. *Libro del arte de cozina*. Madrid, 1599.

Greenblatt, Stephen. *Renaissance Self-Fashioning: From More to Shakespeare*. Chicago: University of Chicago, 2005.

Greer, Meg. "Constituting Community: A New Historical Perspective on the Autos of Calderón." *New Historicism and the Comedia: Poetics, Politics and Praxis*, ed. José A. Madrigal, 41–68. Boulder: Society of Spanish and Spanish-American Studies, 1997.

Grieco, Allan J. "Body and Soul." In *A Cultural History of Food in the Medieval Age*, ed. Massimo Montanari, 143–50. London: Bloomsbury, 2012.

———. "Food and Social Classes in Late Medieval and Renaissance Italy." In *Food: A Culinary History*, ed. Jean-Louis Flandrin and Massimo Montanari, 302–12. New York: Columbia University Press, 1999.

Guerrero Mayllo, Ana. *Familia y vida cotidiana de una élite de poder: Los regidores madrileños en tiempos de Felipe II*. Madrid: Siglo XXI, 1993.

Guerrero Navarrete, Yolanda. "Aproximación cualitativa y cuantitativa a la dieta urbana en el siglo XV." In *Estudios de historia medieval: Homenaje a Luis Suárez*, ed. Vicente Angel Alvarez Palenzuela, Miguel Angel Ladero Quesada, and Julio Valdeón Baruque, 245–65. Valladolid: Secretariado de Publicaciones, 1991.

Guevara, Antonio de. *Aviso de privados*. Madrid, 1673. First published Valladolid, 1539.

———. *Epístolas familiares*. Madrid, 1595.

———. *Menosprecio de corte y alabanza de aldea*. Madrid, 1673. First published Valladolid, 1539.

Guevara, Juan Francisco. *Avisos, y advertmiento de la diligencia, que un señor deve usar en criar los hijos*. Naples, 1602.

Gutiérrez Nieto, Juan Ignacio. "El campesinado." In *La vida cotidiana en la España de Velazquez*, ed. José Alcalá Zamora, 43–70. Madrid: Ediciones Temas de Hoy, 1989.

Haranburu Altuna, Luis. *Historia de la alimentación y de la cocina en el País Vasco: De Santimamiñe a Arzak*. Alegia (Gipuzkoa): Hiria, 2000.

Heal, Felicity. "Food Gifts, the Household and the Politics of Exchange in Early Modern England." *Past and Present* 199 (May 2008): 41–70.

Bibliography

Hernández de Maceras, Domingo. *Libro del arte de cozina*. Salamanca, 1607.

Hernando, Josep. "Els moralistes i l'alimentació a la baixa edat mitjana." In *Alimentació i societat a la Catalunya medieval*, 271–93. Barcelona: Institució Milà i Fontanals, Unitat d'Investigació d'Estudis Medievals, 1988.

Izquierdo Benito, R. *Abastecimiento y alimentación de Toledo en el siglo XV*. Cuenca: Universidad de Castilla-La Mancha, 2002.

Kallendorf, Hilaire. *Sins of the Fathers: Moral Economies in Early Modern Spain*. Toronto: University of Toronto Press, 2013

Kelleher, Marie A. "Eating from a Corrupted Table: Food Regulations and Civic Health in Barcelona's 'First Bad Year.'" *e-Humanista* 25 (2013): 51–64.

Krausman Ben-Amos, Ilana. "Gifts and Favors: Informal Support in Early Modern England." *Journal of Modern History* 72, no. 2 (June 2000): 295–338.

Krondl, Michael. "Food Systems: Pepper, Herring, and Beer." In *A Cultural History of Food in the Renaissance*, ed. Ken Albala, 45–62. London: Bloomsbury, 2012.

Ladero Quesada, Miguel Angel. "La caza en la legislación municipal castellana, siglos XIII al XVII." In *En la España Medieval: Estudios dedicados al Profesor Julio González González*, 193–221. Madrid: Universidad Complutense, 1980.

Lapeña Paul, Ana Isabel. "Notas en torno al sistema alimentario en un monasterio altoaragonés en la Edad Media (el caso de San Juan de la Peña)." In *XIV Jornades d'estudis historics locals: La Mediterrania, area de convergencia de sistemes alimentaris (segles V–XVIII)*, ed. María Barceló Crespí and Antonio Riera y Melis, 379–92. Palma: Institut d'Estudis Baleàrics, 1996.

Laudan, Rachel. *Cuisine & Empire: Cooking in World History*. University of California Press, 2013.

Ledesma, Francisco de. *Documentos de la buena crianza*. Madrid, 1599.

Lera de Isla, Angel. "Cuando Madrid se hizo Corte: La famosa Ronda de Pan y Huevo." *Revista de Folklore* 19 (1982): 3–6.

Levi-Strauss, Claude. "The Culinary Triangle." In *Food and Culture: A Reader*. 3rd ed. Carole Counihan and Penny Van Esterik, 40–47. New York: Routledge, 2013.

Libros de acuerdos municipales de Santander, siglo XVII. Ed. Rosa María Blasco Martínez. Vol. 1. Santander: Concejalía de Cultura, 2002.

Lobera de Ávila, Luis. *Vergel de sanidad: Que por otro nombre se llamava Banquete de cavalleros y orden de vivir*. Alcalá de Henares, 1542.

Lope de Vega. *La moza de cántaro*. 2nd ed. Ed. Madison Stathers. New York: H. Holt and Company, 1913.

López Álvarez, Alejandro. *Poder, lujo, y conflicto en la corte de los Austrias: Coches, carrozas y sillas de mano, 1550–1700*. Madrid: Ediciones Polifemo, 2007.

López Iglesias, Florentino. "Oficios y actividades de las mujeres ovetenses en el antiguo régimen." In *El trabajo de las mujeres, siglos XVI–XX: Actas de las VI jornadas de investigación interdisciplinaria sobre la mujer*, ed. María José Matilla and Margarita Ortega, 50–56. Madrid: Universidad Autónoma, 1987.

López López, Roberto J. *Comportamientos religiosos en Asturias durante el Antiguo Régimen*. Oviedo: Silverio Cañada, 1988.

Luján, Néstor. *La vida cotidiana en la España del Siglo de Oro*. Barcelona: Planeta, 1989.

Magagna, Victor. "Food and Politics: The Power of Bread in European Culture." In *A Cultural History of Food in the Early Modern Age*, ed. Beat Kümin, 65–86. London: Bloomsbury, 2012.

Mantecón Movellán, Tomás Antonio. *Contrarreforma y religiosidad popular en Cantabria: Las cofradías religiosas*. Santander: Universidad de Santander, 1990.

Manual de mugeres en el qual se contienen muchas y diversas reçeutas muy buenas. Ed. Alicia Martínez Crespo. Salamanca: Ediciones Universidad de Salamanca, 1995.

Manuppella, Giacinto, ed. *O "Livro de Cozinha" da Infanta D. Maria de Portugal, primeira edição integral do códice português*. Coimbra: Universidades, 1967.

Martín, José Luis. *La mujer y el caballero: Estudio y traducción de los textos de Francesc Eiximenis*. Barcelona: Universitat de Barcelona, 2003.

Martínez García, Luis. *La asistencia a los pobres en Burgos en la Baja Edad Media: El Hospital de Santa María la Real (1341–1500)*. Burgos: Diputación Provincial, 1981.

Martínez López, José Miguel, ed. *Historia de la alimentación rural y tradicional: Recetario de Almería*. Almería: Instituto de Estudios Almerienses, 2003.

Martínez Martínez, María José. "Hacia la configuración del modelo alimentario feudal en la Murcia Bajomedieval: Transformaciones y nuevas realidades." In *XIV Jornades d'estudis historics locals: La Mediterrania, area de convergencia de sistemes alimentaris (segles V–XVIII)*, ed. María Barceló Crespí and Antonio Riera y Melis, 349–70. Palma: Institut d'Estudis Baleàrics, 1996.

Martínez Montiño, Francisco. *Arte de Cozina*. Madrid, 1611.

Mas i Forners, Antoni. "L'alimentació de la mà d'obra assalariada en l'agricultura mallorquina del segle XIV: L'exemple de l'Alqueria Masnou." In *XIV Jornades d'estudis historics locals: La Mediterrania, area de convergencia de sistemes alimentaris (segles V–XVIII)*, ed. María Barceló Crespí and Antonio Riera y Melis, 523–28. Palma: Institut d'Estudis Baleàrics, 1996.

Mennell, Stephen. *All Manners of Food: Eating and Taste in England and France from the Middle Ages to the Present*. Oxford: Basil Blackwell, 1985.

Micón, Francisco. *Alivio de los sedientos, en el cual se trata de la necesidad que tenemos de bever frío y refrescado con nieve, y las condiciones que para esto son menester*. Barcelona, 1576.

Mintz, Sidney. *Sweetness and Power: The Place of Sugar in Modern History*. New York: Viking, 1985.

Monardes, Nicolás. *La historia medicinal de las cosas que se traen de nuestras islas occidentales*. Seville, 1574.

Bibliography

Montanari, Massimo. *Cheese, Pears, and History in a Proverb*. New York: Columbia University Press, 2010.

———. *El hambre y la abundancia: Historia y cultura de la alimentación en Europa*. Barcelona: Crítica, 1993.

———. "Introduction." In *A Cultural History of Food in the Medieval Age*, ed. Massimo Montanari, 1–18. London: Bloomsbury, 2014.

———. "El papel del Mediterráneo en la definición de los modelos alimentarios de la Edad Media: ¿Espacio cultural o mar fronterizo?" In *La alimentación mediterránea: Historia, cultura, nutrición*, ed. F. Xavier Medina, 73–79. Barcelona: Icaria, 1996.

Montandon, Alain, ed. *Dictionnaire raisonné de la politesse et du savoir-vivre du Moyen-Age à nos jours*. Paris: Editions du Seuil, 1995.

Monzón, Francisco de. *Libro primero del espejo del príncipe christiano*. Lisboa, 1544.

Moreno de la Torre, Antonio. *Diario de Antonio Moreno de la Torre, Zamora 1673–79: Vida cotidiana de una ciudad española durante el siglo XVII*. Ed. Francisco Javier Lorenzo Pinar and Luis Vasallo Toranzo. Zamora: Instituto de Estudios Zamoranos Florián de Campo, 1990.

Motis Dolader, Miguel Angel. "Alimentación y comensalidad: Rito y necesidad substancial." In *Hebraica aragonalia: El legado judío en Aragón*, ed. Miguel Angel Motis Dolader, 122–31. Zaragoza: Diputación de Zaragoza, 2003.

Muzzarelli, Maria Giuseppina. "Reconciling the Privilege of a Few with the Common Good: Sumptuary Laws in Medieval and Early Modern Europe." *Journal of Medieval and Early Modern Studies* 39, no. 3 (2009): 597–617.

Nalle, Sara. "Self-correction and Social Change in the Spanish Counter-Reformation." In *Religion and the Early Modern State: Views from China, Russia, and the West*, ed. James D. Tracy and Marguerite Ragnow, 302–23. Cambridge: Cambridge University Press, 2004.

Norton, Marcy. *Sacred Gifts, Profane Pleasures: A History of Tobacco and Chocolate in the Atlantic World*. Cornell University Press, 2008.

———. "Tasting Empire: Chocolate and the European Internalization of Mesoamerican Aesthetics." *American Historical Review* 111, no. 3 (2006): 660–91.

Novísima recopilación de las leyes de España. Madrid: Boletín Oficial de Estado, 1992.

Núñez de Castro, Alonso. *Sólo Madrid es corte*. Madrid, 1675. First published 1658.

Ortega López, Margarita. "La participación laboral de la mujer en un señorío aragonés durante el siglo XVIII: El señorío de Luna." In *El trabajo de las mujeres, siglos XVI–XX: Actas de las VI jornadas de investigación interdisciplinaria sobre la mujer*, ed. María José Matilla and Margarita Ortega, 67–77. Madrid: Universidad Autónoma, 1987.

Bibliography

Palmireno, Juan Lorenzo. *El estudioso cortesano*. Alcalá de Henares, 1587.

Parasecoli, Fabio, and Peter Scholliers, eds. *A Cultural History of Food*. 6 vols. London: Bloomsbury, 2012.

Pasamonte, Jerónimo de. "Vida y trabajos de Jerónimo de Pasamonte." In *Biblioteca de Autores Españoles*, vol. 90, 5–73. Madrid: Ediciones Atlas, 1956. Electronic version posted at http://users.ipfw.edu/jehle/CERVANTE/othertxts/VidaPasamonte .htm includes an introduction by Enrique Suárez Figaredo. Barcelona, 2003.

Pennell, Sara. "Family and Domesticity: Cooking, Eating, and Making Homes." In *A Cultural History of Food in the Early Modern Age*, ed. Beat Kümin, 123–42. London: Bloomsbury, 2012.

Pennell, Sara. "Professional Cooking, Kitchens and Service Work." In *A Cultural History of Food in the Early Modern Age*, ed. Beat Kümin, 103–22. London: Bloomsbury, 2012.

Pérez, Martín. *Libro de las confesiones: Una radiografía de la sociedad medieval española*. Ed. Antonio García y García, Bernardo Alonso Rodríguez, and Francisco Cantelar Rodríguez. Biblioteca de Autores Cristianos: Madrid, 2002.

Pérez de Herrera, Cristóbal. *A la catolica real magestad del Rey don Felipe III . . . cerca de la forma y traça, como . . . podrian remediarse algunos peccados, excessos, y desordenes . . . de qᵉ esta villa de Madrid al presente tiene falta*. Madrid, 1601.

Pérez López, Jesús. "Las cuentas de la casa Sala, un ejemplo de distribución de los gastos domésticos en la burguesía (Sant Martí d'Arenys 1659–1662)." In *XIV Jornades d'estudis historics locals: La Mediterrania, area de convergencia de sistemes alimentaris (segles V–XVIII)*, ed. María Barceló Crespí and Antonio Riera y Melis, 453–76. Palma: Institut d'Estudis Baleàrics, 1996.

Pérez Samper, María Angeles. "La alimentación como indicativo de un estilo de vida: El colegio de Cordelles de los jesuitas." In *Profesor Nazario González: Una historia abierta*. Barcelona: University of Barcelona, 1998.

———. *La alimentación en la España del Siglo de Oro*. Huesca: La Val de Onsera, 1988.

———. "Cataluña y Europa a la mesa: Las recíprocas influencias en los modelos alimentarios de la Época Moderna." *Pedralbes* 18, no. 1 (1998): 251–72.

———. "Chocolate, té y café: Sociedad, cultura y alimentación en la España del Siglo XVIII." In *El conde de Aranda y su tiempo*, vol. 1, ed. J. A. Ferrer Benimelli, 157–221. Zaragoza: Institución "Fernando el Católico," 2001.

———. "Cocineras, escritoras y lectoras." In *Espacios y Mujeres*, ed. Marion Reder Gadow, 85–143. Málaga: Universidad de Málaga, 2006.

———. "Estilo de servir a príncipes. La cocina y la mesa de un grande de España en el siglo de oro." *Trocadero: Revista de historia moderna y contemporanea* 12–13 (2000–2001): 315–60.

Bibliography

———. "Privacidad doméstica: La mesa y la servidumbre." In *Ocio y vida cotidiana en el mundo hispánico en la Edad Moderna*, ed. Francisco Núñez Roldán, 83–136. Sevilla: Universidad de Sevilla, 2007.

Perry, Mary Elizabeth. "Las mujeres y su trabajo curativo en Sevilla, siglos XVI y XVII." In *El trabajo de las mujeres, siglos XVI–XX: Actas de las VI jornadas de investigación interdisciplinaria sobre la mujer*, ed. María José Matilla and Margarita Ortega, 40–50. Madrid: Universidad Autónoma, 1987.

Pezzi Cristóbal, Pilar. "Fiesta religiosa y ostentación social: La real congregación del Dulce Nombre de Jesús de Vélez-Málaga y la puesta en escena del paso." In *Ocio y vida cotidiana en el mundo hispánico en la Edad Moderna*, ed. Francisco Núñez Roldán, 271–84. Sevilla: Universidad de Sevilla, 2007.

Piccinni, Gabriella. "Family and Domesticity." In *A Cultural History of Food in the Medieval Age*, ed. Massimo Montanari, 125–42. London: Bloomsbury, 2014.

Piccolomini, Enea Silvio. *Tractado de la miseria de los cortesanos*. Seville, 1520.

Pinheiro da Veiga, Tomé. *Fastiginia: Vida cotidiana en la corte de Valladolid*. Ed. and trans. Narciso Alonso Cortés. Valladolid: Ambito, 1989.

Pons Fuster, Francisco. "Mujeres y espiritualidad: Las beatas valencianas del siglo XVII." *Revista de Historia Moderna*, Anales de la Universidad de Alicante 10 (1991), *Aspectos de la vida cotidiana en la España moderna* 1, 71–96.

Pozzo, Cassiano dal. *El diario del viaje a España del Cardenal Francesco Barberini*. Ed. and trans. Alessandra Anselmi. Madrid: Doce Calles, 2004.

Prats, Joaquín, and Carina Rey. "Las bases modernas de la alimentación tradicional." In *Historia de la alimentación rural y tradicional: Recetario de Almería*, ed. José Miguel Martínez López, 53–61. Almeria: Instituto de Estudios Almerienses, 2003.

Prieto Palomo, Teresa. "El abastecimiento alimentario en el Madrid del siglo XVII: Vida cotidiana de una trabajadora." In *Ocio y vida cotidiana en el mundo hispánico en la Edad Moderna*, ed. Francisco Núñez Roldán. 417–26. Sevilla: Universidad de Sevilla, 2007.

Profeti, María Grazia. "Comer en las tablas: Banquete carnavalesco y banquete macabro en el teatro del Siglo de Oro." In *Cultura alimentaria de España y América*, ed. Antonio Garrido Aranda, 75–114. Huesca: La Val de Onsera, 1995.

Pujol y Bertrán, Anton. "Alimentació i nutrició a Mallorca, segle XVII." In *XIV Jornades d'estudis historics locals: La Mediterrania, area de convergencia de sistemes alimentaris (segles V–XVIII)*, ed. María Barceló Crespí and Antonio Riera y Melis, 371–78. Palma: Institut d'Estudis Baleàrics, 1996.

Real Academia Española. *Diccionario de Autoridades*. Madrid, 1726–1739. http://web.frl.es/DA.html.

Riera i Melis, Antoni. "Estructura social y sistemas alimentarios en la Cataluña bajomedieval." *Acta Historica et Archaeologica Mediaevalia* 14–15 (1993–1994): 193–217.

————. "Jerarquía social y desigualdad alimentaria en el mediterráneo noroccidental durante la Baja Edad Media: La cocina y la mesa de los estamentos populares." In *La alimentación mediterránea: Historia, cultura, nutrición*, ed. F. Xavier Medina, 81–107. Barcelona: Icaria, 1996.

————. "Pobreza y alimentación en el Mediterráneo Noroccidental en la Baja Edad Media." In *XIV Jornades d'estudis historics locals: La Mediterrania, area de convergencia de sistemes alimentaris (segles V–XVIII)*, ed. María Barceló Crespí and Antonio Riera y Melis, 39–72. Palma: Institut d'Estudis Baleàrics, 1996.

Ródenas Vilar, R. *Vida cotidiana y negocio en la Segovia del Siglo de Oro: El mercader Juan de Cuéllar*. Valladolid: Junta de Castilla y León, 1990.

Rodríguez Molina, J. "La alimentación en el antiguo Reino de Jaén, siglos XV–XVI." *Boletín del Instituto de Estudios Giennenses* 148 (1993): 35–112.

Rodríguez-San Pedro Bezares, Luis Enrique. *La universidad salmantina del Barroco*. Salamanca: Ediciones Universidad de Salamanca, 1986.

Rodríguez Villa, Antonio. *Etiquetas de la Casa de Austria*. Madrid: Jaime Ratés, 1913.

Saavedra, Pegerto. *La vida cotidiana en la Galicia del Antiguo Régimen*. Barcelona: Crítica, 1994.

Sala Balust, Luis. *Constituciones, estatutos y ceremonias de los antiguos colegios seculares de la Universidad de Salamanca*. 4 vols. Salamanca: Secretariado de Publicaciones e Intercambio Científico de la Universidad de Salamanca, 1962–1966.

Salsete, Antonio. *El cocinero religioso*, ed. Victor Manuel Sarobe Pueyo. Pamplona: Gobierno de Navarra, 1995.

Sánchez Moya, M. "El ayuno del Yom Kippur entre los judaizantes turolenses del siglo XV." *Sefarad* 26 (1966): 273–304.

Santamaría Arnaiz, Matilde. *La alimentación de los españoles bajo el reino de los Austrias: La Sala de Alcaldes de Casa y Corte, las fuentes literarias, los colegios mayores y el papel sanitario de boticarios y médicos*. 2 vols. Madrid: Universidad Complutense, 1988.

Santos, Francisco de. *Día y noche de Madrid*. Madrid: Consejería de Educación y Cultura, 1992. First published Madrid, 1666.

Sarasúa, Carmen. *Criados, nodrizas y amos: El servicio doméstico en la formación del mercado de trabajo madrileño, 1758–1868*. Madrid: Siglo XXI, 1994.

————. "Upholding Status: The Diet of a Noble Family in Early-Nineteenth-Century La Mancha." In *Food, Drink, and Identity: Cooking, Eating, and Drinking in Europe since the Middle Ages*, ed. Peter Scholliers, 37–61. Oxford: Berg, 2001.

Sendra i Beltran, María del Pilar. "Variacions en l'evolució de la dieta alimentària dels monjos benedictins a la fi de l'edat mitjana." In *XIV Jornades d'estudis historics locals: La Mediterrania, area de convergencia de sistemes alimentaris*

Bibliography

(segles V–XVIII), ed. María Barceló Crespí and Antonio Riera y Melis, 417–27. Palma: Institut d'Estudis Baleàrics, 1996.

Serra i Clota, Assupta. "Comportaments alimentaris i factors socioeconòmics en el món rural català a la baixa edat mitjana." In *XIV Jornades d'estudis historics locals: La Mediterrania, area de convergencia de sistemes alimentaris (segles V–XVIII)*, ed. María Barceló Crespí and Antonio Riera y Melis, 529–42. Palma: Institut d'Estudis Baleàrics, 1996.

Serrano Larráyoz, Fernando. "Aproximación a la alimentación del ejército navarro durante la guerra castellano-navarra (1429)." *Príncipe de Viana* 58, no. 212 (1997): 567–88.

Serrano Larráyoz, Fernando. *La mesa del rey: Cocina y régimen alimentario en la corte de Carlos III "el Noble" de Navarra (1411–1425)*. Pamplona: Institución Príncipe de Viana, 2002.

Simón Palmer, María del Carmen. *La alimentación y sus circunstancias en el Real Alcázar de Madrid*. Instituto de Estudios Madrileños, 1982.

Simón Palmer, María del Carmen. "Las bebidas en el Palacio Real de Madrid en tiempo de los Austrias." In *Comer cultura: Estudios de cultura alimentaria*, ed. Antonio Garrido Aranda, 155–71. Córdoba: Universidad de Córdoba, 2001.

Soto, Juan de. *Obligaciones de todos los estados, y oficios, con los remedios, y consejos mas eficaces para la salud espiritual, y general reformacion de las costumbres*. Alcalá, 1619.

Spivakovsky, Erika. "La Princesa de Eboli." *Chronica Nova* 9 (1977): 5–48.

Sreenivasan, Govind. "Food Production." In *A Cultural History of Food in the Early Modern Age*, ed. Beat Kümin, 13–28. London: Bloomsbury, 2012.

Talavera, Hernando de. *Breve y muy provechosa doctrina de lo que deve saber todo christiano*. Granada, 1496.

Teresa of Ávila. *Camino de perfección*. In *Obras completas*, vol. 1. Madrid: F. Gonzalez Rojas, 1902.

Torquemada, Antonio de. *Coloquios satíricos*. In *Nueva Biblioteca de Autores Españoles*, vol. 7, ed. Marcelino Menéndez Pelayo, 486–581. Madrid: Bailly-Baillière é Hijos, 1905–1915.

Torremocha Hernández, Margarita. "Las noches y los días de los estudiantes universitarios: Posadas, mesones y hospederías en Valladolid, s. XVI–XVIII." *Revista de Historia Moderna*, Anales de la Universidad de Alicante 10 (1991), *Aspectos de la vida cotidiana en la España moderna* (I), 43–70.

———. *La vida estudiantil en el Antiguo Régimen*. Madrid: Alianza Editorial, 1998.

Torres, Miguel. "Producción y comercialización del vino en el Mediterráneo." In *La alimentación mediterránea: Historia, cultura, nutrición*, ed. F. Xavier Medina, 197–205. Barcelona: Icaria, 1996.

Bibliography

Valles Rojo, Julio. *Cocina y alimentación en los siglos XVI y XVII*. Valladolid: Junta de Castilla y León, Consejería de Cultura y Turismo, 2007.

Vassberg, David. *Land and Society in Golden Age Castile*. Cambridge: Cambridge University Press, 1984.

Vigil, Mariló. *La vida de las mujeres en los siglos XVI y XVII*. Madrid: Siglo XXI, 1986.

Vinyoles i Vidal, Teresa. "Alimentació i ritme del temps a Catalunya a la baixa Edat Mitjana." In *Actes: 1r Colloqui d'Història de l'Alimentació a la Corona d'Aragó*, 115–51. Lleida: Institut d'Estudis Ilerdencs, 1995.

——— . "El rebost, la taula i la cuina dels frares barcelonins al 1400." In *Alimentació i societat a la Catalunya medieval*, 137–66. Barcelona: Institució Milà i Fontanals, Unitat d'Investigació d'Estudis Medievals, 1988.

Visser, Margaret. *Much Depends on Dinner*. New York: Grove Press, 1986.

Vizuete Mendoza, J. Carlos. "La dieta alimenticia en la religiosidad femenina de San Clemente de Toledo." In *Las mujeres en el cristianismo medieval*, ed. Angela Muñoz Fernández, 247–58. Madrid: Asociación Cultural al-Mudayna, 1989.

Wunder, Amanda. "Women's Fashions and Politics in Seventeenth-Century Spain: The Rise and Fall of the Guardainfante." *Renaissance Quarterly* 68, no. 1 (Spring 2015): 133–86.

Yelgo de Vazquez, Miguel. *Estilo de servir a príncipes con exemplos morales para servir a Dios*. Madrid, 1614.

INDEX

Page numbers in bold type refer to glossary terms.

Index

moriscos, 37, 72, 76, 172–73, 212. *See also* Muslims

Muslims, 26, 72–73, 73–78, 107, 192n87. *See also* moriscos

mutton and lamb, 32, 70, 184n85. *See also* meat

Muzzarelli, Maria Giuseppina, 126

Nalle, Sara, 73–74

New World foods, 109–10, 180n19, 198n35. *See also* chocolate

nobility: diet of, 31, 32–33, 111–12, 131, 166–68, 176, 182n28; fasting (or not) by, 137, 139; origins and categories of, 102, 103–4; special privileges of, 127–29, 129–32, 176; status and status anxieties of, 9, 101–13, 122–23 126–27, 132–33. *See also* despensas; fasting; gluttony and overindulgence; hunting; royalty; sumptuary laws

de Nola, Ruperto, 26, 27, 28, 64, 73

Norton, Marcy, 110–11

Núñez de Castro, Alonso, 165

nuns. *See* convents

nutmeg. *See* spices

offal. *See* despojos (organs and offal)

oil, olive, 79–80, 138

Olivares, Countess of, 13, 108

olla podrida ("rotten pot"), 13, 30, 73, 212. *See also* stews and pottages

oranges. *See* fruit

organ meats. *See* despojos (organs and offal)

de Osuna, Francisco, 59

ovens, 16–17, 43, 181n21. *See also* bakers

overindulgence. *See* gluttony and overindulgence

de Palafox y Cardona, Jaime (archbishop of Seville), 143

panter (bread server and procurer): responsibilities of, 18

pan y vino. See bread; wine

partridges, 31. *See also* poultry

peaches, 18, 39. *See also* fruit

pears. *See* fruit

peasants: diet of, 24, 31, 32–33, 34–35, 141, 175; education of, 90; hunting rights of, 130–31

Pedro I (king of Portugal), 51–52

Pérez, Antonio, 127, 139

Pérez, Martín, 75, 171

Pérez de Herrera, Cristóbal, 34

petitions for charitable assistance. *See* charity

Philip II (king of Spain), 52–53, 57, 66, 108

Philip III (king of Spain), 56–57, 119, 125, 132

Philip IV (king of Spain), 55, 57, 103, 132, 166

Pia Almoina of Barcelona, 38

Piccolomini, Enea Silvio. *See* Pius II (pope)

pigs, 32, 78. *See also* pork

Pinheiro da Veiga, Tomé, 14, 56, 171

Pius II (pope), 124, 141

Platina. *See* Sacchi, Bartolomeo (Platina)

playhouses: as places to eat and drink, 41

plums. *See* fruit

poison, 172–73, 208n154

poor. *See* peasants; urban poor

pork, 32, 69–70, 74, 75, 76, 78–80, 141; lard, 7, 79–80, 192n103. *See also* meat

235

CPSIA information can be obtained
at www.ICGtesting.com
Printed in the USA
LVOW11s2206230117

521934LV00001B/161/P

9 780803 290815